After-Death Communication

... a wonderful book which delves into the many extraordinary experiences the bereaved so often experience but are afraid to discuss. Dr. LaGrand's book will provide comfort and hope to those bereaved who have experienced any kind of ADC. I highly recommend this book not only to the bereaved themselves, but to caregivers and counselors alike.

—Catherine M. Sanders, Ph.D., Executive Director
The Center for the Study of Separation and Loss
Author of *Grief: The Mourning After*

This book makes a significant contribution toward both enlarging our understanding of bereavement and validating the experiences of the bereaved. In a careful, thoughtful way, LaGrand reminds us of the many ways we try to make sense of loss and maintain a spiritual connection to the deceased. The author is to be commended for synthesizing a wealth of material and breaking new ground.

—Kenneth J. Doka. Ph.D.
Professor of Gerontology, College of New Rochelle
Author of *Disenfranchised Grief*

After-Death Communication *is a timely publication that will speak to many of us. In very straightforward, accessible writing, the author has put together a clear, well-reasoned book on a topic of widely and rapidly growing interest. LaGrand makes a solid case for multisensory experiences that will resonate to all but the most skeptical. A helpful final section addresses how we might deal with a bereaved person having an after-death communication experience.*

—J. Eugene Knott, Ph.D., Past President
Association for Death Education and Counseling

Dr. LaGrand's book presents a very thorough and balanced investigation of after-death communications. We highly recommend it to everyone who works with the terminally ill and the bereaved. Those who have had an ADC will certainly benefit from reading its many points of view.

—Bill Guggenheim and Judy Guggenheim
Authors of *Hello From Heaven!*

"I saw my dead son standing in the hallway near the stairs to his bedroom. He was wearing a favorite hat. I wanted to believe he was happy."

In this moving and compassionate work, a pioneer in after-death communication (ADC) research guides you through one of the most astounding and empowering of human experiences. *After-Death Communication: Final Farewells* is based upon over ten years of solid research and is backed up by hundreds of documented case studies.

- Restore your hope and faith, and ease the process of mourning
- Learn how to assist and support someone who has an after-death contact
- Assess whether your own ADC experience was an authentic contact
- Explore the nine different types of contact experiences
- Learn how others have used their contact with a deceased loved one to heal their grief and go on with their lives
- Read documented case studies of after-death contact collected by an accredited bereavement counselor

About the Author

Louis E. LaGrand is Distinguished Service Professor Emeritus at the State University of New York, College at Potsdam, and Adjunct Professor of Health Careers at the Eastern Campus of Suffolk Community College.

A certified grief counselor as well as a trainer of hospice volunteers, he is the author of five books and numerous articles. His two most recent books, *Coping With Separation and Loss as a Young Adult* and *Changing Patterns of Human Existence*, are based on his ten-year study of the loss responses of youth. *After-Death Communication* is the result of over fifteen years' interest in the extraordinary experiences of the bereaved.

Dr. LaGrand is a founder and past president of the board of directors of Hospice of St. Lawrence Valley, Inc. and a member formerly on the board of directors the Association for Death Education and Counseling (ADEC). He is also a member of the Institute of Noetic Sciences, and of the American Society for Psychical Research. He presently serves on the bereavement team of Sarasota Memorial Hospital.

As a counselor, educator, lecturer, author, and media guest, Louis E. LaGrand brings the fruits of over thirty-five years of experience, research, and compassion to the lives of those who mourn a loved one. With an open-mindedness often missing in his profession, he encourages clients and counselors alike to accept the healing value of communication with departed loved ones.

Dr. LaGrand and his wife Barbara reside in New York and Florida.

To Write to the Author

If you wish to contact the author or would like more information about this book, please write to the author in care of Llewellyn Worldwide, and we will forward your request. Both the author and publisher appreciate hearing from you. Llewellyn Worldwide cannot guarantee that every letter written to the author can be answered, but all will be forwarded. Please write to:

Louis E. LaGrand
c/o Llewellyn Worldwide
P. O. Box 64383, Dept. K405-7
St. Paul, MN 55164-0383, U.S.A.

Please enclose a self-addressed, stamped envelope for reply, or $1.00 to cover costs. If outside the U.S.A., enclose an international postal reply coupon.

After-Death Communication

FINAL FAREWELLS

Louis E. LaGrand, Ph.D.

1997
Llewellyn Publications
St.Paul, Minnesota, U.S.A. 55164-0383

FIRST EDITION
First Printing, 1997

Cover photograph: D. Jeanine Tiner
Cover design: Lynne Menturweck
Editing and book design: Ken Schubert

Library of Congress Cataloging-in-Publication Data

LaGrand, Louis E.
    After-death communication : final farewells / Louis E. LaGrand. --
1st ed.
        p.   cm.
    Includes bibliographical references and index.
    ISBN 1-56718-405-7 (trade paper)
    1. Death--Miscellanea. 2. Spiritualism. 3. Consolation.
I. Title.
BF1275.D2L34   1997
133.9'01'3--dc21   97-9262
                                                                    CIP

Printed in the United States of America

Llewellyn Publications
A Division of Llewellyn Worldwide, Ltd.
P.O. Box 64383, Dept. K405-7, St. Paul, MN 55164-0383, U.S.A.

To Steve

TABLE OF CONTENTS

Acknowledgments xi

Preface xiii

One. The Bereaved and the Extraordinary 1

Two. The Extraordinary Is Ordinary 9

Three. The Contact Experience During Grief 23

Four. The Intuitive Experience: Sensing the Presence of the Deceased 37

Five. Postmortem Presence: The Visual Experience 53

Six. Auditory Contacts: Hearing the Deceased 71

Seven. Connections Big and Small: Animals and Birds 87

Eight. The Experiences of Touch and Smell 99

Nine. Symbols and Symbolic Thinking 115

Ten. Third-Party Contacts 127

Eleven. Dreams of the Deceased 139

Twelve. Skeptics All 157

Thirteen. Helping a Person Who Experiences a Deceased Loved One 171

Author's Request 191

Endnotes 193

Suggested Reading 201

Resource Guide 203

Glossary 209

Index 213

Permissions 217

ACKNOWLEDGMENTS

For anyone writing on a subject which has more than its fair share of skeptics, I heartily recommend surrounding yourself with as many people as possible who are open to viewpoints other than those considered conventional. While difficult to arrange or orchestrate, I have been fortunate to find people in my family and outside of it who have been generous with their patience, understanding, and willingness to discuss unconventional and inexplicable subjects which are easily denied or dismissed as irrelevant.

First and foremost, I owe a debt of gratitude to all those who willingly shared their treasured stories with me and allowed me to question them at length about details and personal meanings derived from their experiences. It is my hope that their openness will encourage others to view their extraordinary experiences with greater conviction and come to believe that they have truly received a gift.

I am indeed grateful to all those who read various parts of the manuscript and for their suggestions, especially Professor Darryl Crase of the Department of Human Movement Sciences and Education at The University of Memphis; Dr. Helen B. Tulis; Dr. Norman Licht; Beverly Christianson of the Cutchogue Public Library; Professor Dan Giancola of the Eastern Campus of Suffolk Community College; Professor Jan Londraville of the Department of English at the State University of New York College at Potsdam; and Kathy LaClair of the Crumb Memorial Library at the State University of New York College at Potsdam.

Also, special thanks to Elisabeth Kubler-Ross; Reverend Andrew Greeley; Jo Coudert; Joan Wester Anderson; John Bramblett; Richard Morsilli; Dennis McCarthy; Jane Nichols; Andrew MacKenzie; Ken Czillinger; Barbara Bartocci; Tom Hurley; Francis Vaughan; Willis Harman, President of the Institute of Noetic Sciences; and Professor David Fontana, President of the British Psychological Society.

Most of all, I am indebted to my family, who has encouraged me in this project from the beginning, and especially my wife and best friend Barbara.

What Is After-Death Communication?

After-Death Communication (ADC) is an exciting new field of research which focuses on a variety of extraordinary experiences in which a person believes he or she has been spontaneously contacted by a deceased loved one. It is important to emphasize that the living person is not actively seeking to make contact with the deceased; the experience does not in any way involve a psychic. Instead, it is the deceased (or the unconscious or perhaps a Supreme Being) who seems to reach out to the bereaved and in doing so provides much-needed comfort and solace. Although a contact experience may occur at any time, it commonly takes place when one is grieving the death of a loved one and becomes the basis for the bereaved person to deal with the loss and go on with life.

ADCs include sensing the presence of the deceased, feeling a touch, smelling a fragrance, hearing the voice or seeing the deceased, and meeting the loved one in a vision or dream. Messages are also received in symbolic ways, such as finding an object associated with the deceased, unusual appearances or behavior of birds and animals, or other unexplainable happenings which occur at or shortly after the moment of death. Several combinations of the above phenomena may occur within weeks of the death or over a period of years.

ADCs have a long and eventful history, but the nature of the experience has caused many who feel they have had contact with the deceased to maintain their silence. They seldom share the experience with others out of fear that they would be considered in need of professional help. It is only recently, with the openness displayed toward miracles, the paranormal, and near-death experiences, that people have been willing to speak about these helpful contacts. Andrew Greeley, the well-known author and researcher at the National Opinion Research Center, found that 42% of adults responded in the affirmative when asked whether they "felt as though you were really in touch with someone who had died." (This figure does not include children who also report the experience.) It is estimated that nearly fifty million people have had a contact experience. New interest in the phenomena has skyrocketed in both the general public and in professional caregiving circles.

ONE

The Bereaved and the Extraordinary

*That almost two-thirds of the widows in the American popula-
tion have had some "contact" with a dead person (presumably
their spouses) is perhaps less surprising than the fact that two-
fifths of the population who are not widowed also report such
contact.*
— Andrew M. Greeley in "Hallucinations Among the Widowed"
Sociology and Social Research 73, October 1988

*We have already seen in earlier chapters how the experiencing
of the dead for people in antiquity seems to have been a very
much more natural and accepted phenomena than for ourselves; the greater the development of civilization, the more this
faculty faded.*
— Ian Wilson in *The After-Death Experience*

"I saw my son standing in the hallway near the stairs to his bedroom," she said
haltingly. "He was wearing a favorite hat. I wanted to believe he was happy."

At that moment, I was in the home of Mrs. Lucas, listening to a grieving
mother whose thirty-four-year-old son had died of AIDS ten days earlier. Having
developed a warm, trusting relationship over many years, and having visited with
her and her son several times during his illness, I felt comfortable in her presence.
Now, she wore the drawn look of a combat soldier who had just returned from an
extended tour of duty on the front lines. But though she was clearly exhausted,
she was calm and collected as she told me what else he was wearing on that
eventful evening. As she spoke, her steel gray eyes carefully searched my own for
any hint of disbelief.

Naturally, I wondered if she really saw her deceased son. If it was true, what
had caused it? Had she hallucinated as a result of the medication she had been

taking? Was it possibly a sign of divine intervention? A projection from Mrs. Lucas' subconscious mind? It might even have been her subjective imagination at work or plain old wishful thinking. I could have summarily dismissed Mrs. Lucas' experience, and at worst been called a skeptic by a true believer in After-Death Communication (ADC).

But then, if I had to explain what had taken place between this mother and her son, I would note that such experiences are not uncommon and seem to be part of the hidden lives of many bereaved people. I was not astonished by her remarks because I regularly ask the bereaved if they have had any unusual experiences involving their deceased loved ones, and have found that this is often the case. The experiences of these people are the core of *After-Death Communication* and the subject of the chapters that follow.

Readers will find that this book explores several categories of ADC. The incident I have described is only one of nine types of extraordinary phenomena that appear with surprising regularity. And that is a major reason I have written this book—to assist those who are mourning and believe they have had a contact experience with a loved one who has died. As a family member, friend, or relative, it is quite likely, sooner or later, that you will be confronted by someone you care about who is grieving and reports an extraordinary encounter relating to a deceased loved one. It would be natural for you to assume this person is being consumed by grief and the emotions accompanying loss. But there is mounting evidence that calls this common assumption into question.

So whether you are a concerned friend or family member, or an interested caregiver curious about how the deceased seem to help survivors, you will find that After-Death Communication is a subject rich in resources serving to affirm life, create new beginnings, gently assist the bereaved in letting go of the past, and open a window to the future.

How to Use this Book

Although I have tried to sequence the information, there is no problem if you wish to jump ahead to read various sections of this book. In fact, I encourage it. You can always go back later and read the book in its entirety. Therefore, if you are one of the millions who have had an extraordinary experience involving a deceased loved one and want to find out more about others who have had similar experiences, start with Chapter Four, "The Intuitive Experience." Chapters Four through Eleven deal with a wide range of unusual experiences, as well as some conventional (and not so conventional) explanations for their occurrence.

If a relative, friend, or someone in your immediate family thinks he has had a contact experience and you are unsure of what to believe, or if you are a person who neither denies nor affirms the existence of such phenomena, begin with Chapter Twelve, "Skeptics All." Then follow with Chapter Two, "The Extraordinary is Ordinary." These two chapters will help you sort out your thoughts about extraordinary experiences. They will also moderate the exaggerated cultural view of the unusual and place it in a healthier supportive context.

Should you feel comfortable with your present views on extraordinary phenomena but have little or no insight into the grief process and how the contact experience unfolds, start your reading with Chapter Three, "The Contact Experience During Grief." Here you will find a brief explanation of what to expect from someone who is dealing with a major loss, insights on the individuality of grief, and thoughts on how an extraordinary experience can play a key role in the coping process.

Chapter Thirteen, "Helping a Person Who Experiences a Deceased Loved One" will assist in providing support for anyone who has trusted you with their unusual encounter. It will discuss ways to help the person evaluate what has taken place and decide whether there are normal physical causes to explain it or if it may be a valid spiritual experience with important insights for the mourner. Here you will also learn the details of how I responded to Mrs. Lucas' description of seeing her son.

Finally, as time permits, it is a good idea to re-read various sections to refresh your memory, then discuss the material with a trusted friend. In this way, you can often gain new insights into the meaning of the experience while strengthening existing beliefs. In any event, you will be better prepared to help yourself or another who is in need of guidance.

The Importance of the Contact Experience

During the past fifteen years, I have been frequently surprised, and sometimes awed, by the numerous ADC encounters involving deceased loved ones. Clients, students, and colleagues have shared their grief with me, and often their unusual stories as well. I have found that their ADC experiences engaged the senses of sight, hearing, touch, and smell as well as the intuitive faculties, sometimes referred to as our "sixth sense." Each story stirred my curiosity and caused me to reevaluate my beliefs about the meanings of these encounters.

Plainly, the magnitude of behavioral changes that took place in the bereaved were immediate and difficult to ignore. Their unexpected contact provided them with a sense of comfort—in many cases, a new awareness and profound peace. The contact also marked a turning point in the mourning process. Grief and the contact experience had become attitudinal forces for integrating major loss into their lives. You may think I am exaggerating the importance of the contact experience: I only wish there were words to portray its meaning to the bereaved.

It may interest you to know that many bereaved people have also had dreams of the deceased which, when openly discussed, bring healthy changes in their mourning. Unusually vivid and lifelike, the dream is often interpreted by the dreamer that the loved one is in good health and survivors should not worry about him or her. Strikingly, a wide variety of extraordinary experiences have not only brought about dramatic changes in the course of one's grief, but have even inspired survivors to accept their tragic losses and begin new lives of hope and fulfillment.

Despite such encouraging effects, relatively little attention has been given to the extraordinary experiences of survivors in the literature on grief. For the most part, the boundaries of reality are still defined by what we think we know about the laws of nature and our vast universe. Some books on bereavement fail to mention contacts with the deceased in any context. By contrast, much time and attention has been given to the emotions of anger, guilt, and depression as they shape the grief response. These emotions are shown to be common responses to loss and are eventually dealt with, if the grief is not complicated by other factors such as over-dependence on the deceased loved one. Paradoxically, the contact experience can reduce (and in some cases eliminate) the intensity of these very emotions.

In spite of the lack of attention, ADCs frequently become a hidden source of immense anxiety when the bereaved do not feel secure in talking about their experiences and are left to themselves to ponder the meaning of the encounter. Even so, the contact experience can still be an immense springboard to accepting change, reordering priorities; even bringing one to a meaningful reconciliation with grief and traumatic loss because of the creation of a healthy inner representation of the deceased.

Not surprisingly, most social scientists and educators are of the opinion that various contact experiences of the bereaved generally play an insignificant role, usually as part of the yearning and searching phase of grief.[1,2] ADC is considered to occur primarily with widows and parents of deceased children, and is easily explained away as part of the inability of survivors to let go of the deceased early in the grief process. Regrettably, however, there are all too many instances in which the bereaved need opportunities to freely express and discuss the reality of their unusual encounters. Such discussions about the extraordinary need not be limited to the offices of professional counselors. Indeed, all members of the bereaved's support systems—especially family members and friends—should be prepared for the possibility of emotion-filled exchanges on the topic. These exchanges should be welcomed, assuming you understand the variety of contact experiences that can occur and have not prejudged the mourner or the experience.

Some support persons tend to waver in their beliefs about their ability to provide comfort when confronted with a "story" they deem eerie or mysterious. They become fearful of the bereaved even to the point of questioning their sanity. But that scenario need not happen if family members and friends are aware that the event is common and recognize its potential for comforting the bereaved. As might be expected, mourners find increased trust, support, and solace when they are tactfully encouraged at the appropriate time to share the extraordinary experience with a non-judgmental listener who is familiar with these events. Such a constructive dialogue will strengthen their belief. Consequently, a fundamental practical result ensues—the strengthening of bonds between mourners and their support systems—a condition that all who help survivors agree is desirable.

For instance, while collecting data for this book, I was interviewing a woman who had had an unusual experience. Near the close of our conversation she said, "You know, I feel better already. I can talk to you about this knowing you won't put me down." I had, by my actions, simply acknowledged that the event could possibly have occurred (not whether it was real or imagined), and she responded as though a huge weight had been lifted from her shoulders.

> Almost all societies, it seems, believe that, despite a bodily death, the person not only lives on but continues his relationships with the living, at least for a time. In many cultures these relationships are conceived as wholly beneficial.
> —J. Bowlby, "Loss," Attachment & Loss, Vol. 3
> New York: Basic Books, 1980.

In our journey, there are numerous questions to ponder which may sometimes lead us to places that lack neatly packaged answers. Consider with me, in succeeding chapters, such questions as the following: Is searching behavior (that time of pining and hoping for the return of the loved one) the sole reason behind the many extraordinary events that take place? Should your bereaved friend or relative be encouraged to accept the contact experience as a positive message, i.e. to go on with life? And if the experience is a negative one, how should it be dealt with? Additional pressing queries to be addressed are as follows:

- Should you tell a bereaved person to look for signs that the deceased loved one is okay?
- Should the bereaved be told to pray for such indicators?
- Should the experience be discounted or minimized and explained only in scientific terms?

Finally, we have to confront two vexing issues. Is maintaining a relationship with the deceased, based on an unusual contact, detrimental to concluding the work of readjusting to life without the loved one? And why is it that all mourners do not have the experience?

Let me emphasize at the outset that I have not teethed on the extraordinary, the unusual, or paranormal phenomena: I have had no yen for the unfamiliar or the unknown. In fact, for the greater part of my professional life I could, at best, be classified as a hopeful skeptic. I assumed, like many others in my profession, that the phenomena of experiencing the presence of the deceased in any manner or form was clearly the result of the stress of bereavement—until I began to hear and see startling results which could not be conveniently explained away as merely auditory or visual hallucinations. Perhaps, as some people believe, they were natural happenings given the circumstances under which they occur.

I should tell you that I have been trained in the scientific method and hold a dutiful respect for science. It has brought us a long way—but not far enough, because its method of exclusive reliance on the five senses for gathering data is constrictive to the rich evidence of subjective experience. Thus, science rules out information which is not physically verifiable—and most contact experiences are richly spiritual rather than physical. Still, there is room for science and the spirit to accommodate each other. In particular, there is a pressing need for family members, caregivers, and educators to understand contact phenomena exclusively from the point of view of the grieving survivor.

Lest this discussion appear to be overly optimistic, or a product of my own wish fulfillment, I must tell you that I have grieved the deaths of my parents, a brother who died of cancer, my younger sister, my infant daughter (from Sudden Infant Death Syndrome), and a number of friends, but I have not had an extraordinary encounter with any of them. For that matter, I have never had a paranormal or mystical experience of any kind.

So how did this book evolve? *After-Death Communication: Final Farewells* is the product of four major pursuits. First, the collection of written reports from bereaved survivors over the past decade. Second, my clinical experience as a grief counselor in private practice. Third, discussions with colleagues and experts in the bereavement field, who if pressed, will tell you many unusual stories about clients—which (off the record) they do not classify as simply illusions. And fourth, an examination of the literature, including articles and biographies, which deals with the subject of ADC.

Finding Meaning in Death

As anyone who has suffered the loss of a loved one knows, the search for meaning is an integral part of the grief process.[3] Esoteric deliberations frequently provide a sense of meaning and reassurance for the survivor. In particular, most survivors, consciously or unconsciously, search for answers to questions like: "Why did my loved one have to die? Why did this have to happen to me? How could God allow this to happen?" Values and beliefs are challenged. Plausible answers to such puzzling philosophical or theological questions, as well as new conceptions of life and death, have often been triggered by conversations about the survivor's unexpected experience.

The preceding is not meant to imply that a support person should use any discussion of the topic as an opportunity to influence the bereaved to adopt a specific belief. However, I have seen many individuals who have used their alleged contact with the deceased to accept the loved one's death, change their perceptions of reality, strengthen their faith, or reinforce their belief that they will see their loved ones again. The many case studies in this book attest to that very fact. Life is no longer ordinary for grieving survivors—it takes on new significance.

Oddly enough, scientific "wisdom" suggests that all extraordinary phenomena experienced by the bereaved are merely imaginative, coincidences, or at best the product of hallucinations and misperceptions.[4,5,6] That is, the bereaved are seeing, hearing, feeling, and sensing things that clearly do not exist. So much of what we will be talking about makes little sense in rational terms to the scientific community, even though the phenomena occur consistently among the bereaved. Is it wise to explain away all such encounters and their comforting after-effects as wishful thinking or figments of an imagination strained by tragedy of loss?

My main point is this: There are many uplifting thoughts which evolve from a contact experience (whether provable or not) that can help a mourner during the difficult transition period. However, benefits often hinge on whether or not support persons can overcome the monumental conceptual barriers which isolate the contact experience as an aberration or a sign of instability. People who say they have seen or conversed with their deceased loved ones, or have received a sign that they live on, are not in need of professional assistance. In general, their experiences are not myth or folk tales. The truth may be that we do a great disservice to them by minimizing and wasting such an important opportunity to help them better cope with adversity.

So much for the negatives. In the chapters that follow, this book will offer alternative explanations to the question of origin or cause of the experience. It will do so by exploring the extraordinary through the eyes of the bereaved, and will consider their interpretations and suggestions with greater validity than is usually the case. Accordingly, we will examine nine manifestations of the extraordinary in the lives of the bereaved, the messages conveyed, and the experience's effects on the lives of the grief-stricken.

Through the years, it has become clear to me that there is a great need for education about this phenomena at all age levels; that it should be taken seriously; that the cloak of psychological insignificance should be cast aside; that mourners and their support networks should openly discuss the experience when it occurs. Undeniably, the main reasons for such an adventure may well be the greater insight to be gained with regard to who we are, how we fit into the vast and wondrous universe in which we live, and whether consciousness survives bodily death. More significantly, however, the immediate knowledge gained will be a source of hope and comfort for many grieving individuals.

So let's begin our journey by turning to the task of normalizing the extraordinary. Although we have been taught that extraordinary phenomena (like the emperor's new clothes) do not exist, there is really too much evidence to the contrary.

TWO

The Extraordinary Is Ordinary

. . . some of the most important modern studies indicate that people do have experiences from outside the space-time world and that these do not represent regression or mental deterioration.
—Morton T. Kelsey in *The Other Side of Silence*

Evidence of seemingly paranormal goings-on come in from all over—from many different fields, from many different belief systems, and from all corners of the world. . . . What we are learning about paranormal phenomena flies in the face of everything we have been taught about the nature of reality.
—Bernard Gittelson in *Intangible Evidence*

Consider the following contact experiences: one visual, one through a dream, and one through the sense of touch. They are typical of the kinds of extraordinary events that take place in the lives of the bereaved. All three individuals are convinced—as I am—that the experiences occurred as they have said.

The Dog and I Saw Him

Eighteen-year-old "Maria" (in the interests of confidentiality, names and places have been changed when a first name is used) was grieving the unexpected death of her father Frank, who had been killed two weeks before in a freak industrial accident. She lived with her mother and brother in a two-story colonial house in a rural section of northern Maine. One evening, within two weeks of his death, she walked into the living room after helping her mother clean up the supper dishes when it happened. "I came into the living room and there was my father just standing there," she said, as wide-eyed as the day it happened. "I was startled. My dog saw him too and started barking as he always did when my father came home. In an instant he was gone and the dog went over to the spot where

9

dad had been standing and kept sniffing around for him. I was overwhelmed but I was not scared."

Mom, I'm Okay

Jill's daughter died after a long and painful illness caused by a form of lymphocyte cancer. Her death was the most devastating catastrophe Jill had ever faced, even though she had been told by the family physician to expect the worst. Her grief was intense and prolonged, as it so often is when a child dies. Children are supposed to bury their parents, she thought; parents are not supposed to bury their children.

The intensity of her anguish and pain was nearly unbearable. Then one night she had a dream, unlike any dream she had ever experienced. Her daughter appeared to her, radiant, healthy, and happy. "Mom, I'm okay. Everything is fine. Please don't grieve for me." On awakening, she was filled with joy and new-found energy. The message was a gigantic turning point in accepting the loss of her beloved Sara. Since that experience, she has sensed the presence of her daughter on several occasions.

I Felt His Hand on My Left Shoulder

Sal was twenty-three years old when his grandfather died. They had gone fishing and boating together for years, and Sal's grandfather had taught Sal a great many things about the ocean and respect for the environment. In fact, his grandfather had been like a second father to him, and his death had left a great void in Sal's life—it was inconceivable that he was gone. But Sal's grief took an unexpected turn after the following experience.

> I was alone crying over the death of my grandfather; I believe it was many days after the funeral. I was in my bedroom sitting on the floor, my back against a wall, wanting him back. All of a sudden I felt his hand on my left shoulder—I could feel the weight of it and the warmth. I immediately stopped crying: I felt secure again and warm inside. Somehow, with that brief respite I was able to let him go. I believe my grandfather wanted me to be okay; he let me know he was only in another dimension.

Such unusual experiences—sudden, overwhelming, healing—have been reported by millions of people throughout the world. Thousands of others go unreported because of the survivor's fear of being labeled emotionally unstable. Still, these experiences are part of the mosaic of extraordinary events which occur daily around the globe, something that should not be taken lightly.

Could it be possible that some part of us—call it consciousness, the spirit, the soul or whatever—is indestructible, goes on forever, and continues to experience and be experienced by the living? This belief, more than an echo of the distant past, is held by millions of people and certainly is not of modern origin. Some of the archeological digs in Europe and Asia have turned up 10,000-year-old human remains accompanied by artifacts which were to be used in another life, to sustain the deceased on their visits to the living, or on the journey to a new existence. King Tutankhamen (c.1361–1351 B.C.), for example, whose tomb was found almost intact in 1922, had been buried with a wealth of objects to sustain him in a continued existence. That the living can interact with their deceased loved ones may be the oldest belief in the memory banks of humanity.[1]

The ancients looked to their dreams and their dead for guidance and prophecy. The Koran states that dreams that bring good news are the truest of all. And of course, dreams have for centuries conveyed inspiration to scientists, musicians, inventors, and mourners alike. The results of these dreams include theories, beautiful sonatas, time-saving machines, and changes in how one views the world. In similar fashion, dreams are one of the most frequent modes of communication between survivors and their deceased loved ones. Many religions are replete with history and decision-making based on information received in dreams. Is it possible that the dead are able to help the living and one means of contact is the dream state or are contact experiences simply a function of the overactive mind? In any case, the experience can be beneficial to the bereaved.

In 1621, Robert Burton, in *The Anatomy of Melancholy* wrote the following about unusual experiences in the symptoms of grief exhibited by widows, maids, and nuns: "Some think they see visions, confer with spirits and devils ...." And elsewhere, "... They think they see their dead friends continually in their eyes, observantes imagines...."[2] He concluded that those suffering from melancholy "are almost distracted, mad or stupid for the time, and by fits." While the descriptive language in the modern literature on unusual experiences of the bereaved is somewhat toned down, the essential belief that such experiences are essentially peripheral distractions still exists. For example, in Dr. Beverley Raphael's *Anatomy of Bereavement*, contact experiences are referred to as follows: "These perceptual misinterpretations reflect the intense longing and, like dreams, are a source of wish fulfillment."[3] "Perceptual misinterpretations" is easier to take than "mad or stupid."

The truth, it has been said, is the first casualty of war. And, no doubt, in the endless confrontation between science and the believers in extraordinary phenomena, the truth seems to have slipped away in the conflict. Just ask those who have been visited by a deceased loved one in a dream or have spoken to the deceased who was sitting on the edge of their bed. They will tell you that science says it could not have happened—it had to be the result of internal disorganization and the "need" to maintain contact with the deceased. "But it did happen and it has changed my life," they will respond. The improbable becomes real, the impossible possible. Countless reports of unusual assistance from the deceased abound. A sense of relief fills the air. A new lease on life is found.

Unfortunately, our misconceptions about science and the extraordinary keep us from benefiting from both. But maybe, just maybe, science isn't as on top of the issue as it should be. And for good reason—the scientific method does not lend itself well to examining spontaneous events or intuitive faculties, especially unexpected events associated with grieving survivors or information that is transmitted by means that are unconventional and unexplainable.

Over half a century ago, Sir Arthur Eddington, Professor of Astronomy at Cambridge University, reflected on the incompatibility between the scientific method and unexplainable phenomena. He noted that two faculties of consciousness reveal two quite different perceptions of reality. On the one hand, our eyes are the basis for judging what is considered significant or insignificant. This use of sight could be described as an act of faith—we believe what our eyes tell us is in the here and now. On the other hand, by a similar determination, the mystic utilizes another faculty of consciousness which highlights another reality outside the boundaries of space and time. Although both perceptions originate from consciousness, there is a vast difference in the methods that determine actual existence. He concluded that "It would be wrong to condemn alleged knowledge of the unseen world because it is unable to follow the lines of deduction laid down by science as appropriate to the seen world; but inevitably the two kinds of knowledge are compared, and I think the challenge to a comparison does not come wholly from the scientists."[4]

The highly speculative nature of the unseen does not diminish the fact that extraordinary phenomena and our intuitive faculties have always played major roles in the development of civilizations and their philosophies. Nowhere is this more apparent than in extraordinary religious revelations. Christianity, Judaism, and Islam, for example, flourished in part through visions, miracles, and apparitions. The apostles were witnesses to a variety of extraordinary phenomena. Both Buddha and Mohammed had paranormal experiences before launching on their religious ministries. Hunches, the creative unconscious, intuitive wisdom—all agents of non-physical reality—continue to aid in the growth of the individual and the understanding of the mysteries of the universe.

Albert Einstein, famous author of the Theory of Relativity, Otto Loewi, who showed that nerve impulses were both electrical and chemical in origin, and Friedrich August von Kekule, the Flemish Professor of Chemistry, whose visions revolutionized chemistry, all had extraordinary episodes preceding their discoveries. Here is a partial description of Kekule's initial vision of molecules which resulted in establishing that benzene has a "ring" structure. He was riding on a streetcar and dozed off:

> *I fell into a reverie, and lo! the atoms were gamboling before my eyes... Now, however, I saw how, frequently, two smaller atoms united to form a pair; how a larger one embraced two smaller ones; how still larger ones kept hold of three or even four of the smaller; whilst the whole kept whirling in a giddy dance. I saw how the larger ones formed a chain.*[5]

Although this description of Kukele's dreamlike state reads more like someone who is hallucinating, it was the beginning of a discovery (coupled with other dreams that he had) that brought great insight in understanding the molecular building blocks of benzene. It was considered by many to be one of the greatest discoveries in the field of chemistry up to that time.

Alfred Ribi, Director of the C. G. Jung Institute, in Zurich looks at our intuitive abilities this way: "Intuition is a function kept outside of science, but only as long as you are not aware that most of the creative investigations in science are instigated by intuition."[6]

Welcome to the Extraordinary Wars. There is much wisdom in Ribi's words, even though most of us are brought up to believe that either a thing can be explained in a causal and rational way, or it does not exist. Be assured that hunches, non-physical reality, and intuition are as much a part of the human condition and the extraordinary as they are of science. They are all integral factors in the development of civilizations.

Defining the Extraordinary

Since the extraordinary means so many different things to professionals and non-professionals alike, it is prudent to examine the various definitions of the concept and then define how I intend to use the term. First of all, I must emphasize that there is a great lack of standardized terminology to describe the unusual experiences of the bereaved. Some people believe the phenomena is natural, others supernatural or spiritual, and still others that it is psychic or paranormal. Consequently, everyone uses words and phrases that have their own personal meaning. Because there appears to be an interface of the spiritual and the psychic realms, we will examine two words: *extraordinary* and *paranormal*.

The word *extraordinary* is defined as "beyond what is ordinary, out of the regular or established order." Synonyms for the word are uncommon, exceptional, inconceivable, incredible, and phenomenal. What some of the bereaved experience is all of that and more, for at times these synonyms would be apt descriptions of ADC phenomena. If you consult a dictionary of psychology, a common definition of the paranormal states essentially that it is an event which occurs "along side of or beyond the normal" or a "claimed occurrence of an event or perception without scientific explanation." In short, paranormal or extraordinary events have no logical explanations which fit the well-established scientific world view. The typical definition of the paranormal includes examples such as ESP (extrasensory perception), which is the ability to communicate in ways other than using normal sensory faculties.

ESP commonly includes clairvoyance, telepathy, and precognition. Clairvoyance is the ability to acquire information about objects or events at great distances as they are unfolding; that is, to look ahead and see by means not involving the known senses. Telepathy (originally called thought transference) is usually defined as the transmission of information between two people by some means other than by normal sensory perception. This is one commonly accepted explanation for many ADC exchanges. Precognition is the ability to randomly predict the future in a way other than through logical inference. A fourth psychic ability, psychokinesis, is the use of the mind to affect matter as in moving objects, inducing rapid healing, producing an image on unexposed film, or affecting the electrical circuits of machinery. These four processes are collectively referred to as psi phenomena. Psi is the twenty-third letter in the Greek alphabet, and is commonly used in the scientific community to indicate the unknown.

The existence of psychic abilities as aspects of the human mind have caused a great deal of conflict and confusion among scientists simply because in the context of scientific materialism, psi cannot be explained by the electrical circuitry or biological structure of the brain. These abilities may act like physical forces, but they are not physical forces. Nor do they seem to be limited by space or time. They somehow exist apart from the brain. Or as Charles Tart, Professor of Psychology at the University of California at Davis and a pioneer researcher in altered states of consciousness put it: "Mind does not equal brain."[7] Such a concept is not new in scientific circles. In the 1970s, Wilder Penfield, the physician-philosopher and father of neurosurgery, published *The Mystery of the Mind*, in which he argued that some aspects of the mind are independent of the brain.[8] After fifty years of studying the brain he concluded that there is what could be called a spirit. Of course, such a reversal from the materialistic point of view he had previously espoused drew much criticism from colleagues and friends alike. However, there is mounting evidence to suggest that mind may be primary and brain secondary in all creative functioning and not the other way around, as has been taught for years.

In this framework, our definitions of what is extraordinary or paranormal are expanding. The paranormal experience is defined by others to include déjà vu experiences (the feeling you are somewhere you have been before, but there is no way you could have been there), mystical experiences (coming into contact with a unifying force, with a Presence, the Absolute, with God), and contact with the dead experiences (which includes hearing the deceased, post-mortem presence, and a host of other interactions). Once more, the definition I have just given for mystical experiences is the classical description. Modern use of the term includes almost any encounter which brings about a spiritual experience as interpreted by the person reporting the situation. Some of these experiences are a result of "becoming one with nature" or in finding relief from stress.[9]

It is not necessary here to examine a whole range of other ostensibly paranormal phenomena such as levitation, remote viewing, near death experiences, and faith healing, to name a few. There is a worldwide cornucopia of extraordinary phenomena that is not easy to simply explain it all away as the work of crazies, charlatans, or plain dishonest types.

I could go on with other difficult-to-verify phenomena which often fall under the umbrella of the paranormal or extraordinary, but let's consider how I am using the terms in this book. By my definition, extraordinary experiences of the bereaved refers to the spontaneous contact by the deceased loved one of the survivor. That is, the survivor is not attempting to communicate with the deceased by any overt means, such as a seance. In no way are we talking about summoning spirits or the Spiritualism of the Victorian Age. The survivor is essentially a spectator, and experiences the deceased loved one either directly or indirectly by way of a sign, apparition, the senses, intuition or through a third party. I will usually refer to these experiences as contact experiences. Otherwise, I will indicate the general use of the terms "extraordinary," "paranormal," or "ADC" (After-Death Communication) where necessary.

Let me emphasize one point: The non-seeking behavior of the survivor is important to understand. Although survivors are under emotional duress and often have not been able to accept the deaths of their loved ones, they are not actively trying to engage the deceased at the time of the experience. However, some do pray for a sign that their loved one is all right. Yes, I am aware of the argument that it is precisely the survivor's refusal to accept the death which pre-cipitates the need to experience some indication that the person still lives. Nev-ertheless, most contact experiences occur spontaneously, without warning, and at times when the survivor is not thinking about the deceased; it is essentially a pleasant surprise helping the survivor rethink the loss experience.

> *Americans express a belief in the existence of paranormal, psy-chic, ghostly, and otherworldly experiences and dimensions to a surprising degree. These beliefs ... are almost as common among Americans who are deeply religious in a traditional sense as in those who are not.*

—George Gallup Jr. and Frank Newport
The Skeptical Inquirer, Winter 1991

Frequency of the Extraordinary and the Paranormal

Just how frequent is contact with the deceased experienced? Let us begin to answer this question by first looking at the frequency of extraordinary phenomena in general, and then turn to contact with the dead as our primary focus. Let me reassure you that I have no intention to present a typical academic review of the literature. However, a brief overview of some of the pertinent studies and major findings will be useful in establishing the universality and normalcy of what are generally considered to be sporadic oddities by the general public.

A considerable amount of research has been done on a national and interna-tional basis with regard to belief in the extraordinary and the incidence of para-normal phenomena experiences. In the early 1980s Erlendur Haraldsson, a psychologist at the University of Iceland, and his colleague Joop Houtkooper uncovered a widespread belief in and experience of psychic phenomena in thirteen countries in Europe and in the United States.[10] The 18,000-plus sample of respon-dents, all interviewed face to face, were drawn by standard sampling methods, and were representative of the adult populations of each participating country.

The findings were both impressive and unexpected. For example, in the U.S. and Italy, 60% of respondents reported some type of psychic experience (defined as telepathy, clairvoyance, and contact with the dead). Norway, at 24%, had the lowest number of people who made such claims. For Europe as a whole, nearly half of the people polled (46%) had one or more of the three types of occurrences. These figures are up from previous studies and may indicate that people are more willing to discuss their experiences under research conditions.

In 1987, Andrew Greeley (yes, that Andrew Greeley) and his colleagues, in a national survey conducted at the University of Chicago's National Opinion Research Council (NORC) found that two-thirds of all adults (67%) in the United States reported having experienced ESP.[11] Are all of these people in Europe and America deceiving themselves? Or is it possible that we have yet to discover a mode of communication that is inherent to everyone in the universe?

Let's turn now to the prevalence of reported contact with the dead. Prior to the Age of Enlightenment (1700–1800), the contact experience, along with occult practices, was considered part of received knowledge, and commonly accepted.[12] With the founding of the Society for Psychical Research (SPR) in 1882 in London, some of the earliest studies of the contact experience were to begin. The founding was a historical event, for it signaled specialization in the study of the paranormal.[13] The SPR and its American counterpart, the American Society for Psychical Research (ASPR), founded in Boston in 1882, attracted the leading physicists, philosophers, and psychologists of the times. William James, Sigmund Freud, F. W. H. Meyers, Sir William Barrett, Eleanor Sidgwick, Sir Oliver Lodge, Carl Jung, and the Cambridge University professor Henry Sidgwick all claimed membership at one time or another. The distinguished members reflect the rigorous methodology employed in research conducted by the SPR. Not to be overlooked is the fact that many members of the Society were also skeptics of the phenomena, adding to the organization's credibility. The first major study undertaken by the SPR was The Census on Hallucinations (in this study, hallucination was simply defined as sensory contact with an absent person). The project was international in scope. The major goal of the Census was to determine how many people had experienced sensory hallucinations while awake and in a sound state of mind, and under what conditions. The study was based on survey results from France, Great Britain, Germany, Russia, Italy, and the United States, and involved over 17,000 respondents.[14] Ten percent of those interviewed said they had had a hallucination while completely awake. They included visual, auditory, and the sense of touch contacts as well as the sense of presence of a person who could not be seen. Of particular note was that nearly twice as many apparitions of the living were reported as compared to the dead.[15]

In 1948, D. J. West published a report on a mass-observation questionnaire on hallucinations and found that 14% of his respondents reported one or more contacts.[16] Ten years later, Marris reported that 50% of the seventy-two young London widows he interviewed said they had experienced contact with their dead spouses.[17] In Japan, Yamamoto reported that all but two of twenty Japanese widows he and his colleagues interviewed had sensed the presence of their deceased husbands.[18] Back in the U.S. in the '70s, Palmer and Dennis, Kalish and Reynolds, and Greeley reported contact experiences of 16%, 17%, and 25% in their respective studies.[19,20,21] Greeley's study involved a representative national sample.

In one of the few in-depth studies, involving 227 widows and sixty-six widowers, Rees reported that almost half of the people interviewed had illusions or hallucinations of the dead spouse. These experiences lasted for many years. In addition, young widows and widowers were less likely to have the experience than those over forty, and the incidence of contact was particularly associated with a happy marriage and parenthood. The vast majority of respondents said they were helped by their contacts (82.4% who spoke to the deceased, 78% who visually hallucinated, 73% who sensed the deceased's presence, and 66.7% who thought they heard the deceased).[22]

Primary care physician P. Richard Olsen and associates interviewed forty-six widowed residents of two nursing homes in North Carolina.[23] In answer to the question, "Have you ever experienced your husband with you in any way since his death?" twenty-eight widows (61%) said "yes." Of the twenty-eight, twenty-two reported visual experiences, fourteen reported auditory experiences, six reported tactile experiences, nine said they had felt the presence of the deceased, and five said they talked with their husbands. Twenty-four of the twenty-eight widows who experienced a deceased spouse described it as a good experience.

In 1984, as part of NORC's General Social Survey, Greeley asked respondents how often they "felt as though you were really in touch with someone who had died."[24] Of 1,445 people polled, 42% said they had a contact experience. It is worthy of note that nearly two-thirds of the widows in the American population have indicated they have had a contact experience. Of equal significance is the fact that two-fifths of those who are not widowed but have experienced the death of a loved one also report the experience. This should not be lightly regarded.

Keeping in mind that the General Social Survey represents a probability sample of the American population, it is quite clear that a large number of people are reporting extraordinary experiences, whether they are real or not. And some of the smaller studies tend to back up the national study on a proportional basis. The overall numbers alone should merit a closer look at what is going on. In any event, the experience is not remote or trifling but is rather frequent.

Furthermore, it appears that people in countries with quite different cultural traditions about death and dying have similar contact experiences with the deceased. The event is normal, not strange or unusual as we are constantly encouraged to believe. Of particular significance is the observation that most individuals accept the experience as helpful.

Before turning to an examination of those who have such normal experiences, let us conclude our brief run of studies with Andrew Greeley's astute observation:

> *What has been "paranormal" is not only becoming normal in our time—it may also be health-giving.... That has not made the news welcome to the routine scientist. There's an understandable resistance to studying phenomena, however benign, whose nature we really don't understand.... It would be easier, certainly, to deny that these experiences exist. But the data show clearly that they do exist, that people experience them in great numbers—and that they could even change the nature of our society.*[25]

Some rather stimulating observations from a well-respected researcher who has no philosophical or religious ax to grind, only a sociological one.

Who Believes In and Experiences the Extraordinary?

At this point, it might be important to consider just who the individuals are who say they have experienced deceased loved ones. As a middle-aged woman once asked me: "Are these people kooks, religious fanatics, or just plain crazy?" Well, as you take a close look at the various populations involved in the studies you may be mildly surprised. Although some studies indicate that equal numbers of both sexes experience the event, the overall evidence suggests that more women report the event than men. Men may be more likely to dismiss the experience as purely imaginary, and more conscious of appearing strange by even discussing the subject. However, members of both sexes and all ages report the phenomena. Because many of the more recent studies have focused on widows, there is a tendency to think that women have the experience almost exclusively. Not so.

In my own collection of anecdotal data I have had students, nurses, housewives, college professors, secretaries, counselors, and others of various ages and both sexes who reported a contact experience. In fact, there is evidence that strongly suggests that the majority of those who have contact with the dead are people from all walks of life, both young and old, and not widowed.[26]

Types of Contact with the Dead

Over the years, I have catalogued nine types of contact experiences. I will briefly introduce them here and follow with a short description of each. In succeeding chapters, each will be discussed at length. This classification is based on the contact of the bereaved person by the deceased.

- The Intuitive Experience
- Postmortem Presence
- Auditory Contacts
- The Presence of Birds and Animals
- Tactile Experience
- The Sense of Smell or Olfactory Experience
- Symbols and Signs
- Third-Party Experiences
- Dreams of the Deceased

The Intuitive Experience. This experience involves a feeling that the deceased is present and in some instances watching over the survivor. It may occur when a survivor is alone or with others. Several mourners may sense the presence at the same time. Sometimes the presence is sensed in conjunction with the appearance of an insect or animal in an unusual place. It could occur with a wild animal appearing in one's backyard for the first time or a butterfly coming to rest on one's chair or table.

Postmortem Presence. This experience is visually oriented, and commonly involves seeing the deceased sitting in his or her favorite chair or standing in a familiar place within the house. It has also been reported by those who have experienced the deceased immediately after death when the survivor has not yet been notified of the death. Sometimes the deceased is seen by more than one person and in different places.

Auditory Contacts. Sound-based experiences occur in a variety of settings in which the survivor may hear the footsteps, breathing, or laughter of the person who died. In some instances, a loved one and the deceased carry on a conversation. It may also involve hearing a door opening at a time when the person normally came home, or the actual voice giving encouragement, advice, or warnings. It may be music associated with the deceased, or in some instances communication may occur without words being spoken.

Birds and Animals. These creatures are common means through which the deceased may communicate with a survivor. Usually, such a bird or animal was of particular interest to the deceased, and its presence or behavior at an unusual time or place is interpreted as an indicator of a comforting message. Sometimes it is interpreted as an answer to a prayer.

Tactile Experiences. Touch-based contacts take the form of an embrace, the feeling of a touch, or the clasping of hands. Often the Tactile Experience is combined with verbal or nonverbal communication as well as being a major component in vivid dreams.

The Sense of Smell Experience. This is usually associated with the scent of something the deceased wore, such as perfume, cologne, or a flower. Sometimes, the odor of delicious baked goods that the deceased used to make fills the room when there is no source of the food odor to be found. Many other aromas associated with the deceased such as pipe tobacco or bath powder may be involved.

Symbols and Signs. Objects such as clocks, rainbows, or personal objects of the deceased are commonly involved with the contact experience. Their presence or absence at a particular time is interpreted as a communication from the deceased or from God. The object could be a Christmas ornament, a sand dollar, a picture frame found in an unusual place, or a possession of the deceased.

Third-Party Experiences. These involve a third person who has little or no information about the relationship between the survivor and the deceased, but becomes a primary messenger to the survivor. Often the third person is a young child, and his or her behavior conveys a meaningful message to the bereaved. In some situations, a near-death experience results in helping a survivor when the loved one finally dies.

Dreams of the Deceased. Such dreams are common ways in which survivors receive information that the deceased is all right, and that the survivor should not worry. These dreams are vivid and have a particular quality quite unlike a normal dream. Sometimes several people will have the same or a similar dream about the same deceased person.

Birds and animals as well as symbols are in some respects indirect contacts. That is, the deceased are not seen or heard, but the circumstances of the contact reflect thoughts, feelings or behaviors associated with the deceased. Nevertheless, they can provide information which is as supportive to the bereaved as any of the direct contacts. Often dismissed by empiricists as coincidence or chance events, indirect contacts forge links to the deceased which sustain survivors throughout the course of their grief work, and in some cases for the rest of their lives.

There are probably as many variations of these nine categories of contact experiences as there are mourners, and many contact experiences include a combination of direct or/or indirect contacts. Although many specialists on grief would say that all of the above are essentially the products of searching behavior (looking for the deceased to return, coupled with the refusal to give up the past), most of those who experience a contact say they were not consciously looking for a return or a message in the form in which they received it.

At this point a reasonable query presents itself. In what contexts do these contact experiences occur? This naturally brings us to the grief process and an examination of when the experience takes place. We begin the next chapter by focusing on the important resource for recovery from loss which grief represents and then examine how the contact experience frequently evolves.

THREE

The Contact Experience During Grief

Just as one might have to turn the whole body around in order that the eyes should see the light instead of darkness, so the entire soul must be turned away from this changing world until its eye can bear to contemplate reality.

—Plato

Hallucinations of both the visual type and the auditory type are included in this list of normal behaviors because hallucinations are a frequent experience of the bereaved....With all of the recent interest in mysticism and spirituality, it is interesting to speculate on whether these are really hallucinations or possibly some other kind of metaphysical phenomena.

—J. William Worden in
Grief Counseling and Grief Therapy

What is grief? Grief is the universal human response to loss. Although still considered by some as a sign of weakness, it is a natural, healthy, yet painful internal process. More specifically, grief is the emotional and physical response to any meaningful loss or change. It is significant that we emphasize the physical component, because every cell in the body is affected by our emotions. In fact, there is impressive evidence that over a period of time the continuous stress of grief compromises the immune system. Or, as medical researcher and physician Dr. Irving Oyle offers: "You cannot have a single thought in your head which is not instantaneously translated into a bodily sensation. If you have a pessimistic or a catatoxic thought, you make adrenaline instantaneously. You have a worried or frightened thought, you get a squirt of adrenaline. That's the connection between mind and matter."[1] Thus, grief affects our entire being.

A cursory examination of grief shows that we grieve over many things besides the death of a loved one. For example, the breakup of a love relationship, the loss of a job, the destruction of a home by fire or natural disaster, a geographical move, the incarceration of a loved one, a divorce—these and other losses can bring intense grief. Ultimately, all relationships end in loss and separation. Life and grief are inseparable.

The grief process has always been an integral part of dealing with change, and at root it is a sign of caring. But although it is a normal occurrence—as well as a gift for dealing with all of the abrupt changes and tragedies of life—it is likely the most misunderstood process that every individual is bound to experience. Grief is a gift because it is a healthy pathway to reconciliation with inevitable change. It is misunderstood because the culture still teaches us that grief should be contained, not shared. Yet it is in sharing our grief that we endure.

Consequently, we all need clear-cut and basic information about grief early in life if the process of grieving is to be a stepping stone and not a stumbling block. I dare say as an adult that you would not suddenly hop on a bicycle and go for a ride unless as a child you had learned some lessons, had developed the necessary skills. Yet most of us deal with losses in adult life without the skills or tools to manage catastrophic change. Thus, education about coping with loss—a life-long project for all of us—could also lead us to developing a healthy coping style as well as a healthy perspective on the place of the extraordinary in the grief process. Learning about loss is as normal as eating, sleeping, or breathing.

Let's Define Some Terms

Before we get too far, keep in mind that grief, mourning, and bereavement are three terms that are commonly used interchangeably when talking about loss and transition, but which in fact have different connotations.

Earlier, I said that grief is a process of experiencing loss and change. The key word here is process, an ongoing mental and physical process of experiencing a host of emotions, social changes, and reactions associated with loss. One may shed many tears and recall many memories, for it is essentially an internal personal experience. And the intensity of the grief response depends on the personal and symbolic meaning of the loss to the mourner, which is why each grief response is so highly variable.

Mourning, on the other hand, is the sharing of that internal experience with another as one takes action to adapt to the absence of the loved one and establish a new identity. Mourning is also manifested in the wearing of clothing or insignia (athletes often wear the initials or number of a deceased teammate on their athletic uniform) to indicate the outward expression of sadness. Although everyone grieves, not everyone mourns.[2] Yet mourning is a very natural and healthy way to cope with loss regardless of its type or duration. Mourning is one of the essential processes of reconciliation with the loss experience; it facilitates the release of pent-up emotions and the stress associated with confronting massive change. As stated earlier, grief is not merely a mental process, but is expressed through every cell in the body—so too with mourning. However, all too many people grieve and keep the process internal, hiding what is really taking place, which results in paying a heavy price both physically and mentally. While mourning is a painful process of learning to adapt and live again without the deceased, its purpose is to gradually lead to reinvestment in life.

One final point about mourning: The expression of emotion when mourning is only the beginning. There are many other thoughts and memories which have to be reviewed and dealt with in order for the mourning process to culminate in a healthy remembrance of the deceased and for the mourner to embrace life once again. For example, what symbols and memories will be retained? What type of a relationship will be established between the mourner and the deceased? And what will the mourner have to do for himself or herself that was formerly taken care of by the deceased?

Our third commonly used word, bereavement, is the objective state of loss and change. One is bereaved when a loved one dies, a home is destroyed, a valuable item is stolen, or a child leaves home. The term does not necessarily imply emotion but rather a condition of loss.

Grief work is one other term we need to examine, as it is often used by writers and counselors and I will be using it frequently in the chapters ahead. It describes the work of establishing new routines, priorities, and even beliefs in order to create an orderly environment which no longer includes the physical presence of the deceased—it is slowly undoing the ties that bind. Mourning and grief work are related. In fact, grief work is at the very core of the mourning process. As one does his or her grief work, the process of mourning begins to change. Furthermore, grief work includes the withdrawal of our emotional investment (not our memories) in the deceased and the establishment of a different relationship with the person. It demands that we gradually stop anticipating events and routines that normally included the deceased. This is perhaps the most difficult task for most people, because the anticipation of future events with our loved ones is a source of much joy and satisfaction. Nonetheless, the essence of grief work is the necessity to initiate new routines, behaviors, and traditions. Grief work is hard work.

You Can Cope with Loss

Having completed our tour of definitions, let's examine three critical concepts about loss and grief that we all need to learn as children from the significant adults in our lives. They can prove useful in coping with traumatic change as well as open us to understanding the place of the contact experience in the healing process.

First, I would like to strongly suggest, as unlikely as it may sound, that we can prepare to deal with the deaths of loved ones long before those deaths occur. This preparation need not be morbid at all, if we would come to the realization that death, change, and grief are conditions of existence, an integral part of being human. There are no exceptions—no one escapes those conditions. I need not tell you that preparation will not take away the pain of loss. However, I do know one inescapable truth: Preparation will limit, in some cases eliminate, unnecessary suffering.

So many people are excessively anguished because they have lived in a conspiracy of silence about what is a part of being human. The results are catastrophic—an endless burden of unfinished business. Some survivors are left guessing about the wishes of the deceased, others are racked with guilt and depression over issues that could have easily been settled before the loved one died. Still others threaten suicide in the mistaken belief they have nothing left—all because of years of silence. So how do we prepare? Preparation begins by talking about death just as we talk about any other topic. It means considering death as a teacher about life and its brevity. When a child asks questions about death that you are uncomfortable with, refuse to dismiss the inquiry with a "That's morbid" or "Stop talking about such nonsense." If you don't have the answer, tell the child you will find out and continue the dialogue. Education about death starts with adults who will actively listen. The refusal to talk about death in an open manner and the refusal of so many of the bereaved to relate contact experiences when they occur is based on fear. It is never too late to begin dialogue—even when a death occurs and you are grieving—although the earlier in life it can begin the better. Bob Deits in *Life after Loss* makes a very practical observation when he says, "As soon as you decide there are things you can do to prepare for life's inevitable losses, you have begun to take charge of your own destiny."[3] Preparation is simply a way of having some control over how you will deal with a part of life that has to be faced. So make a commitment that you will not pass on your fears to your children, that you will muster the courage to teach them that death is a part of life.

The second concept I place great emphasis on is that it is all right to shed tears or not to shed tears when death or other losses occur. Crying is a form of communication and should be facilitated. We do a terrible disservice to our children in this regard by sending the wrong message early in life that crying is a form of weakness. I am reminded here of a speech given by psychiatrist Elisabeth Kubler-Ross and her example of how parents inadvertently teach children that they should not cry. She asked us to recall the admonition of our parents saying, "You want something to cry about? I'll give you something to cry about." Does that sound familiar? It does to most of us.

Whether male or female, tears are the universal human communicator of sorrow as well as joy. The act of crying, as millions of people will attest, discharges tension. Studies have shown that crying is not only emotionally healthy but possesses physiological merit as well. Tears of sorrow, for example, appear to contain products of the stress response that the body disposes of through the act of weeping.[4]

And what if you don't cry when loss occurs? For any reason, be it the way you were reared or the nature of the emotional attachment to the deceased, it is still acceptable. You may express your sorrow in other ways. We should not judge the depth of one's sorrow by the flow of tears, for that is to misjudge. As healthy as crying may be, some mourners will have to find other means by which to assuage their pain. For some, it will be found through greater participation in ritual or in the help provided to others in the first few days of intense grieving.

Finally, I would like to suggest that many mourners, whether male or female, must give themselves permission to grieve, to mourn, and then to go on with their lives. Of course, this is easier said than done. But since grief is the other side of the coin of love, then your grieving is a symbol of love shared. If you choose to love, as we all do, you automatically choose to grieve. There is a reason to grieve and you have every right to express that reason, to celebrate and honor the deceased loved one. You do not have to grieve silently, nor is the goal of your grief work to forget the person. On the contrary, you must now establish a new relationship with the loved one who died. Often this relationship is facilitated by the contact experience, which brings untold relief and allows a survivor to go on with his or her life.

A key component in giving yourself permission to grieve is to realize that it is okay to feel what you are feeling, that there is nothing abnormal with feeling the way you do, and, most importantly, that you are going to get through your grief, whatever it takes. This is a commitment you make to yourself and your loved ones—you will make it through your grief eventually.[5] Surely, it will be a long and arduous task. It will be painful and it is necessary to experience the pain. But life will be meaningful again.

A Glimpse at Grief

What is nor[mal grief]—or as counselors call it, an uncomplicated grief reaction? Normal grief [includes] a wide range of behaviors, emotions, physical sensations, and thoughts. [The though]ts, which Worden refers to as cognitions, include a variety of contact phe[nomena]—for example, the sense of presence of the deceased and hallucinations. [Obviou]sly, those who are classified as experiencing complicated grief are subjec[t to simi]lar responses, but with a major difference. Complicated grief implies tha[t mour]ners have become "stuck" in their grief, and their grief work has ground to a halt. They are unable to continue the process of assimilating their losses into their lives. They have been unable to let go of the past with love and reinvest in life and new routines.

Small griefs are really not small, not if they're yours. Significant loss is defined in each individual's heart, and who is to say what is significant? No matter what we've lost, if it wounds us enough to trigger the grief stages, then we must allow ourselves to mourn. If we don't suffer and share our sadness, it will hide inside our psyche like a canker.

—B. Bartocci, "Little Griefs Still Matter,"
Woman's Day, September 1, 1994

Small Griefs and Big Griefs

We often fail to realize how frequently people grieve because of what we may consider a small loss. We forget that a loss depends on our perception of an event and perceptions vary immensely. Truly loss, like beauty, is in the eye of the beholder. Thus, some people do not think that loss of money, an ability, self-respect, or faith and trust in someone are valid sources of grief. But in fact, we grieve over small losses in our own individual ways. Someone who loses his ability to see or hear or has difficulty breathing because of pulmonary disease will grieve these losses in very deep ways. Although we associate grief with big losses like death and divorce, there are people around us all of the time who are silently grieving changes in their lives.

I should emphasize here that there is a very wide range of normalcy in the grief process. Again, the operational word here is "process." Grief is not an event which comes and automatically ends after a given period of time—it is ongoing and reappears for many even years later. Unlike earlier assumptions about grieving, current theory suggests that not everyone experiences despair and depths of depression. Some others are able to integrate the most catastrophic losses into their lives due to their belief systems.[7] Therefore, grief may be brief or prolonged, intense or wavering, immediate or delayed, even erratic and repetitious—and all quite normal.

It is clear that grief is not static, but rather a dynamic interplay of many social, physical, and emotional forces. For example, examine a short list of factors influencing how one mourns when a loved one dies:

- Cause of death
- Socioeconomic status
- Age
- Family support
- Sex
- Unfinished business
- Previous loss experiences
- Unresolved anger
- Overdependence on the deceased
- Physical health
- Religious beliefs
- Cultural differences

Grief, therefore, is highly individual because there are differing emotional investments, social variables, and expectations among mourners—especially within a particular family. In fact, there may be as many grieving and mourning styles as there are lifestyles. Not everyone cries. Not everyone becomes angry or guilt-ridden. Not everyone is touched by reactive depression. Grief is sometimes borne lightly. What used to be considered pathological grieving is now assessed as normal.

On the other hand, some mourners suffer from chronic or delayed grief reactions; they are bewildered with the massive changes to be faced. There may be extreme anger or guilt concerning the deceased or another family member, or they are unable to express certain feelings about the deceased. Usually, these suppressed feelings surface in disguise as bodily aches, pains, illnesses, or anger toward others. They are experiencing a form of complicated grief.

Finally, grief does not really progress in set, predictable stages. However, in order to study the process, experts have to propose various models or stages for better understanding and suggest support strategies. In this vein, there are general characteristics of grief which can be clearly identified. Rhode Island therapist and writer Therese Rando suggests that all grief responses fall into three broad categories or response sets: Avoidance, Confrontation, and Accommodation.[8]

Shock, numbness, disbelief, and denial are often prevalent in the Avoidance phase when one is face to face with the unthinkable. Most authorities agree that these are among the universal reactions of the early days and weeks of grieving. Confrontation, on the other hand, includes the highly charged emotional states of anger and rage. The mourner offers resistance. At this time, anxiety, yearning, pining, despair, a sense of helplessness, sleep disturbance, and confusion are usually present. Guilt and depression may also present themselves. In the Accommodation or re-establishment phase, the business of reordering priorities, accepting the loss, instituting new routines, dealing with fatigue, and reinvesting in life become major goals of the adjustment process. In any event, it is worthy of note that recipients of a variety of spontaneous contacts with deceased loved ones, whether considered to be grieving in a complicated or an uncomplicated way, have been helped to adapt to their losses because of their experiences.

To briefly summarize, remember that your grief or the grief of the person you are giving support to is one of a kind and may or may not include some or many of the descriptions we have reviewed. Any number of modifying factors, as well as the unique character of the relationship with the deceased loved one, will contribute to the grieving process. With this in mind, we are ready to examine how the contact experience often unfolds.

The Place of the Contact Experience in the Grief Process

To better understand the conventional view of where and why the contact experience occurs, let us turn to the work of John Bowlby, the well-known British psychiatrist and researcher in the field of personality development. He has suggested a four-phase model of the grief process:[9]

- The phase of numbing
- The phase of yearning and searching
- The phase of disorganization and despair
- The phase of greater or lesser degree of organization

The phase of numbing, being the initial reaction to hearing the news of the death, lasts from hours to several days, and is characterized by intense distress, a feeling of "this can't be true." One is stunned, as though suddenly thrown into an unreal world. For some, this may eventually lead to panic, anger, and intense emotion. Nonetheless, according to Bowlby, the initial state of affairs sets the stage for yearning and searching for the deceased loved one which manifests itself in preoccupation with his or her image. Specifically, the search often culminates in "a sense of his actual presence, and a marked tendency to interpret signals or sounds as indicating that he is now returned." The sense of presence, although occurring among members of both sexes, has often been reported by widows as being most comforting to the point that they deliberately attempt to invoke the deceased loved one's presence when they are feeling sad and in need of support.[10] The yearning and searching phase is in full swing as the bereaved is said to be alternating between two states of mind: the realization of the death with hopeless yearning, and the disbelief of its occurrence and the hope that all is not lost.

It is believed that the search for the deceased may be consciously or unconsciously conducted. Some individuals are very much aware of the purpose of their behavior; others are not. Accordingly, the search is compelling and the recovery of the lost loved one most important, although the motivation to continue the search wanes over time. It is further suggested that the search is revealed in dreams about the deceased which occur in about half of widows and widowers. Children of all ages (including adult children) may also experience the search for their parents through dreams. In general, a great variety of emotional behaviors are features of the yearning and searching phase. As Bowlby concludes... "restless searching, intermittent hope, repeated disappointment, weeping, anger, accusation, and ingratitude are all features of the second phase... and are to be understood as expressions of the strong urge to find and recover the lost person."[11]

Let me emphasize that the vivid dreams of the deceased as alive and well, hearing familiar sounds of him or her coming up the steps or putting the key into the lock, and interpreting other sounds as related to the person as if alive, are all considered a normal part of the grief process by most professionals. But they are only considered to be artifacts of grief, not real events. That is to say, this phenomena, while common, is an expected result of the memory of these repetitious events when the person was alive.

As a result of the foregoing description of the phase of yearning and searching, we can now address the question with regard to specific times for a contact experience to occur. Searching behavior may go on for months or years—it is impossible to place specific time boundaries on the experience. However, it is safe to say that any survivor may have contact within minutes of the death, may have the experience once or several times over several years, or may not experience any contact at all. Can we assume that if a survivor is subject to a contact experience five years after the death of a loved one, that he, the living survivor, is still searching for the lost person? Any answer to the question will be controversial at best. I would argue that the contact experiences of the bereaved, coming as they do without warning, may occur at any time after the death of the loved one and are not particularly bound to any time frame or phase of grieving. While this is contrary to current theory, there is good reason for it. Some people have reported contacts within minutes of the death, when they were not present at the death bed or even knew the loved one had died, then never had further contact. Others have engaged the deceased months or years after the death, or have had a series of contacts during several months or years.

What the Contact Experience Is Not

At this point, we can begin to understand the state of mind in which a bereaved person may not accept that the loved one is actually gone, never to return. Consequently, one must test his disbelief in the hopes that a mistake has been made and the loved one will reappear. After all, we have been subtly taught not to accept the reality of death and may readily use denial as a delaying tactic to give us time to assimilate what appears to be otherwise incomprehensible. For many, though not all, looking for signs that the loved one is still around is absolutely essential for going on and trying to complete their grief work. Here is where expectancy in general and the imagination in particular come into play.

It is quite common to expect to see or hear an individual in a specific place or associated with a specific set of circumstances when one has seen or heard that person in those surroundings hundreds or thousands of times over the years. The expectation is simply automatic and habitual. Perhaps the most common example of this expectation is seeing a person from a distance who looks like the deceased loved one, hurrying to get to the person before she gets lost in the crowd, only to discover that it is someone else very much alive. This is not what we will call a contact experience.

Another situation which occurs again and again is the feeling that you are sure someone has just walked by into the next room or passed by your window, and you believe it is your loved one. Peripheral vision, which varies from person to person, can often pick up movement or shadows out of the corner of the eye which are often misinterpreted. Sanders has called this the "flicker phenomenon." But when one turns to look, hoping it will be the deceased, nothing is there.[12] This also will not be labeled as a contact experience.

A similar indicator that someone might be present happens when you look at a drawn venetian blind that is not completely drawn closed or there is a slight opening between the side edge of the blind and the side of the window frame. If you move left or right when looking at these small openings, it appears as though something on the other side of the blinds is moving. In this case, seeing is not believing, although one may entertain the thought that it may be the deceased. These are circumstances that we will not consider in our discussions.

Last, but certainly not least, are any experiences which suggest that mourners should take some type of drastic action or place themselves in harm's way. Any experience of this nature implies the immediate need to obtain help from a friend or a professional counselor (depending on the nature of the event) as soon as possible. Keeping silent about such negative experiences can only be detrimental to the mourner and prevent one from doing the work of grief.

What if You Experience the Extraordinary?

It is not unusual for people who do not believe that consciousness survives death in some sort of after-life existence to have a contact experience. Of course, after such an experience a strengthening or change in beliefs often ensues. At the same time, there are also individuals whose religion suggests not only praying for but praying to the deceased loved one. In this vein, one may believe that the deceased is with God and can intercede on behalf of the survivor. In either case, when one is suddenly confronted with the extraordinary, the rush of thoughts and feeling can be overwhelming.

How should you interpret your experience? As a gift, a blessing? Or perhaps a haunting or a scare? The very nature of the event most often will answer these questions. Here are some guidelines to consider when dealing with the aftereffects of the experience that may assist in your interpretation:

- As soon as time permits, write down what you have experienced. Be as detailed as possible, indicating what time the contact occurred, what you were doing and/or thinking prior to the experience, what message (explicit or symbolic) you received, and what may have caused it to happen. All of this can ultimately help in your final interpretation of the event. Another reason for putting the event on paper is to counter one of the criticisms leveled by skeptics. They insist that much of the important detail surrounding the contact experience is forgotten over time and the story is unintentionally changed or filled in with information which seems to best fit the desired outcome.

- Remember that regardless of the nature of your experience, you are not "losing your mind." Whether you think it was a real post-death visit or a hallucination, whether you interpret the event negatively or positively, most professional therapists agree that it is not abnormal to have a contact experience after the death of a loved one. Yes, you are distraught over your tragic loss and you may be filled with confusion, despair, guilt, and/or hopelessness, but your unexpected event should be placed in perspective—it has happened to millions of others. So don't fear you are losing your sanity. No one knows for sure why some survivors have the experience and others do not. There is some evidence to suggest that the deceased often appear to those who are in most need of support in dealing with their loss, to finish unfinished business, and to give reassurance that love is eternal and that death never breaks the bond.

- Share the experience with a trusted friend or relative to obtain another viewpoint. As with any subject or event that challenges your state of mind and proves stressful—or is an occasion for joy—find someone with whom you can unburden yourself. This is particularly important considering the major stress you are already having to deal with. The choice of your confidant should obviously be guided by trust. But there is also another consideration: Is he or she a non-judgmental listener, someone you could tell anything to? You are in need of a sounding board at this time, not someone who jumps to conclusions. Take your time in making this choice; there is no need to rush. Be specific and detailed in explaining what happened. Describe to your listener the physical setting in which the experience took place. Tell him or her what you were doing before the event occurred and your frame of mind. Then listen to your confidant's response before you share your feelings. Carefully gauge that response before taking the next step.

- Express your deep feelings and emotions regarding the event, if you are convinced it is safe to do so. It is one thing to tell someone that you have had an unusual experience. That can be a release in itself. But it is quite another to open your heart and mind by sharing what it really means to you. Let your confidant know the effect the experience has had on you. If you feel you will be too vulnerable and fear your friend may be frightened by your reaction, or think you are becoming excessively troubled, then seek his or her initial reaction first. That is, say what you experienced but withhold your interpretation until you are satisfied that it is safe to continue. If the listener's response and body language is threatening to your beliefs about the event, you can then choose to end the conversation and seek help elsewhere. Don't be discouraged, just try someone else.

- If your confidant has been neutral, noncommittal, or accepting of your view of the experience, at the appropriate time ask for an opinion from your listener about what he/she thinks the experience means. Obtaining opinions from another can be most helpful in sorting out what has happened. But keep in mind it is only an opinion, an alternative among many alternatives which may help you to interpret the event or add something to your own interpretation. Sometimes a good listener can come up with an idea that immediately feels right and gives you a message that you had failed to see.

- Carefully examine alternative explanations. There are many possible explanations for the extraordinary events that occur when one is grieving. Your confidant will not have all of them at his or her command, which means you may have to seek additional help before deciding what your experience means, if anything. I have included a number of different interpretations in later pages, and my list is by no means complete. On the other hand, you may be comfortable with the way you have already interpreted the experience, convinced that its vividness and message was either real or imagined. Go with your heart; your deep inner self knows. Only you can decide. In either case, get on with your grief work and use the experience accordingly.

- Accept repetitive events. It is not unusual to have more than one or a series of extraordinary events. It could be a repeat of the same experience or an entirely different one. Quite possibly, you could have a combination of legitimate contact experiences and others which can be explained as natural or misinterpreted happenings. Whether it is a repetitive dream, sound, or vision of the deceased loved one, it is not an aberrant or atypical experience when grieving. (Caution: If the event suggests you should harm yourself or another in some way, this is not a contact experience, and it is essential that you seek professional assistance immediately.)

- Seek professional counseling. There are a number of instances in which a certified grief counselor can help in interpreting an extraordinary experience. In some instances, it may help to know that what you experienced could be real, that others have been through it, or that sometimes the event may have no significance whatsoever. A counselor may be needed if you are unable to share the experience with anyone else but feel you must talk about it. In choosing a counselor, don't hesitate to ask if the counselor has been specifically trained in grief counseling. Even then, I regret to say that some counselors have difficulties accepting anything of an extraordinary or paranormal nature and may dismiss the event as meaningless. If there is not a specialist in your area, contact the Association for Death Education and Counseling (see notes and references section), and that organization can help you find someone in a nearby city or town.

- You make the final decision. Never give up your right to decide what happened and how to interpret it. Regardless of the qualifications of the counselor or friend who gives you an opinion, go with your intuition and heart after carefully weighing the possibilities. Remember that this is your grief work, your event, your decision to live with. Most importantly, you know the relationship you had with your deceased loved one better than anyone else, and you can assume your deceased loved one knows that too.

During your considerations, you may have doubts and receive some skeptical input from friends or professionals, which is to be expected. There is a strong tendency toward reductionistic thinking, which can be countered in part by turning inward and listening to your inner wisdom. Authentic messages and messengers possess an encompassing characteristic—they will always draw you and those you love into a greater circle of love. Let that be your guide in your deliberations about your experience.

We turn now to one of the most frequently occurring contact experiences—the sense of presence of the deceased, often referred to as the intuitive experience.

FOUR

The Intuitive Experience:
Sensing the Presence of the Deceased

Intuition is increasingly recognized as a natural mental faculty, a key element in discovery, problem solving, and decision making, a generator of creative ideas, a forecaster, a revealer of truth…. There is a growing conviction that perhaps we ought to trust the hunches, vague feelings, premonitions, and inarticulate signals we usually ignore.
  —Philip Goldberg in *The Intuitive Edge*

It often happens that an hallucination is imperfectly developed: the person affected will feel a "presence" in the room, definitely localized, facing in one particular way, real in the most emphatic sense of the word, often coming suddenly, and as suddenly gone; and yet neither seen, heard, touched, nor cognized in any of the usual "sensible" ways.
  —William James in *The Varieties of Religious Experience*

The intuitive sense of presence of the deceased loved one, which may occur at any time during or after the grief process has run its course, is one of the most self-reinforcing and frequent encounters reported by the bereaved. As William James states in the opening quote of this section, the sense of presence has no association with the senses as we are accustomed to using them. Still, when criticized by those who scoff at the suggestion that the deceased person was present, those reporting the experience will respond with something like, "That's their opinion; I know what I experienced." Or, "As soon as I walked in, I felt a presence like I had never felt before. I knew it was her." For the bereaved, the ring of truth cannot be denied. Where, then, does this conviction of knowing come from, if not through the normal channels for processing information from the outside world?

37

The only answer, it seems, is that it comes from that "other sense," our intuition. Intuition defies current logic and reason, although each of us is endowed with intuitive abilities. We often sense when something is not right with a friend or have a "gut feeling" that we should take a specific course of action. Like all faculties, its level of development varies among individuals; however, our intuitive abilities are neglected by the educational system and most individuals, as is so much of nonphysical reality. Once again, this neglect can be traced to the difficulty in cornering and studying the process with precision and accuracy. Intuition possesses that same characteristic of spontaneous appearance which favors the contact experience. Yet everyone has intuitive ability and often uses it unknowingly.

By definition, intuition is said to be "the direct perception of truths, facts, or information independent of any reasoning process." The emphasis here is on the fact that there is no reasoning or logic involved; there is a direct knowing. It is a form of nonlogical thinking which has been the basis for numerous discoveries and creative works throughout history. In ordinary descriptions, people will say they "just knew," they "had a hunch" or "a funny feeling," and then made a decision based on that intuitive event.

> *The moment of truth, the sudden emergence of a new insight, is an act of intuition. Such intuitions give the appearance of miraculous flashes, or short-circuits of reasoning. In fact they may be likened to an immersed chain, of which only the beginning and the end are visible above the surface of consciousness.*
>
> —Arthur Koestler, *The Act of Creation*
> New York: The Macmillan Co., 1964.

It is often very disquieting, yet clearly evident on later analysis, that there appears to be no conscious or rational sequence of thought leading up to an intuitive insight. As though turning on a light bulb, all of a sudden we are face to face with our "knowing" and as hard as we might later try, we are unable to turn on the intuitive light by command. There are no rules to invoke this wisdom, although some books (see Flora Davis' *Inside Intuition* and Francis Vaughan's *Awakening Intuition*) purport to show that it can be integrated into rational thinking. But although intuition is part of our complex thinking processes, we must wait for it to arrive on the scene. I accentuate this spontaneous characteristic because it poses a very critical question which we will deal with momentarily. But first let us examine a typical intuitive experience involving a deceased loved one.

I begin with the description of an event which took place in the late 1800s simply to show that the intuitive encounter is nothing new and has been reported as a rather natural occurrence since time immemorial. The man involved in the extraordinary event was absorbed in reading a book, fully relaxed and in good spirits, and, significantly, was not thinking of any of his friends.

> *...when suddenly without a moment's warning my whole being seemed aroused to the highest state of tension or aliveness, and I was aware, with an intenseness not easily imagined by those who had never experienced it, that another being or presence was not only in the room, but quite close to me. I put my book down, and although my excitement was great, I felt quite collected and not conscious of any sense of fear. Without changing my position, and looking straight at the fire, I knew somehow that my friend A. H. was standing at my elbow.*[1]

This sense of presence was augmented by a visible appearance of his friend when he turned his eyes to his left. However, what is of interest to us in our discussion of intuition are these characteristics of the experience: it came without warning, there was no fear, and he knew it was his friend.

How did he know? Was it a function of that murky faculty called intuition? We will see shortly. Now let us return to the question of spontaneity and ask, "Where does this way of knowing called intuition come from?" As is often the case, there is more than one answer to the question. We will look at two opposing viewpoints. Conventional wisdom says that this unusual ability, which anyone can develop, is part of the highly creative unconscious mind. According to Jung, founder of analytical psychology, the unconscious is a treasure trove of wisdom, experiences, and knowledge. It possesses infinitely more information than the conscious mind, and has better sources of information available to draw from than sense perceptions.[2] There are some who believe that intuition and so-called psychic ability are closely related, and that we call it intuition because the term is more acceptable than psychic or psi. That is to say, "extrasensory perception, clairvoyance, and telepathy are part of the intuitive function."[3] Intuition, then, may well be an undeveloped extrasensory function. Here is an example from a young man who shared the following intuitive experience with me.

Edgar's father had been ill for several days and was in a hospital in another state. One evening, upon retiring, Edgar had been lying in bed for about fifteen minutes when he received an intuitive insight he did not want to believe. He bolted upright, turned to his wife and said, " My father died." He spoke with conviction, with a sense of knowing which he did not want to accept. They talked about it for a while, but neither wanted to deal with it further or make a long-distance telephone call and upset the family if it were not true. Eventually they drifted off to sleep. At 6:15 the next morning, the telephone rang: it was Edgar's brother with the news that their father had died during the night. His father was not expected to die that evening, and in fact was scheduled to undergo tests the following day. Edgar was unable to explain why he had received the intuitive message the previous evening.

Was it intuition, telepathic communication, or simply a dreaded thought he blurted out in that twilight time just before dropping off to sleep? There is much theory available to argue for each of those possibilities. But let's turn to a second explanation for the origin of this elusive faculty: that it is part of the way one receives guidance from a spiritual source.

Goldberg suggests that intuition and rational thought go hand in hand and that in dealing with complex questions, incomplete information, or unfamiliar subject matter, "we are dependent on intuition to tell us whether we are on the right track."[4] Furthermore, it is generally agreed that intuition manifests itself in a variety of ways: a sensation or feeling, a sudden picture in the mind's eye, a dream, a "light bulb" solution, or an inner voice. Any of these manifestations of intuition, it could be argued, may well be inspired by a spiritual (some would call it divine) source in many instances—just as it is argued that intuitive ability is basically a part of rational thinking and that it can be worked on and developed.

In like manner, many individuals believe that what science calls intuition is in reality a part of the Kingdom of God within. By whatever name it is called, there is an intelligence in each person which solves problems, provides information to act on, as well as answers to the difficult problems in life—and it eludes scientific scrutiny. Through the ages, this intelligence has been referred to as common sense, Infinite Wisdom, the Inner Guide, the Universal Mind, the Supreme Spirit or the Holy Spirit. In the Bible it is found in the passage, "Do you not know that you are God's temple and that God's spirit dwells in you?" (1 Corinthians 3:16). Intuition, in this sense, leads some people toward an all-knowing Divine Consciousness. It is a reminder that we are more than physical parts and electrochemical circuits. As frequently experienced, it is an obvious bridge between the known and the unknown.

Having examined two possible sources for intuition, the unconscious mind and a power of divine dimensions, we are still unable to physically locate its source. While intuition may reside in the brain, there is no scientific proof that it is produced by the brain. The same can be said of consciousness—there is no incontrovertible evidence that it originates in the brain, as is commonly believed. To suggest, without proof, that it is a function of the brain is like saying that the symptoms of a disease are the origins of the disease. That consciousness and intuition exist is not questioned; where they come from is very much a matter of debate and opinion.

> *Pure intuition at the spiritual level is non-dualistic and non-symbolic. It is a state of imageless awareness, in which there is no duality between the knower and the known, between consciousness and its objects. This level of reality cannot be described in words, since words invariably posit duality, or separation from what is described.*
> —Frances E. Vaughan, *Awakening Intuition*
> New York: Doubleday, 1979

The intuitive experiences I have found in my research have been profoundly thought-provoking in relation to the universal questions: Who are we? and Why are we here? Let's start on this quest with Jana's experiences involving the unexpected death of her infant daughter. I begin with her most recent experience.

"You Did the Right Thing, Mom"

I had just finished speaking with Dr. LaGrand on the phone, having responded to his ad in Bereavement Magazine. We shared our stories. I was amazed at the "non" coincidence of our infant daughters dying of SIDS. The conversation was one of (from my perspective) instantaneous trust and a wish to share. After I hung up the phone, my kitchen changed in the quality of the light (it was late at night). It took on the light that I now associate with her presence; it took on a clarity in the edges of the surfaces. I was filled with her presence. I stood for some time in a place of infinite peace.

My daughter said to me, not in human words, but I knew her to say, "You did the right thing, Mom. You are supposed to meet him." Then the kitchen changed. The sense of peace in that circle clicked off, and I felt happy, but the usual kind, not the big one.

Her death is not an accident. I since have been accepted at a school for counseling. I am changing careers and I will move from volunteer peer support of bereaved parents to a professional therapeutic counseling role. I am going home. I feel a sense of comfort and peace with this new path which I never felt in my work in the business world. My daughter lives as a presence of love and wisdom and an access to the larger circle of life.

This experience took place nearly six years after the death of her daughter. Notice that her intuitive experiences have been occurring in an ongoing manner. In particular, it is interesting that she knew what her daughter said although there were no words spoken. Also, through her daughter's death she has found the way to a new career. Her earlier experiences also proved important in the way she has dealt with her daughter's death, as suggested in the following.

"She Was There"

I was dressing my other children, two and four years old, to meet their father for our annual family photo and I was missing my first child who would have been six and a half. As I was putting their coats on I stopped. There was a clarity to the objects in the room. The edges got, not sharper in a harsh way, but more clear. I heard my kids but I was aware of a presence, a silence. She was with me as I bundled her siblings up in their coats; she was there. I was existing in two planes, parallel planes; one silent, infinitely aware and at peace, one frantic, scrambling to dress two kids late for an appointment. Then it was gone.

She was there. She will always be a part of me and a part of my family. She came to my consciousness for a moment—limited and unaware as it is—to remind me of that fact. I smiled and hurried to our appointment very contentedly.

Again, as with my other experiences, this was a reminder of the power of love, the meaning of death as only a gateway to infinite peace and harmony. This, as all the other visits from my baby, remind me of the big picture and help me to focus my life on healing, love, and service to others.

The brief sense of presence is striking, particularly in the way it impacts on Jana's outlook and commitment. Using the sense of presence as a tool for seeing the "big picture" is a powerful way for her to find meaning in death and strengthen her philosophy of life.

In the third description, she further clarifies the meaning she has drawn from her daughter's death through these contact experiences.

"She Lifted my Burden"

I had pulled into my driveway with the children in the back of the car in their car seats. I let them out to play in the back yard and I stayed in the car watching them play and crying about a very serious problem regarding my family and my childhood that I am struggling to come to grips with. I was just so burdened and despairing that I prayed to my daughter. I asked her to help me. As I looked from the driver's seat, out over my children in the grass, out over the tree tops past the clouds behind the sky, there was a sense of her. I felt her merging with me, her coming to me, me going to her in a sort of a tunnel, still aware of all around me but at ultimate peace. She lifted my burden.

Each experience with her presence is accompanied by a kind of clarity, a silence, a feeling of time infinite and still. It represents to me the God force of harmony and hope. I believe that my love for her is at times bigger than my feelings of loss and I am able to tap into that circle of love because my soul is open for a moment to its power. The message I receive is this: she is ever present, ever embracing of me and her family. I know to trust the power of healing love she can bring to my life. The experience was a reminder, five and a half years after her death, of the eternal love of the soul.

In this passage, it is clear that the bond of love between mother and daughter is so strong as to have transcended death. The sense of presence fills Jana with the power of love, which sustains her in dealing with the problems of everyday life. The concept of a circle of love that she can become a part of is a healing force which minimizes the physical separation between them. Significantly, love is often mentioned by survivors as the reason the deceased loved one makes contact with them. In some instances, no words are spoken or messages received, just a reminder that they are loved. This is illustrated in the experiences of Marsha, who, in the middle years of her life, has been sustained from time to time by the presence of both of her grandfathers.

"There Is No Death"

From time to time, since the deaths of both of my grandfathers, I have had the feeling of the sense of their presence in my bedroom just before going to sleep. This has happened numerous times with both grandfathers. (My grandmothers are also deceased.)

I think relaxing after a hard day opens my mind and I think my grandfathers loved me greatly and felt a special bond with me. I don't receive a message. I just feel they are near, standing next to the bed. It makes me feel reassured that maybe they're looking after me. The experience reinforces my belief that there is no death, only transformation.

Reassurance is a consistent product of the intuitive experience, whether or not there is verbal communication between the deceased and the survivor. The mind-easing effects of the sense of presence of the deceased loved one is an antidote for insecurity. With both Jana and Marsha, the intuitive experience has reaffirmed their belief that their loved ones live on, that consciousness does not end when death occurs.

In 1956, C. S. Lewis, English author and professor of Medieval and Renaissance English at Cambridge, married Joy Davidman, an American poet. A brilliant writer, he had been a confirmed bachelor. Three years later, she died of cancer. In *A Grief Observed*, Lewis wrote of his experience of confronting his devastating loss, and tells of the sense of presence of his wife and the intimacy he felt because of it. We see in this piece the typical scholarly resistance to the unseen.

I said several notebooks ago, that even if I got what seemed like an assurance of H's presence, I wouldn't believe it. Easier said than done. Even now, though, I won't treat anything of that sort as evidence. It's the quality of last night's experience—not what it proves but what it was—that makes it worth putting down. It was quite incredibly unemotional. Just an impression of her mind momentarily facing my own.[5]

Lewis felt that the event was rather unemotional, matter of fact, as he said, like getting a telephone call. Despite the lack of emotion or the sense of love that is usually present, the event was for him confirming and comforting. As he remarked, "Wherever it came from, it has made a sort of spring cleaning in my mind." What Lewis refers to as spring cleaning, others who have had similar contacts might call transformative, inspirational, or even invigorating. And then his interpretation goes to the heart of the matter with his closing remarks which lay bare his deep feelings about the presence of his beloved wife.

One didn't need emotion. The intimacy was complete—sharply bracing and restorative too—without it. Can the intimacy be love itself...? If so how many preconceptions I must scrap! ... It would, if I had a glimpse be—well, I'm almost scared of the adjectives I'd have to use. Brisk? cheerful? keen? alert? intense? wide-awake? Above all, solid. Utterly reliable. Firm. There is no nonsense about the dead.[6]

What a wonderful way to look at intimacy: as being solid, reliable, and firm, void of emotion as we know it. Notice that there was, as he put it, a mind-to-mind contact; a presence that was clear and unassailable. It is interesting that this scholar describes the sense of presence as contact of the mind of the living and the mind of the deceased. Something good had happened, although he would not allow himself to revel in its potential benefits. This is far from an uncommon reaction. Not surprisingly, as we reread his description of the event, there is a hint that what occurred in those restorative moments was not only challenging to his intellectual defenses, but had actually broken through that barrier. He had experienced something he had not thought previously possible.

We have examined four personal accounts of the sense of presence of the deceased. In each one, it is clear that the person is convinced of the reality of the presence in some form. There is personal meaning in the experience, a good feeling about the contact, and inherent trust in the mystery of the unseen. There is reassurance, relief, a sense of peace. Last, but not least, love seems to permeate the relationship. This attribute and the intimacy that accompanies it seems to be especially present between twins, who commonly enjoy many unexplainable moments of "knowing" something about the other when the five senses are not involved.

Twins and the Sense of Presence

The sense of presence of a deceased twin has been a salient factor in many surviving twins' ability to deal with grief work. In many instances, the sense of presence has helped the living twin avoid danger or deal with a fearful situation. I am familiar with two instances involving the deaths of twins in which both the remaining living twins received direction and strength from the deceased others.

The first situation, which occurred nearly a year and a half after the death, involved a surviving twin who was in combat in Korea. He was often assigned to a forward post watching for the enemy. "I was never alone at that forward post," he said. "My twin was with me. He was there. His presence was of great help at a difficult time." In the second incident, a young woman avoided a serious automobile accident when her deceased twin's presence caused her to take a different, longer route to her home. The shorter route would have taken her across a flooded bridge which collapsed at the time she would have made the crossing. Such anecdotes, though difficult to corroborate, provide another avenue of research to determine how the deceased are able and willing to help the living. I have mentioned these two incidents to bring another dimension of the puzzle of the intuitive experience into view—the special bond of caring between living twins that persists in death. The bond seems to be unbreakable, just as it is between close friends, parents and children, or grandparents and grandchildren. In a later chapter, I will tell you about a premonition of my mother's death that my twin sisters experienced.

Lifelong Sense of Presence

Although most individuals who sense the presence of their deceased loved ones do so generally in the early months or years following the death, there are a few cases in which the survivor experiences contact with the deceased loved one whenever faced with frightening situations. Such is the case of a young woman I met in the hospital who had immigrated from Jamaica. Her father died when she was three years old. What she remembers most about the event is her mother's sadness. But her father's presence has been continuous. She tells it as follows:

"I Know He is Around Me"

Any time I feel fear I immediately sense the presence of my father—and it goes away. Once I was alone in the subway wait-ing for the train and I saw a sinister-looking man at the other end of the platform. He just looked as though he was up to no good. He started walking toward me and I froze. I couldn't move. He came right up to me and I was afraid, but I couldn't run.

All of the sudden I felt as though I was holding on to my father's hand. I felt protected. The scary-looking stranger stared at me and then I saw fear in his eyes. For some reason he was afraid and walked away. I always feel the presence of my father in fear-ful situations. I am more accepting of his death because I know he is around me when I need him.

Since coming to America, this young woman has had numerous instances in which she was fearful and apprehensive. Each time, she has always had this per-ceived presence to guide her. Some would say it was her guardian angel, but she believes it is her father, helping her in her adjustment to America just as he did when she was growing up in Jamaica.

Several People Sensing a Presence

The sense of presence has also been experienced by more than one person at the same time. My first awareness of this phenomena came a number of years ago from a colleague. It was completely unsolicited. I believe he shared it with me simply because he knew I was a bereavement counselor, and he wanted to obtain my reaction to this puzzling event.

Jim and his wife had been informed of the death of his father and left the next day to attend the funeral, which was held several hundred miles away. It was a hurried trip as well as a sad one. They arrived on a Monday and the funeral took place the following day. Jim explains what happened:

"We Felt the Presence of My Father"

It was a beautiful summer day. If you had the choice, it was the kind of day you would pick to be outside working on your house or going on a camping trip. It was a day my father would have loved. Jane and I had driven to the funeral by ourselves, and we were on our way back to my aunt's house. The traffic was heavy in the city and we had just pulled up and stopped at a traffic light. The windows in my car were open, and as we were sitting there waiting for the light to change, a Monarch butterfly flew in and perched on the dashboard. We both looked at it and then at each other. Simultaneously, we felt the presence of my father as though the butterfly heralded his coming. His presence lasted only a few moments, as though he were saying good-bye.

The symbol of the butterfly and its change from one stage to another adds another dimension to this intuitive experience. My colleague and his wife were happy with their momentary gift, which altered the somber mood of the day.

The second incident of more than one person sensing the presence of the deceased was related to me by a woman who had been in the nursing profession for over thirty years. It took place back at the home of relatives after a wake. Having been invited back to the house for refreshments, she was joined by a few other close friends. This is what happened.

"Do You Feel What I Feel?"

We were all a little tired. Before Angela could get to the cookies and put the coffee on, Alice, Marie, and I went into the living room and sat down on the big couch. It was so inviting to our tired old legs. The conversation was not continuous and during a brief lull I had this feeling that Matt was there in the room. I tried to shrug it off. As I turned to my left to look at Alice and Marie, they were both looking at me, wearing the most unusual expressions. The silence seemed forever until I said: "Do you feel what I feel?" Almost in unison they nodded their heads and said: "Yes." We all felt he was there.

There are also many instances, perhaps more than we suspect, when only one person in a group or a large crowd senses the presence of the deceased. The question of why some people in a group may have the experience and others do not is not easy to answer. It may very well be a product of the type of relationship that previously existed between the survivor and the deceased, or the assistance one needs in dealing with the loss of the loved one. Whether the bereaved is alone or with others, it is apparent that the intuitive experience causes the recipient to reflect on the possible continued existence of the deceased in the world of the unseen.

Intuitive Awareness of the Death and Presence

The last type of intuitive experience I will consider involves sensing the death of a loved one before the survivor "knows" the death has occurred. These experiences are, to say the least, some of the most dramatic encounters and among the most difficult to explain using typical cause-and-effect theory.

Sensing the presence of the deceased before being told of the death may be accompanied by hearing or seeing the person. This is illustrated in the following account which comes from fifty-year-old Fred, an agnostic, who experienced the deaths of three friends in this unusual way.

"A Saying of Good-Byes"

In three separate and unrelated deaths of close friends over a ten-year period I sensed the presence each time, saw one, and heard (inside my head, not an actual voice) my friends tell me they were dead. Each experience was a matter-of-fact declaration, without emotion on their parts. They seemed to be in some transitional period, a saying of good-byes, and then on to a new phase of awareness. Each experience occurred, as far as I could determine, at about the time of the person's actual death.

For each of my experiences I was in the northeast United States. One friend died in Oregon in an undersea diving accident; one was murdered in Manhattan; one was struck by lightning in

Rome, Italy. In each case I had to contact others to find the cause of death.

I would like to add that paranormal experiences have been quite frequent in my life—not everyday things, but they occur often enough to me so that I wonder why they are (whatever they may be) considered so bizarre by some people. My feeling is that awareness of, and communication with, other spheres is a relatively normal, but mostly repressed phenomenon. But what do I know?

My friends saying good-bye seemed like almost normal happenings. The message I have received from my experiences is an awareness and existence of some kind of after death. Also, as a result of these experiences, my grieving for these friends (and for others) was not severe and not lengthy. I am simply left wondering what life after death consists of—not whether or not it exists.

What I found unusual about Fred's remarks, more than any of the people I have interviewed, was his calm acceptance of these encounters as being quite normal and that the experience is common but repressed by most of us. This was reinforced by his belief and expectation that even under the circumstances of death close friends would say good-bye. Of course, what makes his experiences especially interesting is that his three friends were in good health, he was miles from them at the times of their deaths, and he had not been thinking about them.

Most important for our consideration are the results of the experiences in terms of the nature of his grief work. His wondering about the existence of life after death and the intensity and length of the grief process were less than he had previously experienced early in life. The intuitive awareness of his friend's deaths, call it psychic awareness if you must, have been a powerful catalyst for change in his behavior.

The significance of saying good-bye should not be underestimated as an influential factor in how one goes on with life and is able to integrate the death of a loved one into a world which abruptly changes. Not only do Fred's remarks speak to this point, but so do those of twenty-two-year-old Nancy, who tells us about her unusual good-bye to her grandmother.

"My Ritual Was Her and My Way of Saying Good-Bye"

During the summer of my senior year in college, my grandmother was hospitalized with a sudden illness. We were not able to spend as much time together as we would have liked; nevertheless, we shared a special closeness. She always kind of knew when I was in trouble. Since my family and I maintained minimal contact with each other, I never really knew how sick she was, or what was going on.

I remember it was a warm and settled evening that summer, and I was out running. I just got this sense, almost a heavy feeling, that I needed to complete a ritual, that I seek a cemetery. I found a small, old graveyard on a country road and stood in it for about twenty minutes. I don't remember feeling much except that I was in the right place. If I hadn't gone there I would have been disrespectful to my grandmother.

Later, I found out she died that day. I realized my ritual was her and my way of saying good-bye to each other, a private exchange. It actually helped me cope with her passing since I felt I had been given an intimate and private opportunity to say good-bye.

Nancy's interpretation of her need to find a cemetery as a way to show respect for her grandmother is unusual to say the least, although on learning of the death she realized she had been drawn there to say good-bye. At first blush, I am baffled at this young woman's intuiting that she should find a cemetery while she is out jogging. It would seem that such a thought would be the furthest thing from her mind. Yet, once she found one, she knew she was in the right place. From what place does such a directive originate? Whatever the source, what is highly significant is the experience was real for Nancy and the occasion to say good-bye assisted her in her grieving.

The Spiritual or Mystical Experience

Although the words "spiritual" and "mystical" are interpreted in a variety of ways, I have used the words here to denote contact experiences which directly involve one's religious beliefs and the deceased loved one. The following two experiences illustrate this concept: both took place in a church setting.

The first event involves a sixty-eight year-old woman I'll call Phyllis. Her husband had died after a long illness which had been extremely demanding on her. They had been a devoted couple with strong family values and commitment to their Christian faith. She continued to attend church each Sunday, knowing that her faith had sustained her throughout her ordeal and convinced it would continue to do so no matter what happened. One Sunday during the service, Phyllis had an ecstatic sense of presence of her husband. Here is how she tells it:

"My Husband and I Were Entwined within the Body of Christ"

> *It was during the part of the Mass when the priest consecrates the bread and wine into the body and blood of Christ. Instantly, I felt my husband and I were entwined within the body of Christ. We were one. I sensed his presence and realized God had given me a gift. I knew that my husband was happy and waiting for me. It helped me so much at the time. Since then, I try to remember exactly what happened and experience it again.*

This type of contact experience has great significance for the mourner. It is unequivocally clear to her that the deceased loved one is with God, happy, and at peace. In addition, the mourner knows they will be together again, reunited with Christ. The experience is a perpetual source of strength and sustains the survivor through the difficult transition from wife to widow and beyond.

The second example of the sense of presence occurring when one is at prayer took place when a priest in his early forties was attending a retreat. His brother died fifteen years prior to the experience.

"I Was Comforted and Felt a Deep Peace"

> *I was making a retreat. While meditating in the chapel I looked up. It was as if the roof of the chapel opened up and I had an intense experience of my brother's face. I sensed his presence through the comforting smile on his face. I was comforted and felt a deep peace. I don't know what caused this to happen within me but the message I received was that my brother is alive. There is life after death. It also helps me to be open to the experiences of others and not close my mind and heart to what they experience.*

Not only did this priest receive reinforcement of his religious beliefs and help in his ongoing grief work, but the experience afforded him an avenue of insight in his counseling of the bereaved.

What can we conclude about the variety of intuitive experiences which occur so commonly? Based on my interviews I would offer the following:

- All who sense the presence of the deceased are convinced the experience is real, they did not imagine what took place, and they received a meaningful personal message. Because the bereaved did not believe the events were products of confusion or despair, they are most likely to assume the sense of presence of their deceased loved ones originated from an outside source.

- Generally, the event occurs without warning. Although some people feel that certain circumstances may trigger the process, in most instances the sense of presence comes at unexpected moments.

- The event often brings overwhelming joy and peace to the bereaved. Not surprisingly, existing beliefs about seeing and some day being reunited with the deceased are reinforced, or similar new beliefs result. Marveled one woman: "I now have come to realize that there is something else after life on this earth."

- The sense of presence of the deceased can occur at any time. It may be immediately after the death, or months or years later, though it most often seems to occur in the first week following the death. Some have reported that up to six months or a year later they have continued to sense the presence of their loved one.

Let us move on to another intriguing and very controversial contact experience— postmortem presence, or seeing the deceased—which, although less common than the intuitive experience is equally interesting in terms of the variations in which it occurs.

FIVE

Postmortem Presence:
The Visual Experience

The tea-party question, "Do you believe in ghosts?" is one of the most ambiguous which can be asked. But if we take it to mean "Do you believe that people sometimes experience apparitions?," the answer is that they certainly do. No one who examines the evidence can come to any other conclusion.
—Professor H. H. Price., quoted in Andrew MacKenzie's
Hauntings and Apparitions

We must assume our existence as broadly as we in any way can; everything, even the unheard-of, must be possible in it.
—Rainer Maria Rilke

I once heard a hospice nurse, with eighteen years of experience in helping people with life-threatening illness, tell a large audience the following story. Two young children, a girl and a boy from the same family, were in a very serious traffic accident. The boy died as a result of his injuries. Later at the hospital, the little girl was asked if she wanted to know what had happened and how the accident had occurred. She replied that she already knew because her brother had been there and told her everything.

What was equally striking to me as I listened was the manner in which this nurse related the details of the story, which had happened less than forty-eight hours earlier. Her gentle demeanor was matter-of-fact, sincere and without pretense, as though this type of conversation between siblings was as common as enjoying a conversation with an old friend. Through the years, she had been a witness to so many of these revealing stories that it was not extraordinary to her at all, simply a natural human response under the circumstances; something to be expected. It was obvious to her that the little girl's brother knew she would be upset at his absence and death, really visited with her, and that was that. Nothing to be alarmed about. This hospice nurse is not atypical, not by a long shot. If you are interested in finding down-to-earth professionals willing to talk about death and death-related visions, go to a presentation given by a certified hospice organization as part of their community education program. One person in particular who can be most helpful is the Bereavement Coordinator or Director of Bereavement Services. These are individuals who have direct contact with survivors through the bereavement follow-up program conducted by every hospice for family members of the deceased. You will find that death is viewed as a part of life and not apart from it. The world paradigm of hospice volunteers and nurses is most often diametrically opposed to the conventional world view of the general public. The former do not view death as signaling the end of reciprocal love or life between the deceased and their survivors. Not infrequently, however, the latter may fluctuate in the struggle between believing or not believing stories which suggest something else exists beyond this life. Similar viewpoints like the hospice nurse's persist with the subject of postmortem presence. There is no contact experience more provocative than those involving visions and apparitions of a deceased loved one. Hospice personnel are well aware of that controversy.

Let me emphasize that the postmortem experience is not limited to surviving children. Adults and children of all ages have had contact experiences with deceased loved ones involving the actual presence of that person, usually in what they interpret as normal bodily form. In some cases, the deceased appears in two or three-dimensional form. In others, the upper body or the face is seen, sometimes surrounded by a white light. With rare exceptions, one of which we will be discussing, the deceased looks whole and in good health. Of course, of all types of extraordinary experiences which may occur when a person is mourning, the visual or postmortem experience is usually cause for judging the mourner as unstable or in need of professional care. The reason for this judgment is that we are talking about ghosts, visions, and apparitions, which conjure up all sorts of suspicions, fears, and apprehensions. These unfortunate dynamics are something that is part of our cultural heritage.

Visions of deceased loved ones (or for that matter, those who are still living) are judged abnormal by today's standards. However, as history constantly reminds us, visions have been an integral part of the development of civilizations and the bedrock of many religious organizations, not to mention their role in the dramas of discovery and invention. Still, there is a special stigma attached to seeing things that cannot be held in one's grasp or ordered up for visual inspection again and again. In fact, many visions are denied by those who experience them out of fear that they may indicate mental deterioration or insanity. And those who have them will tell you that it is not easy to find someone who will openly listen when they wish to talk about them.

I submit that a large number of people who have visions are not suffering from acute anxiety attacks or schizophrenia, labels that are conveniently overused. I know it must be discomforting to those who are unable to believe in the reality of visions to have to entertain the slightest possibility that they are anything else but fantasy. Nevertheless, Joan of Arc's vision of angels before going into battle, Paul's vision of heaven and his being felled on the road to Damascus, as well as the Swedish scientist and mystic Emanuel Swedenborg's vision of a devastating fire which was actually taking place hundreds of miles away have not been considered fantasy by many historians. In fact, it is quite clear that St. Paul's vision was a significant factor in the spread of Christianity, and a major force in changing the face of Western civilization. Still, labeling visions as a product of dementia becomes a secure feeling when one's perceptions of reality are challenged.

But visions may be nothing more than the flip side of dreams. Dreams and visions are closely linked: the latter simply occur when we are wide awake. There are untold numbers of dreams—thoughts in picture form—which result in action when the dreamer awakens. The same holds true with visions. They are motivating, they change behavior, they save time and heartache, and interestingly, they result in peace of mind, a goal most of us consciously or unconsciously strive for.

Here is an example. Tom Hurley is the Director of Membership Education at the Institute of Noetic Sciences in Sausalito, California, a research foundation and educational institution which is in the forefront of consciousness research. His mother died unexpectedly of a massive heart attack and he was left with unfinished business, compounding his deep sorrow and loss. He flew back home for the funeral and to be with the family. His unusual experience occurred at the wake.

"I Exalted in My Mother's Liberation"

A Catholic wake service was held for my mother three days after she died. My mother's one request—expressed long before her death—had been that a rosary be said at her wake. (In the Catholic tradition, a rosary is a series of prayers dedicated to Mary, for whom my mother felt a special devotion.) A nun who had been a close family friend led the rosary. In the middle of it, a simple, extraordinary thing occurred. I saw my mother's spirit rise from her body. The room suddenly glowed with light, and I was filled with joy, peace, and a sense of wonder. A moment earlier I had ached with a sense of loss; now I exalted in my mother's liberation. Later, my wife Sarah asked if I had experienced anything unusual during the rosary. To my surprise, we discovered our experiences had been virtually identical.[1]

The next afternoon at the funeral Tom also experienced the sense of his mother's presence and received a second gift. "In a moment of sudden, unexpected communion with her, I saw that she had known who I was in this life, in some essential, intuitive way no words could express, and that she knew of my love for her. And I knew who she was. My sense of unfinished business vanished." Thus, in two very brief episodes, a major obstacle to going on with his grief work had been overcome. Love won out. He had received an important message: Their love was reciprocal after all. He was at peace.

Visions, Dreams, and Apparitions

If visions are the flip side of dreams, what are apparitions and ghosts? The main difference, it has been suggested, is that an apparition is a one-time appearance, while a ghost appears more than once in the same general area.[2] Obviously, these terms are often used interchangeably and may diminish the accuracy of reporting unusual phenomena—a hazard of confronting the difficult-to-explain. One distinction which is sometimes made between the three terms involves the origin of the phenomena that they purport to describe. It appears that visions are generated from within while it can be argued that apparitions and ghosts are seen "out there." Of course, there are some who say that all three originate from within the individual, and still others who counter with the belief that all are processed through the mind after having been received from an outside source. In particular, there are a number of people who believe that visions come directly from God.[3] There is little agreement as to cause and effect. Hence, each of us has to decide whether visions, apparitions, and ghosts are realities from without—part of nonphysical or spiritual reality—which we process like any other sensory experience, or are generated within the conscious and unconscious mind of the individual. Perhaps it is part of both. In any event, let me suggest that all three are means by which the nonphysical world communicates with the bereaved.

To further our discussion of the visual contact experience, I should call your attention to the confusion of hallucinations with the three terms just mentioned.

Regrettably, the term *hallucination* carries a negative and intimidating connotation in the minds of most people as it implies mental illness or drug use. There are a variety of definitions for the term. A standard dictionary calls it "an apparent perception for which there is no external cause." It is also defined as "suffering from false notions." William James suggested that a hallucination was a sensational form of consciousness, as though a real object was there, but there is no real object. When I was teaching a course on Drug Studies at the State University of New York, a common definition within the drug culture was "seeing sounds and hearing colors." The recent scientific literature labels all contact experiences involving a visual sighting of the deceased as hallucinatory, which typically implies pathology. That is, it labels all such experiences as false notions. This prevailing characterization programs many bereaved people who have a visual experience to quickly dismiss it as a product of an overworked imagination. Others will question their sanity after having the experience. But a significant number of these contacts happen spontaneously and in a manner that is perfectly acceptable to the mourner. They bring the most positive results imaginable when not negatively labeled. The notable change in the survivor's grief work is immediate. One is spared months or years of suffering or learning to adjust because of a single short-lived experience. In truth, psychology has no other language with which to describe the visual experience other than calling it a hallucination, a word that perpetuates a negative image for a very positive event. At the same time, it is interesting that those who use the term in their research studies of the bereaved report that they find the experience benign, giving comfort and solace—yet it is officially described as an abnormal function of the brain due to the stress of grief. Some counselors even instruct their grieving clients to dismiss such occurrences from their thoughts.

The Most Common Visual Experience

There are several types of death-related visions that have been reported by countless loved ones and friends of those who have died. G. N. M. Tyrrell, a reputable scientist and former president of the Society for Psychical Research (SPR) has offered four group classifications of such apparitions. Those in group one are called crisis apparitions, which occur at the moment of death or shortly after. Group two encompasses postmortem apparitions, which are seen twelve hours or more after death. Group three apparitions are continual apparitions, seen many times over a long period. (These are considered as ghosts by many parapsychologists.) The fourth category refers to apparitions of the living. There have been many reports of appearances of the living in one location when they have been documented as being somewhere else.[4] Although apparitions of the deceased may occur many years later, the most common vision or apparition which I have found appears to take place within the time frame of three or four weeks to several months after the death of the person. The place of appearance is usually in the familiar surroundings of the home. These appearances would fall into Tyrrell's category of postmortem apparitions. Here are three examples. In the first, a college student I'll call Tina sees her father in the hallway of her home.

"He Didn't Look like He Did before He Died"

The funeral was finally over. It had been a long day. That evening I took a shower to try to relax. I got dressed and came out of the bathroom to make a warm drink in the kitchen. As I turned to the right I saw my father standing at the end of my hall. He had had several strokes before he died and was partially paralyzed. He didn't look like he did before he died. He was vibrant and healthy and looked the way he did before he was ever sick. He stood there a few seconds, smiled, and gently faded away. I think he wanted me to know he was going to heaven and that his pain was finally over. This experience helped me because I knew he was finally happy and not suffering anymore.

Tina, who had just turned twenty, was not at all surprised by her father's appearance. She had been very close to him and was glad to see him so healthy, since his long illness had dimmed her memory of how active he used to be.

The second example comes from the oldest subject I have interviewed about a contact experience, eighty-two-year-old Doreen. I spoke with her in the room in which she saw her husband about seven months after his sudden death. Doreen was alert, decisive, and, I must admit, a bit defensive. I mention that because as she ushered me in and we sat down, before I could ask a single question, she started with, "I want to tell you I never believed in this sort of thing." Here is her account of Ted's visit to her.

"He Was Always Caring"

I knew Ted since I was nine years old. We were childhood friends and I later learned, when I was sixteen, after our first date, he told one of his friends that someday he was going to marry me. We finally did get married in 1935—fifty-seven years of marriage. We had a good life and a great relationship. He was a salesman, humorous, and the type who could keep the party going. But as he got older he developed asthma and once when he went into the hospital for some routine tests, the doctor discovered that he had gallstones and had to have an operation.

I figured everybody can have a gall bladder operation. Well he had it, and it was successful, but he developed an infection and they had to go back in again a second time. The reason for the second operation was they couldn't control the infection (He had been in intensive care for three weeks). I should have known it was more serious, but the doctor and the nurse didn't think it was real serious either. At least that's the impression they gave me.

I used to go in every day and stay from 10:00 A.M. until 4:00 P.M. One day, I had just arrived home and they called and said to come right back because he was having trouble breathing. He died before I could get back because he couldn't get enough air. The last thing he had said to me before I had left two hours earlier was "You've been so good to me and for me." I don't know if he had a premonition that his time had come or not, but I didn't expect his death.

The day I had the apparition, I was sitting right in this chair reading the paper. It was about 4 o'clock in the afternoon. For some reason, I glanced over the top of the paper and saw Ted floating in a vertical position right across the doorway between this room and the kitchen. He was about three feet off the ground. I saw him from the knees up, his feet couldn't have been touching the floor. It didn't take long for it to happen but I sort of sat there in shock. Normally, I would have poo-pooed all of this but I definitely did see it. He was dressed and looked good. There wasn't much color to it all; he was sort of like in a vapor. I could understand it if it happened right away after his death because it's all on your mind. This was several months later.

I think he's still checking on me and making sure everything is okay. He was always caring, watching to see that everything goes right. You know, things have worked out very nicely. I always say my prayers each night. He's there and God is there with me. I am content with my life.

Doreen maintains a very active lifestyle. She volunteers at a little store operated by the town in which she lives, plays lots of bridge, and goes out on dates. But she does not want to marry again.

In this third example of a postmortem vision, a grieving sister, who I will call Allie, not only sees her deceased brother, but is given encouragement by him.

"Allie, Everything Is All Right"

My brothers had always watched over me and I really had become too dependent on them for some of the things I should have been doing for myself. My brother Phil had been killed in the automobile accident which also involved my oldest brother who was seriously injured but survived. I was very close to Phil and could not accept what had happened. I was beside myself with grief. One evening, several days after his death I just passed out from all the stress and trauma. When I opened my eyes Phil was standing over me and said, "Allie, everything is all right."

Because it was so hard for our family to accept his death I believe he wanted everyone to know he was now at peace, he was OK. But he came to me when I was in special need.

In each of these incidents, survivors interpreted the experience to mean that they should go on with their lives. Significantly, Allie's vision occurs after having passed out. She could not have been seeking his appearance in her temporary blackout. The implication was that Phil knew the difficulty his family was having accepting his death, and was there to ease the burden. His appearance to his sister may be viewed as simply another example of the opening anecdote of this chapter involving the two small children—he was doing what was expected. In a similar way, Doreen was completely surprised with Ted's visit. She had been out for most of the day, came home, and decided to read the newspaper. Her grief work, according to her own evaluation, was going well. She had accepted Ted's death and was not thinking about him at the time he appeared. But his appearance convinced her that he was still concerned and wanted her to know. This was comforting for her.

Despite their importance, not all visions of the deceased are accepted by survivors. Sometimes survivors are scared by the appearance and fear they may be losing their sanity. This is what happened to Laura (not her real name) several years ago. I learned of it after speaking to a group of professional caregivers at a college on the topic of grief support. My speech included some information on how to deal with someone who experiences the extraordinary. It never fails that after introducing the topic of the unusual experiences of the bereaved as a normal part of the grief process, someone will approach me or send me a note regarding a personal experience. In this instance, a middle-aged woman waited until most of the other participants had left the room and came up to me with great anxiety in her eyes. Here is the account of her experience as she shared it with me with much feeling.

"I Thought I Was Losing My Mind"

My father committed suicide. We were all so upset, destroyed. We couldn't understand what would drive him to do such a thing. About three days later, I went over to his house to organize his possessions and take care of his clothing. As I was walking up the driveway to the house, I looked up at the large glass-enclosed front porch—and he was standing there as big as life. I was scared. I thought I was losing my mind. He was there for only a short period of time and when I looked again, he was gone. It was a chilling experience and has caused me lots of problems. What do you think of this?

This woman (who was an acquaintance of mine, though not one I expected to share her inner fears with me) was very concerned that there was something wrong with her mind. She was in desperate need to hear that what had occurred was not at all an indicator of a mental disorder; that it happens to many people; that her father's presence could very well have been his attempt to ease her suffering. Normalizing the experience was a significant step for her.

Sometimes the deceased will be seen in a favorite reclining chair or at the table, even sitting at the foot of the bed. According to Carl Sandburg, Mary Todd Lincoln told her White House nurse after the death of little Willie that the child "...comes every night and stands at the foot of my bed, with the same sweet adorable smile he always had."[5] Her visions ended after a short period of time, having fulfilled an important function. It is also common that the deceased looks healthy or indicates that he or she is whole again. This is what happened to Beverly, whose husband had died of a heart attack after having severe angina pains for several years. "I knew my husband was always in a lot of pain and would try to hide it from me," she said. "One evening, when I was home alone, he was suddenly there with me in the living room. He looked so good and alive. He stretched out his hands and said, 'See I have no more pain.' I was so relieved and for a moment happy because he was happy."

In many visual experiences, the person is seen in vivid detail, which includes clothing, gestures, and facial expressions. He or she arrives suddenly and is gone just as suddenly. Occasionally there is a reappearance, as happened with Darlene. Her father had died unexpectedly from a heart attack. He had left the house to go fishing and was later found on the beach with his fishing tackle at his side. It was 2:00 A.M. when a detective knocked on Darlene's door to inform her of his death. The succession of appearances of her father (Tyrrell's "continuous apparitions") began shortly after his funeral and continued for several weeks. Here is her account.

"I Didn't Know What to Believe"

I would wake up to the doorbell ringing at 2:00 A.M. The first time it happened I thought that someone else had died. I put on my bathrobe and went downstairs to answer the door. As I opened the door and peeked out there stood my father. He was dressed in his red checkered shirt and his fishing hat just as he was on the last day when they found him on the beach. He wore that smile I always loved. But as soon as I opened the door all the way, he was gone. This went on for several weeks; it would be 2:00 A.M. I would hear the doorbell, put on my robe, go down and open the door, and he would be there smiling and then vanish. I didn't know what to believe, although it didn't really alarm me. Finally, I talked to a friend at my church who had a similar thing happen to her. She helped me a lot. A short time later it stopped.

Darlene accepted the series of appearances of her father, but told me she was perplexed at why they occurred, since the same repetitive pattern was followed each time. She wondered, after his third or fourth appearance, if there "was something I was doing to cause them or if I perhaps was fantasizing." It was fortunate that she was able to find someone at her church to talk with who had a very similar experience with the death of a loved one. Because Darlene was a professional caregiver, her questioning of the experience was thorough and ongoing.

Proof or Fantasy?

Darlene was in good company. None other than Carl Jung, who was very interested in the extraordinary and believed that by way of the collective unconscious we all share a common bond with those who have gone before us, questioned the one-time appearance of his deceased friend. In his autobiography *Memories, Dreams, Reflections*, he writes about his postmortem apparition and his hesitancy in accepting what was happening to him.

Jung had been lying awake one evening reviewing the events of the previous day which were dominated by the funeral of a friend who had died unexpectedly.

He had been deeply moved and saddened by the death. Without warning, he suddenly sensed the presence of his friend standing at the foot of his bed. At the same time, Jung felt that his friend had made a gesture to follow him out of the bedroom. The inner visual images were at first considered nothing more than mere fantasy. But he toiled with the problem that if it was not a fantasy and it really was his friend standing there, he would be showing great disrespect by not responding to him. In either case, he had no proof. So he gave his friend the benefit of the doubt and reacted as though the event were real.

In his imagination, he followed his friend as he walked out of the bedroom, up the road to his friend's house, and into his study. Very methodically, he watched as his friend climbed on to a stool and showed Jung the second of five books with red bindings lying on the second shelf from the top. At that point the vision ended.[6] The next day, he went to his friend's widow to ask if he could look something up in his library. Though Jung was not acquainted with the library, everything was in place as it had been in his vision—the stool under the bookcase and the five books with red bindings. The title of the second book was *The Legacy of the Dead* by Emile Zola. The contents had no meaning or interest for Jung but in recalling the experience he said that, "Only the title was extremely significant in connection with this experience."[7]

We can only speculate what Jung believed was so significant about the title. Perhaps one legacy of the dead is their ability (the source of which is unknown) to communicate with the living. Perhaps the message his friend wanted to get across was that his appearance, vision, or apparition—whatever we might call it—was real; that the dead live on. There was personal meaning for the living in Jung's vision of his friend.

Some critics challenge the idea that visionary messages of any type could be considered valid. They insist that the power of suggestion and expectancy on the part of the mourner is the catalyst behind why one sees the deceased. Although a host of visual experiences occur when the mourner is not thinking of the return of the loved one, it is difficult to explain away experiences in which the deceased speaks and gives advice.

Judy Tatelbaum, in *The Courage to Grieve*, provides an excellent illustration of a woman whose deceased father appeared at the foot of her bed on several occasions, and each time was laughing. This was disturbing to her, and when trying to figure out why he was laughing "...she suddenly 'heard' him say as he might have when alive, 'Laugh a little. Don't take this grief so seriously.'"[8] Thereafter, her father's visitations ended.

What Is the Meaning of the Visual Experience?

For an outsider looking in, perhaps the most intriguing question to be asked is "What is the meaning of these unbidden appearances of the deceased to the living?" Certainly, the question has been asked many times. Putting the hallucination theory aside for now, most survivors who experience the deceased loved one believe the answer is quite obvious: their loved ones are very concerned about how they are adjusting to their deaths. They want their survivors to realize they are all right and to accept their deaths. Certainly, this is not unreasonable. It could very well be their task to draw the living into greater love for each other as well as to say "our love is eternal even though we are separated." In this realm, the deceased are very much concerned about the living and their relationships. Perhaps the deceased, by their appearances, are attempting to alert their loved ones not to be discouraged, that there is a much broader meaning to existence, and that "we will meet again." For many survivors, the thought that they will someday be with their loved ones—based on the interpretation of their visual experiences—is a powerful ally in the management of grief. They receive a feeling of empowerment which transcends any sense of isolation or abandonment.

Of course, those who have not had a visual or any other contact experience are reluctant to agree with such a sentimental assessment. I regret to say that the prospect of the deceased helping the living is also seen by some of the most respected parapsychologists as a far too simple reason for visions and apparitions.[9] This is reflective of our recent history in which few things are not deemed useful or acceptable unless they are complex, costly, or time consuming. Most scientists and many parapsychologists cling to the traditional explanation for seeing the deceased: hallucinations. Their theory is based on the following reasoning:

> *...apparitions act in a way that one would expect them to act if they were the products of our own thinking. For instance, if apparitions are really spirit entities, how could they not only appear clothed but be accompanied by dogs, walking sticks, or even a horse and carriage? If apparitions are taken to be proof of spirit persons, then surely they must be taken to be proof of spirit shirts and trousers.*[10]

Regardless of the perspective of those who need proof to accept the visual experience as valid, for now, one point should not be overlooked: the overall results of the experience are genuinely positive and encouraging for the bereaved. Lest we forget, what makes people happy again and able to go on with their lives is what goes on in their heads, not what others tell them they should be doing, thinking, or accepting.

Could there be other explanations for why the deceased engage the living, assuming one believes that some of their appearances are in fact real? A number of parapsychologists believe that the many thousands of apparitions which have been reported throughout recorded history could be regarded as proof that consciousness survives bodily death and that there is another realm of existence (perhaps the reason for Jung's vision?) I will add to the meaning of the visual experience later when we examine various explanations for all of the extraordinary phenomena which is associated with bereavement.

> *As I examined the cases, I began to realize that visionary experiences are very similar to near-death experiences. Indeed what are often called in medical textbooks grief-induced hallucinations are not hallucinations at all but normal brain processes that happen to be visionary.*
>
> —Melvin Morse, *Parting Visions.* New York: Villard Books, 1994.

Crisis Apparitions

Using Tyrrell's terminology of crisis apparitions, that is, appearances of the deceased at the moment of death or shortly after, we venture into some of the most compelling experiences of all. I use the word *compelling* because in these contacts the survivor sees the deceased before he/she is notified of the death. In some instances, the deceased and the survivor had made a pact to attempt to let each other know if something happened to one or the other, if they were separated. Some visions occur with no verbal response received from the deceased. Others include an auditory as well as a tactile contact. Here are two examples of documented visual experiences occurring at or shortly after the moment of death. The first comes from one of the earliest written accounts of a crisis apparition collected by the SPR (Society for Psychical Research) and reported to the Literary Committee.

Russell and Oliver Colt were brothers in every sense of the word. They were very close and concerned about each other's welfare. At nineteen years of age, older brother Oliver had already become a lieutenant in the Seventh Royal Fusiliers and was about to face a grim yet heroic combat experience in the Crimean War. Russell missed his brother, and they corresponded frequently. On receiving a letter in which Oliver was obviously dejected and not feeling well, Russell wrote back in an attempt to lift his brother's spirits, saying that if anything were to happen to him, "he was to let me know by appearing to me in my room." That Oliver received this letter was later confirmed by a clergyman assigned to the company. He was thrust into battle shortly afterward, and within a few hours of the storming of the Redan he was placed in command when the captain fell mortally wounded. Thus, he had to lead the men in the next charge. In doing so, he sustained several wounds, but kept advancing until he was finally struck by a bullet in the right temple, which ended his life. He fell among a large number of his men already dead in a half-kneeling posture, propped up by their bodies. This occurred on September 8, 1855. Younger brother Russell tells what happened the evening of his brother's death.

"I Only Know I Shall Never Forget It"

That night I awoke suddenly, and saw facing the window of my room, by my bedside, surrounded by a sort of phosphorescent mist, as it were, my brother kneeling. ... I decided that it must be fancy, and the moonlight playing on a towel, or something out of place. But on looking up, there he was again, looking lovingly, imploringly, and sadly at me. I turned and still saw poor Oliver. I shut my eyes, walked through it, and reached the door of the room. As I turned the handle, before leaving the room, I looked once more back. The apparition turned round his head slowly and again looked anxiously and lovingly at me, and I saw then for the first time a wound on the right temple with a red stream from it. His face was of a waxy pale tint, but transparent looking, and so was the reddish mark. But it is almost impossible to describe his appearance. I only know I shall never forget it. I left the room and went into a friend's room, and lay on the sofa the rest of the night. I told him why. I told others in the house, but when I told my father, he ordered me not to repeat such nonsense, and especially not to let my mother know.[11]

Two weeks later, the family was informed of Oliver's death. Russell's vision of his brother on the day of his death was not only convincing but unforgettable, having occurred within a few hours of Oliver's mortal wounding. Twenty-seven years later, he sent the account to SPR investigators studying the phenomena, although he had honored his father's request for silence on many occasions.

In the second example, the survivor not only sees the deceased, but also hears and is touched by her. And, like the previous experience, there is no previous knowledge that the death had occurred.

David Belasco was a giant among New York's theatrical producers and playwrights at the turn of the century. Although he lived on the east coast, his mother, brothers, and sisters resided in San Francisco. Early one morning, after arriving home from a late rehearsal, he awoke from a sound sleep to find his mother standing near the bed. But she was on the other coast, he thought. As happens with many apparition contacts, his mother spoke to him at length, smiling and saying that everything was all right and that he should not grieve for her. The assumption was that her death was quite normal, no cause for alarm, and was to be accepted without fanfare. Of course, Belasco was riveted on the apparition and was in awe when his mother leaned over and kissed him as she departed repeating his name three times—"Davie, Davie, Davie." He was not sure how long he lay wide awake before he managed to put on a bathrobe and go downstairs. His footsteps had awakened his family. He poured out the story, adding that he was convinced his mother had died. They would have nothing of it and suggested that it must have been a dream.[12]

The next morning, Belasco went to rehearsal. Later, he had lunch with a member of the theater staff who handed him some letters and telegrams he had picked up at the office. Among the telegrams was the news that his mother had died. It was then that the meaning of his experience the previous night was made clear. He had seen, heard, and been touched by his mother. He soon learned that her death occurred at the same time she had appeared at his bedside. It wasn't until years later, when visiting his brothers and sisters in San Francisco, that he was informed that his mother had called out "Davie, Davie, Davie" shortly before her death. Belasco's affection for his mother is reflected in a letter he wrote to a friend. In it he said: "I cannot tell you how close we were—how she seemed always to understand me without words and often seemed to be near me when I was in trouble and needed help."[13] Belasco had been given a final parting gift.

In my own research, a woman I'll call Lisa had the following visual experience which involved her husband's grandfather. At twenty years of age, Lisa had been married less than a year when her husband's grandfather was taken sick and was near death. Her husband was with his family while she remained at home, having to work the next day. Lisa tells us:

"He Cared Deeply for Me"

I had trouble sleeping that night as Richard wasn't at home. I had been tossing and turning for nearly an hour when I saw Richard's grandfather walk past the foot of my bed and go over and stand by the window. I guess you could say I froze and could not put the light on until he stopped by the window. When I put the light on, no one was there. This happened to me three times that night and each time my heart would be pounding.

I think my husband's grandfather did this because he cared deeply for me and wanted me to know he was leaving. He died that night. This experience has helped me to understand and relate when others have told me about their hard-to-believe experiences. I can see that they are credible because of my own experience.

These three crisis apparitions illustrate the variation in relationships in which the deceased loved ones may appear. Sibling and mother-son relationships can be easily assumed to be particularly close. However, one would not expect a spouse's grandparent to make contact with the other spouse as in Lisa's experience unless their was a strong, compelling bond. So much for strict familial ties. But notice that Lisa believes the experience occurred because the grandparent cared about her. As she said, he was perhaps giving forewarning to ease her burden and strengthen her belief that he was going to be all right. The experience would also help her in supporting her husband in his grief work.

Of all visual experiences encountered by the bereaved, none demonstrate credibility more than the crisis apparition. This is especially true when the deceased speaks to the survivor or gives a clear message which is later verified.

The crisis apparition pointedly brings the question of "Why?" to our attention. Why do these events take place? This question begs several others: How is the image of the dying or deceased transmitted to the survivor who has no knowledge of the death? How could the psyche of the survivor possibly conjure up the image of the deceased, if he or she doesn't know the person has died? And why does the event occur in some relationships, but not all?

Any attempt at answering these questions demands throwing out some time-tested laws. Only recently, and very reluctantly, a few scientists have no longer unconditionally accepted linear causality (one thing leading to another) with irrefutable certainty. For example, some accept Heisenberg's Uncertainty Principle, which states that in the quantum world individual events are spontaneous and unpredictable. The concept of matter as the ultimate reality is challenged. (In this regard, you may be interested in reading the work of some of the pioneers in quantum physics like David Bohm, Werner Heisenberg, and Niels Bohr.) In place of the old way of viewing the world comes an idea quite foreign to our way of thinking—that what happens in one place may happen in another place at the same time. Such an occurrence may not be as preposterous as it may seem, if one believes that some contact experiences are in fact spiritual experiences. All sorts of possibilities present themselves if we no longer follow the usually accepted time-space model.

Once the intrusions of the unknown are accepted as independent of space and time, as currently understood, new meaning emerges. But I will leave that decision up to you. Again, what is important is the fact that the contact experience helps survivors go on with their lives. And one final caveat: Under no circumstances should we forget that there is no scientific proof that crisis apparitions, or for that matter all classifications of apparitions, are not possible. The territory is largely unexplored.

In the next section, we examine a rather common contact experience: Hearing the deceased in a variety of different ways.

SIX

Auditory Contacts:
Hearing the Deceased

Many people who hear a voice attribute it to some otherworldly being or to God, as saints and modern-day spiritual "channelers" have done. . . . Alschuler isn't sure of the source of his voice. "Perhaps it's a kind of superconsciousness," he says, "as it tends to deal with high ideals and the relationship to God."
—Patrick Huyghe in "Mind: Voices From Inner Space,"
Hippocrates, July/August 1988

Where there is great love there are always miracles.
—Willa Cather

Hearing the voice of the deceased, music, or other sounds associated with the person is not an unusual experience for the bereaved. In some instances, direct communication takes place between the two, a clear conversation between the living and the dead. There are also a number of interactions in which the deceased provides information that is used to protect the bereaved from harm.

Music, for some, is an answer to an expressed desire for the deliverance of the deceased into the hands of God. One may pray for a sign and hear "celestial music" which could not be duplicated by any high-tech equipment now available in recording studios. I once had a woman tell me that she had a vivid dream about her dead child in which she heard "the most beautiful heavenly music, like I never thought was possible." Through it she received assurance about the safety of her child.

There are also instances in which a survivor is awakened from sleep by the voice of a dying or deceased person. Here is an example from one of the early volumes of *The Journal of the Society for Psychical Research.* It concerns a nurse who worked the night shift and slept during the day in a room provided for her at the hospital where she was employed.

"Darling Peggy Passed Away at 5:30 P.M"

I was startled out of my sleep by a voice which called out my name distinctly, "Margaret, Margaret." I felt positive that someone had been in my room by my bed and rushed out again. I was never called by my Christian name at the hospital....I thought it must have been the maid calling the night nurses, and she had not switched my light on. I got out of bed and looked down the corridor. I did not hear or see anybody. I looked at my clock; it was 5:30 P.M. At breakfast that night I told some of my colleagues about my strange experience and they just joked about it. I went on duty at 10:30 P.M.....The night sister came to me, called me to one side.... She handed me a telegram which said: "Darling Peggy passed away at 5:30 P.M.".... Peggy was my little niece, aged eight years. We were great friends. She was taken suddenly ill and an immediate operation was performed, but she lived only a few hours. When I met my sister I told her what I had experienced, and she told me that the child called out, "Margaret," and she remarked to her husband, "Is she calling herself or Auntie Margaret?" It is a strange fact that the stated time of the child's death on the wire was 5:30 P.M., just about the time I was disturbed from my sleep. I did not know the child was ill; it was very sudden. I cannot describe my feelings as I read the telegram, which reminded me of my strange experience at 5:30 P.M.[1]

How can this be explained? Parapsychologists say that it is simply a form of telepathic communication that can take place between the living or the living and the deceased. Conversely, critics of those who say they have heard the dying or deceased loved ones call their name commonly say these experiences are auditory hallucinations. The same explanation is given when someone reports hearing footsteps, music, or breathing (when alone or lying in bed at night) attributed to the deceased. However, the nurse who heard her formal name called while sleeping had no knowledge of the imminent death of her niece.

On the other hand, critics reason that auditory hallucination may explain many circumstances in which the bereaved expect a loved one to arrive home at a particular time, as he or she did for many years. Thus, having heard the same familiar sounds hundreds of times in the past, memory sets off the sequence of events. We can all see how a conscious or unconscious state of expectation can play a role in misinterpreting sounds and sometimes voices. I recall an experience when I was expecting my wife to return home with my mother-in-law and I wanted to be sure I was ready to help her with a project we had planned. I expected them at any minute, and was vigilantly listening for the car to pull into the driveway. Lo and behold, I heard the car pull in, the doors of the car close, and a conversation between the two—or so I thought. I waited. And waited. No one came to the door. They clearly had arrived home; at least, that's what I thought. I was wrong. What had happened was simply that a next-door neighbor had arrived with a guest and I had misinterpreted their arrival as that of my wife and her mother. Strong expectation played a key role in my mistaken assumption that they were here. Yet at the time, I thought the voices were beyond a shadow of a doubt those of my wife and her mother.

It is rather easy for doubters who demean any type of auditory contact to prove the expectation syndrome, because the sound of the car pulling into the driveway or the key turning in the lock can be quickly verified. The bereaved either sees the parked car or someone walking through the door after it has been unlocked. When no such proof is evident, though, it is simply attributed to auditory hallucinations. Can the same conclusions be reached when it comes to hearing the voice of the deceased? And is the old saw "Seeing is believing" the only grounds for accepting or rejecting an auditory contact?

To begin with, the anticipation of the return of the deceased by the bereaved person (what counselors call the expectation set) is not always in an acute or heightened state; certainly not as alert as I was in expecting my wife and mother-in-law to return from their shopping trip. Not true, you say, since the bereaved is always expecting the return of the loved one. Yes, but it is a rather long stretch of the imagination to imply that all bereaved people are expecting the deceased to give them verbal support. For example, is it reasonable to assume that a mourner who is expecting the return of his deceased loved one would also expect her to tell him that she is at peace, or "please don't grieve for me, I am okay?" Obviously, the nurse who was called by her niece in our opening quote had no reason to be expecting a call, since she did not know her niece was near death. In short, those who experience the deceased through an auditory response have little expectation of the type of messages they hear or the conversations carried on. When one hears or sees something other than what is expected, it is a good bet that something other than fantasy or the imagination is at work.

The Stigma of Hearing Sounds and Voices

Reporting an auditory contact often results in the stigmatization of the bereaved. I say that because many of us have unconsciously held beliefs about people who hear voices or talk to themselves. This behavior is especially disconcerting when we observe someone engaging in it. Regrettably, many people have accepted without question the idea that when someone starts to hear voices there is a problem lurking somewhere. Hearing voices means you're in emotional turmoil. Without a doubt, there are a number of individuals with emotional problems whose symptoms include voices that tell them to do things that are dangerous. However, people who hear voices (or talk to themselves) are not necessarily candidates for psychiatric treatment, although the stigma is not an easy one to shake. This is especially true when the voice or sounds are said to come from the dead, because there is still a cultural taboo about death despite the greater openness of the past two decades.

Plato's teacher Socrates (470–399 B.C.) wrote of the *daimon*, a voice which guided him in decision-making throughout his life. The word *daimon* or *daemon* (demon) originally did not have the satanic connotation that it does today. In fact, Socrates used it interchangeably with Theos or God, from which we derive the word *theology*. He believed very strongly that his daimon had been given to him by a divine source, and it was through this voice that he made many choices which ultimately made him one of the noted philosophers in history. The daimon he listened to was a voice he was convinced came from outside, from a Deity, and directed him toward good and away from evil: it was his moral guide, a source of wisdom. At times he was observed walking down the streets of Athens talking to himself, in actuality talking to his daimon.

Strangely, Socrates reports that his invisible companion was silent when he came to confronting his trial and death sentence. "... the voice has given me no opposition, neither when I left my house this morning, nor when I entered the court." He took this absence of input from his source of wisdom as approval of what was going to happen to him.[2]

When Charles Lindbergh climbed into the cockpit of the Spirit of St. Louis and lifted off from Roosevelt Field on New York's Long Island in May of 1927, he never believed he would receive any assistance in his flight, once airborne. His solo thirty-four-hour sojourn caused him to drift off to sleep occasionally, which would affect the course he had plotted for his trip to Paris. In those days, there was no such device as an automatic pilot to switch on to allow the pilot a break. Lindbergh was later to admit that familiar voices had guided him in those precarious moments when sleep would gain the upper hand, keeping him from veering too far off course and wasting precious fuel.[3]

In the 1981 skywalk disaster at a Kansas City hotel, a woman heard two words that saved her life. First she heard her name called which caused her to look up toward the ceiling, where she saw a large chandelier begin to come loose. Then she heard "run," which she did, and was therefore saved from the collapsing ceiling and staircase. Voices of warning and protection have been heard throughout history.

> *Many readers told me of hearing unexpected, unexplainable music, especially at the time of a death. But they have usually kept silent about it, fearing others would assume it was a grief-induced hallucination.*
> —Joan Wester Anderson, *Where Miracles Happen*. Brooklyn, NY:
> Brett Books, Inc. 1994

At one time in his life, C. G. Jung reported that he had conversed with a voice when he had been especially stressed. He even gave it a name: Philemon, a Greek poet of The New Comedy who lived between 361–262 B.C. At another time, after he had had one of several powerful dreams presaging his mother's death, Jung heard music and laughter.

He had been staying in the Tessin, a mountainous region in the central Alps, when news of his mother's death finally reached him. He packed his belongings and left immediately on the night train. As expected, he was filled with sadness and remorse and was also preoccupied with thoughts of the frightening dream of the previous evening which he believed had forecast her death. Yet although grieving, deep inside Jung did not feel the constant emotional turmoil so often associated with the loss of one's mother, because of a paradoxical experience. All the way home, he heard lively dance music and joyful laughter that would be expected at a gala wedding party. His entire journey was punctuated with the joy of music and laughter alternating with pangs of grief. His sorrow had been tempered by this experience. He had not been plunged into depths of despair or depression.[4]

The bereaved and the famous are among many who have heard voices that have had nothing to do with the contemporary notion that to hear a voice is a sign of emotional illness. Obviously Jung, Lindbergh, and Socrates all had something in common: they heard voices and paid attention to what they were hearing.

We obviously live in a complex world of relations, connections, and interdependencies that are yet to be understood. If every voice that one hears, when no one can be seen to account for it, were doubted, the civilized world would be far behind the stage of development of the present day. Civilizations and religions have flourished because of those who have heard voices, unexpected voices bearing good news. For example, the archangel Gabriel told the Prophet Mohammed that he had been chosen by Allah; John heard the voice of God say, "I am the Alpha and the Omega, the first and the last, the beginning and the end;" and when Moses saw the burning bush and approached, a voice told him to take off his sandals because he was on sacred ground. Jacob, St. Augustine, and numerous others have been spoken to by angels, and Joan of Arc's voices encouraged her in her defense of France. People from all walks of life—athletes, scientists, revolutionaries, military leaders, poets and philosophers—have heard voices without seeing a person in the flesh. And many musicians have heard their music clearly before they wrote their masterpieces. For example, Mozart is said to have heard some of his symphonies as though he were sitting in a famous music hall with a fine orchestra before he put them on paper. Not to be overlooked are the many voices that people have heard and followed which resulted in miraculous healings from crippling disease. Countless lives have been saved by warning voices from deceased loved ones. Equally important, these voices usually emanate goodness to the vast majority of the bereaved who have an auditory experience. Obviously, then, there are life-affirming voices and very meaningful sounds.

But there are also torturous voices and hellish sounds which have been heard through the ages and cannot be fully accounted for. A young man once told me that his aunt said she heard a voice which told her to go to the window and jump out in order to join her son in death. Certainly, when one hears voices that are condemning, abusive, or demanding that something socially unacceptable be done, illness is at hand. These are known as "command hallucinations" and are usually associated with acts of violence.[5]

So let's set aside the assumption that hearing things when no one is around is ipso facto grounds for dismissing them as having been imagined. Could it not be possible (as related by esoteric teachings of both East and West) that we all have an angel, guide, or a "voice" which lovingly points us in the right direction at times, if we are willing to listen? Even though it cannot be physically confirmed, could it be another reality or dream-state we are taught not to accept? The reality of the unseen is not subject to the laws of physics. Nevertheless, it is in the realm of nonphysical reality that we build bridges to rise above and solve some of the complexities of our existence. In the final analysis, it is the context in which a voice or other tell-tale sound is heard which is critical in determining the meaning, importance, and authenticity for any listener.

Types of Auditory Experiences

Auditory contacts usually occur in one of three ways:

- A sound or voice is clearly heard coming from an outside source.
- A sound or voice is clearly heard which appears to come from within the bereaved person.
- An auditory contact in combination with a vision or with a touch from the deceased.

In a large number of these experiences, information is conveyed that the deceased is all right and that there is nothing to worry about. Here are two typical combination events involving hearing and seeing the deceased.

"I Felt Loved, which I Needed Badly at the Time"

When my grandmother died I was having other problems in my life which were causing me great anxiety and I was unable to attend the wake. A few days after her death, I saw my grandmother in my room and spoke with her. She simply came out of nowhere. She said she understood why I was not at the wake and that she would always love me. She also told me that having a baby, even though I was unmarried, was not the worst thing in the world.

I'm not sure why all this happened, other than the fact that Gramma knew I loved her and I needed a great deal of love and understanding at the time. At that point in my life, I was only 16 years old, not really sure of grief, but I felt loved which I needed badly at the time. Yes, I would say it helped a lot. It pulled me out of my depression and the way I felt about myself. Even though she had died, somehow Gramma realized I was in need and came when I most needed her. She changed the way I look at life.

The second example of hearing and seeing the deceased took place on an Indian reservation and was experienced by a young Mohawk woman who was one of my graduate students. The depth of this particular experience made a major impact on this young woman and her beliefs about an afterlife. It occurred in her home and she was able to "see" what her grandmother was describing in the conversation.

"It Was Warmer than Any Hug I've Ever Had Before"

*My Gramma came to me and had me "go with her." She showed
me her farm (the way it used to be) and all her flowers. I saw
where her garden was, all in bloom. She was talking and talking.
I felt so good being with her. She became frustrated as she tried to
tell me something. I couldn't understand (maybe she was speaking
Mohawk).*

*Then I saw that she had piles of family pictures in front of her
and began cutting my brother's face out of all of the pictures. She
said that my brother was going to be hurt in a car or in sports or
something. Then she was gone. I called my parents immediately
and told them all about it. My brother was hurt two weeks to the
day of the vision.*

*I felt happy to see Gramma and was utterly amazed at what
she said. But I have no idea what caused her to come to me. It felt
so warm and good to feel and be with my Gramma. It was
warmer than any hug I've ever had before. It was good.*

It is important to recognize how open these two young women were to their experiences. Both received messages of concern and protection which were uplifting.
They firmly believed in their experiences and the wisdom of their grandmothers.
Now, let's contrast those experiences with those of Diane, a woman I have known
for over thirty years. Her cousin had died unexpectedly. At my request, she wrote
the following account of an incident that occurred shortly after his death.

"Are You Laughing because I'm Mowing the Lawn?"

*I was in my backyard mowing the lawn a day or two after my
cousin had died unexpectedly. I wasn't thinking about anything
in particular when suddenly I heard my cousin laughing. He
seemed to be way overhead and moving toward Mason, where his
parents lived. His laughter caused me to immediately look up and
I responded out loud, "Are you laughing because I'm mowing the
lawn?" He did not answer. I believe my cousin was "on his way"
to "visit" his parents—he chose to go by way of my house. You
know, it gave me a good feeling to hear him laughing. I knew he
was all right.*

Diane's auditory contact took place and was recognized above the hum of a
lawn mower. Of particular note is that she was not thinking of her cousin at the
time, nor had she ever heard her cousin laugh while she was mowing the lawn.

As odd as this event appears to some, it was encouraging to her and gave her peace of mind that her cousin was well. Diane, a highly skilled secretary with a long meritorious career, is a very bright and charming person who is convinced the experience was meant to help her accept his death. She is an excellent example for anyone who has an unusual contact experience that is questioned by others. She knows what it meant to her, and that it was significant and useful. Only she could judge its realism and interpret its meaning.

The first auditory experience that came to my attention occurred some fifteen years ago and was shared with me by Martha, a very down-to-earth college student. It took place in her home, and she was in a fully conscious state when it happened. Even with fatigue from the long hours at her father's wake, difficulty in sleeping since his death, and the stress of the funeral on that dreary Monday morning, she recalled the event clearly.

"Take Care of Your Mother"

After my father's funeral we all came back to the house for something to eat. Many of our friends and relatives had accepted the blanket invitation to gather with us for refreshments. However, so many people came back it was more stress on all of us. I remember thinking that I just had to get away from them for a while, so I decided to go up to my room for a few minutes.

I trudged up the stairs, closed the door to my room and was about to collapse on to the bed. Without any warning I felt a hand on my shoulder and my father's voice say, "Take care of your mother." I looked around expecting to see him, but no one was there. There is no doubt in my mind it was him. It was my father. He was there.

Several months later I was doing some writing on grief and the extraordinary and looked for the student to ask how she felt about her experience now that some time had elapsed. When I was finally able to locate her between classes one day, I asked if she still felt the same about the experience. She looked me square in the eyes and said, "There is no doubt in my mind that this happened. My father was there." She also understood that her father thought she had some responsibility toward her mother. The contact was useful.

Contacts Heard by More than One Person

It is not unusual for more than one person to hear a sound or the voice of a deceased loved one. The experience is often more reinforcing and convincing to the bereaved when another shares it. In the following illustration, not only do the mother and daughter hear the deceased loved one, but their dog acknowledges his presence as well. I interviewed the daughter, whom I will call Karen, several months after her father's death.

"He Was Saying Good-Bye and Going up to Heaven"

My father had a stroke and was hospitalized for a long period of time before he died. We knew he was not getting better but still his death came as a shock. The first night after he died I was sitting in the living room with my mom and Topper our dog. I was doing a puzzle and she was on the couch reading with the dog next to her. It seemed as though we all looked at each other at the same time when we heard my father coming up the stairs with his familiar footsteps. They were very distinct because he had to wear special shoes due to the stroke. I got up out of my chair and went over to the door to open it and Topper jumped down from beside my mother and started sniffing under the door. I opened it but he wasn't there.

I had expected to see him. Mom and I talked about it for quite a while and decided that he was saying good-bye and going up to heaven. My mother also "speaks" to my father whenever things aren't going well or she has a problem. I don't mean that she sees him but she just talks to him.

What is especially impressive about this event is what researchers call collectivity—the fact that more than one person heard the footsteps. In addition, the dog responded as well. Furthermore, it is noteworthy that mother and daughter were able to agree on the meaning of their auditory experience and accept it as a parting gift. Also, the sensitivity of the dog to the sounds of his master's footsteps was especially meaningful for both of them. Karen's mother's conversations with her deceased father are not an uncommon practice. It is not unusual for widows and widowers to "talk" to their deceased loved ones for months after their deaths. Such behavior is highly therapeutic for many and helps them adjust to the absence of the spouse.

These one-way "conversations" sometimes result in decisions and action which assist the bereaved in their grief work. Of course, like anything else, this behavior can be carried too far. If the surviving spouse gives up independence, or postpones asserting independence and beginning a new life, it can prolong the work of mourning and adjusting to the absence of the deceased. On the other hand, such conversations can help one remember what the deceased might have advised them to do in a given situation.

In this second example of collectivity, the narrative is carried out by Jaci, telling about her daughter and her high school track and field coach, who both had the contact with the deceased.

"Mom, Dad Was Here"

My daughter Darby was a freshman in high school and it was late May of 1990. She was on the track team and they were in Massena for the sectional championships, the trials for qualifying for the State Tournament. Darby was the last qualifier, and therefore the last jumper.

I was using the video camera, taping her last jump, when the coach came over to me and said—"Boy, would Al have enjoyed this"— meaning this little freshman competing against the seniors and the best of Section 10. Darby's father was a terrific athlete and firmly believed his daughter was going to be the first girl on the golf team. He was sure she would be able to do whatever she made up her mind to do.

I filmed Darby's last jump and everyone knew immediately it was a good one. In fact at 16' 8" it was the best jump of the season, which meant she was going to the states. When she got up, she brushed down her arms, looked around and even into the air with a really puzzled look on her face.

She came over to me—I started to tell her how proud I was of her when she stopped me by saying—"Mom, Dad was here. I heard his laugh when I landed the jump."

I believed her because Alan's laugh was like no other laugh I have ever heard. Right on her heels was the coach, who is the athletic director, and also Alan's best friend and he said, "Jaci, Alan's here. I heard his laugh." I didn't feel or hear Alan but it certainly made an impact on Darby and Jim. She feels that her Dad was taking such pleasure in what she was doing and he was saying good-bye to her, something he didn't have a chance to do.

Jim felt something different. He thought it was a sign of things to come and that's why Alan laughed. How right he was because when Darby graduated from high school she had her name in the record books for swimming and track (indoor and outdoor) that still stand today. She never lost a long- ump or high jump competition for the next three years.

What is particularly impressive about this auditory experience is the environmental circumstances in which it occurred—outdoors, in the heat of competition with many spectators looking on. The pressure of competition for a young girl against teenagers three or four years older and for the coach who is rooting for her would seem to eliminate the possibility that either of them were thinking of the deceased at the same time his laugh was heard. Although Jaci did not hear her husband on that occasion, she heard him early one morning in an experience which helped bring closure to her grief work, as she tells us in the following account.

"He Was Telling Me He Was Okay"

To understand Alan and a little background of what he was like, I should tell you he was very protective and extremely strong-willed. When he was diagnosed with pancreatic cancer he accepted treatment and went on teaching, coaching basketball, playing golf, and swimming. We have a pool in our backyard right underneath our bedroom window. During the summer, I would wake up at 1:00, 2:00 or 3:00 A.M. and I would hear him swimming laps in the pool. He had left our bed and I had not heard him.

I always went to the window and watched him, and our conversations were always the same—silly. Usually I would inform him that he was trespassing and I was going to call the police. He would tell me that he was just guarding the furniture, the flower garden, or checking out the locks—protecting me. Sometimes he wanted company, and I would go down. Sometimes he just wanted to be alone.

Eventually, Alan was hospitalized away from Ogdensburg for three months, and then we finally brought him home to Hepburn in late November. Alan died in Hepburn Hospital on December 13, 1986.

For the four weeks Alan was hospitalized here in Ogdensburg, I must have somehow conveyed to him that I was nervous staying in the house with just the children. I don't remember saying it in just those words—but I woke up every morning at 3:00 A.M. listening.

About three weeks after Alan's death, I woke up to the sound of someone swimming laps in the pool. It was 3:00 A.M. just like every other morning. I listened for a few minutes and then went to the window. The pool of course was covered, the furniture was put

away—it was very quiet except for the sounds of swimming. I
opened the window and called Alan's name and told him I was
all right—thanked him for watching over us.

The sounds stopped. I closed the window. I never heard the
sounds again and stopped waking up at 3:00 A.M. every morning.
Now with my children on their own and in college, I am not afraid
to stay alone. I realize that Alan was trying to tell me that I would
be all right. He was watching over us. Also, he was telling me he
was okay and it was all right to let go. He was saying good-bye.

This experience helped me in my grieving because I think
Alan felt that the children and I were going to be all right. He was
satisfied and he could go.

Though this experience was real for Jaci, she did not want to tell her children
what had happened because they were young and she was afraid they might think
their mother was in need of help. She felt she had to be strong for them. But it
was clear to her that her husband was letting go with love and the contact was a
signal for her to reassert herself. She knew all along that she possessed the ability
to bring up the children without a father, and that now she too must begin the
process of gradually letting go.

In looking at the possible connection between the two contacts at different
times (one in the winter and one in the spring) Darby and Jim's experience with
Alan's laughter at the track meet could not have been suggested by Jaci's experience, since neither of them knew anything about the sounds in the backyard
swimming pool. It is interesting that both of them immediately came over to Jaci
to report that "Alan is here." They were clear in their convictions of what had
transpired and needed to share it as soon as possible. Neither Darby, Jim, nor Jaci
at any other times in their lives had heard an imaginary voice or laughter as they
did on those days when they experienced Alan.

As comforting and therapeutic as it is for the bereaved to find closure
through an auditory contact, some bereaved persons are still unable to find complete peace of mind. Instead, they are left wondering why the deceased had to die
or how to interpret what the loved one intended by a particular message. Lynn's
story serves to illustrate this dilemma.

"To This Day I Wonder"

It was six months after my mother had died suddenly from a
stroke and without any warning. I was sound asleep when some-
one touched the tip of my nose. (That was the way my mom woke

me up when I was a child. She would wet the tip of her finger and gently touch my nose.) I instantly knew it was her. She looked beautiful standing by the side of my bed. She was dressed all in white and she was surrounded by white.

The first question I asked her was, "Are you with Pop?" (That was my grandfather.) She said, "No. He's waiting for your grandmother." (My grandmother was still living at that time.) Then I asked her if she was with my Aunt Heddy. She replied, "Yes. How did you know?" I told her that I had heard Aunt Heddy's laughter in the background. I asked her many times why she left me. All she answered was, "Everything will be all right." It bothered me for a long time in wondering what she meant. To this day I wonder, although I was able to let her go because of this experience. Nothing that I can remember actually caused this experience, except that I didn't understand why she left me. Despite this nagging lack of understanding, her coming to me helped me very much because I knew she was happy and not alone and that she was still alive in a better place.

This exchange between Lynn and her mother is significant in the length of time that it took. Two or three minutes had passed from the time the conversation started until it came to an end. It is the longest in-depth exchange that I have come across.

During my discussion with Lynn, I asked her if she felt that she had been abandoned by her mother, since her mother left the area in which they both had been living shortly before she died. Her mother knew that her life was coming to an end but did not want to tell her daughter. Lynn was angry because she had not been told. Her anger appeared to be a block to her understanding of what her mother meant that "everything was going to be all right."

Lynn was recently divorced, and did not feel that her life was going well at the time of her mother's appearance. However, after our discussion she saw a new way to look at her mother's message—that her mother was going to be all right and was waiting for Lynn's father. However, she did not find complete closure or an answer to the nagging question of why her mother had left her without telling her that she was going to die soon.

Messages and Meanings

Hearing the voice or sounds associated with deceased loved ones is usually a source of great comfort and insight for the bereaved. Whether the sounds are conversation, laughter, or some significant fleeting sounds, the bereaved share two common responses—relief and reassurance. These responses are idiosyncratic and based on the specific circumstances surrounding the relationship between the deceased and survivors.

Relief is manifested in one of several ways. First, there is often an unspoken belief that the deceased lives on. Second, this belief is a powerful motivation to start anew and begin the task of adjusting to life without the presence of the loved one. Third, a sense of relief comes in the recognition that the loved one is truly in a better place, content, and aware of the survivor's work of adjusting. And fourth, the survivor is usually convinced that the deceased loved one is free of the medical problems and cares associated with the physical body.

Reassurance has long been the antidote for feelings of insecurity. It is manifested in the perceptions of survivors who sense concern for their welfare through the contact with the deceased. In some, there is a feeling that the deceased loved one was being protective and watching over them during the tumultuous change, willingly standing by as a form of support. This feeling of being protected often culminates with the thought, "I can make it. I can endure." By far, the strongest sense of reassurance is found in the reality of the event for each individual, signaling that the relationship bond has not been broken; its nature has simply been transformed. There is a renewed sense of purpose.

We move now to examining another set of phenomena which has provided many bereaved people with motives to go on with their lives; namely, animals and birds that have direct or symbolic associations with the bereaved.

SEVEN

Connections Big and Small: Animals and Birds

Just because coincidences happen in the outer world does not mean that they have to remain there. We can choose to view our coincidences as what psychologist Carl Jung called "synchronicities" or bridges between the worlds of matter and mind and science and the spirit.

—Paul Pearsall in *Making Miracles*

The world around us abounds with coincidental occurrences, some of which are meaningful but the vast majority of which are not. This provides a fertile ground for the growth of fallacious beliefs. We readily learn that associations exist between events, even when they do not.

James E. Alcock in "The Belief Engine," *Skeptical Inquirer,* May/June 1995

Three years ago I received the following letter from a young woman living in the eastern United States, whom I will call Loretta:

Dear Dr. LaGrand:

I saw your name in Giving Sorrow Words, *written by Candy Leightner, regarding your belief about extraordinary experiences after someone has died. I then very much wanted to tell you of mine and hear your thoughts, if possible.*

My husband died six years ago at the age of thirty-five of cancer. He starved to death from stomach cancer.

Last Spring my son and I were at the cemetery at his grave stone. I had planted flowers and wanted to take a picture of them.

87

Two tiny birds were flying close by. They landed on the stone and we watched them. Then one little fat bird flew to my shoulder and sat there while I looked at it. My son was able to take a picture of it. I love birds and my husband often gave me little ceramic birds as gifts because I collect them. I came away from the experience feeling that this was a little miracle, that a wild bird would sit on my shoulder.

Was this perhaps a sign from my husband? I don't know if this letter will ever get to you. I truly hope so. I need something to hang on to and perhaps this little bird can be it. Please, if you get this letter, could you write me a few words on what you think about this.

In responding to Loretta's request I told her that she was fortunate to have had something like that happen to her, and although the scientific community would view the experience as sheer coincidence, she might consider it as a gift, and to be very thankful for it. Furthermore, I suggested that she entertain the possibility that it was a way for her husband to say, "I'm okay; go on with your life."

About a month later, I received another letter from Loretta thanking me for writing and asking if there were any books on extraordinary experiences of the bereaved. Also, she had enclosed two photographs, each showing a little bird sitting on her shoulder. My interest was rekindled and I decided to spend some time finding out what type of bird it could be. My first step was to take the photos to a chemist I knew who was also an expert on birds and ask his opinion. Keep in mind, he was a highly regarded scientist. After examining the pictures he said without hesitation that the bird was a Zebra Finch, that it is often kept as a pet, and it had probably escaped from its cage and been free for some time. Most likely, he offered, it had been used to sitting on the shoulder of its former owner.

His wife, also an avid bird watcher, agreed that the bird was of the pet genre but countered with, "I don't care whether it was a pet or not. It's highly unusual for any bird to fly into a cemetery and sit on somebody's shoulder. Besides, there were two of them. Did they both escape and run off together?" she chuckled. The more important consideration is: What did the experience do for Loretta in dealing with the death of her husband?

From the tone of her first letter it was clear that she missed her husband and needed to find meaning in his death at such a young age. The experience with the bird helped her to strengthen her belief that her husband was okay, that he was with a friend or friends, and that the bond of love was not severed by his death. In researching material for this book, I spoke with her by telephone and she stated:

"When I feel depressed or sad I think about it. It helps me. I can draw strength from it." I also inquired why she had brought the camera to the cemetery on that particular day. The reason was simply that she had been out to the cemetery often (she lived close by), the crocuses were coming up and looked beautiful, so she decided it would be a good idea to take a picture of them. She had brought her son with her, who was fourteen years old at the time. I could only conclude that it was highly unusual, in and of itself, that on the only day she had ever brought the camera to the cemetery, a small bird would sit on her shoulder. Whether we are to believe the event was a coincidence or a healthy contact brought about by supernatural intervention, the result has been a positive one for Loretta, especially in light of the fact that she had been left alone with an eight-year old to raise.

A similar positive interpretation of an experience occurring at a cemetery took place at the burial service for the grandmother of Joni, a counselor at a major university. Joni and her sister had both previously experienced the presence of their grandfather after his death six years earlier. On different occasions, when he had appeared, he had told each of his granddaughters that he was okay and doing well. And they always remembered how much their grandfather had admired black squirrels. Joni picks up the story.

"It Gave Me Hope"

Six years later my grandmother died after a long struggle with cancer. We went up to Toronto for the burial. My grandfather was buried there as well, but none of us had been to his grave as of yet. We were listening to the minister speak from the Bible. It was a cold spring day with snow blowing in the air. Suddenly the sky broke, a ray of sunshine came through, and a black squirrel ran across their graves. My grandfather used to love black squirrels and would point them out to us as kids. Just as suddenly, the black squirrel left the area and the sky closed up again.

I feel my grandfather was letting me know he was okay because it had been a long time since I had seen him before he died. I also feel when my grandmother died, my grandfather was letting me know that he was there to be with my grandmother and that she was going to be taken care of.

It was a calming, reassuring experience for me. It helped me to better deal with my grief and loss. The squirrel represented my grandfather and the sky opening up with sunshine coming through represented that my grandparents would be together in a different world now. It helped me in my grief in different ways. I felt better knowing that my grandfather was there to welcome my grandmother. It also gave me hope that I will be with them when I die.

Were the preceding events simply chance occurrences? Coincidence? Coincidence is much too easy an explanation for all of this. You may find it highly unusual for Joni to draw so many conclusions about her grandparents based on the sky opening and a squirrel darting across a grave—unless it is considered as a form of synchronicity.

Synchronicity

Largely owing to the work of Carl Jung, we can at least proceed a step higher than chance alone in attempts to understand the unexplainable. The term *synchronicity* defines meaningful events that occur simultaneously but are not causally related. That is to say, when two or more events take place at or near the same time, "where something other than the probability of chance is involved."[1] Everyone has experienced synchronicity even though they often dismiss the coming together of certain events as luck, chance, or just plain coincidence. Let's look at a few examples.

If you talk to medical personnel who work in neonatal units, they will tell you that there often seems to be an unexplainable connection between a mother who dies during or shortly after delivery of her newborn and the way the baby responds. What is the invisible bond between the mother who dies this way and the baby who temporarily takes a turn for the worse?

Similarly, it seems highly unusual that we can sleep through all the traffic noises outside our windows or with the television still on, yet we hear our eighteen-year old, who was out with the family car, tip-toeing up the stairs at 12:30 A.M., to our relief. And how can one family member decide on a whim to stop by the home of another family member living miles away, and arrive just in time to provide assistance in a difficult situation? Is it possible that the unconscious mind of one individual could communicate with the unconscious mind of another—and then intrude into conscious awareness?

How can we explain the series of little miracles that took place after Cathy Griffin's snowmobile went off the trail and hit a tree, leaving her bleeding internally and in a coma for a week? A doctor who was cross-country skiing witnessed the accident and resuscitated her; the first car her friends stopped had a telephone; the local hospital had just gotten a CAT scan machine which revealed the internal bleeding; when rushed to a larger hospital she was not supposed to live—but she did.[2]

Where do we start to explain the mysterious collaboration between people and events that culminate in reassurance, hope, and faith in the future? Through the basic belief which underlies the whole idea of synchronicity—the idea that there is a meaningful connectedness between each of us and the universe in which we live. There is an unbroken orderliness, if we predispose ourselves to it. There is unity in all things, something which the ancients and the mystics have been telling us for centuries, and which we have buried in our ravaged environment.

The acceptance of connectedness and order reflects a positive inner attitude. As Jung put it: "An initial mood of faith and optimism makes for good results. Skepticism and resistance have the opposite effect; that is, they create an unfavorable disposition."[3] In short, with faith you see more synchronicities, more meaningful coincidences. Put another way, with faith you see miracles. Believing is seeing.

Make no mistake: I am not implying that Jung did not believe in some form of chance. But he was also convinced that there was something else operating in the universe which was simply incomprehensible to us at this point in time. It was another aspect of nature, not something associated with a Supreme Being. For Jung, causality could only mean physical causality.[4] Of course, it should be noted that no one can prove a synchronistic event any more than one can prove a coincidence. Still, it is a sign of progress that someone of Jung's stature has recognized that something other than chance is operating on a daily basis in the universe. For those of you who have shared your contact experience, your miracle, with another only to be told it was merely a chance occurrence, consider British poet Samuel Taylor Coleridge's view of chance: "Chance," he once wrote, "is but the pseudonym of God for those particular cases which he does not choose to acknowledge openly with His own sign-manual."

We may now proceed to look at Joni's sky and squirrel story in another way. There is no such thing as coincidence. Well, almost. I know with that statement I risk being burned at the intellectual stake by my colleagues. Still, there are too many "daily coincidences" that reflect an order in the universe that we do not completely understand and has absolutely nothing to do with chance. Admittedly, to any empiricist, this concept would be considered purely irrational despite the fact that there is a growing number of Westerners who are living happily and with purpose by such a belief system. Perhaps they are aware that the more we see random coincidence in our lives, the more we isolate ourselves. For many, the idea that every coincidence has meaning is being translated into peace of mind and a new spiritual awareness. The more we become aware of the meaningful coincidences in our lives, the connectedness, the more we begin to see the contact experience in an altogether different light. Everyone is the recipient of a large number of synchronicities (some would call them little miracles) throughout life which turn out to fulfill very specific purposes (some of which we are not too happy with at the time they occur). Many are hardly recognized by the recipients because of their fast-paced lives. Who is in the habit of watching for synchronistic events to unfold in life? Nonetheless, they are part of a much larger scheme. The contact experience, presenting through birds or animals (as well as symbols, which we will be addressing in Chapter 10), is one of many synchronistic events which do attract the attention of those who are open to the possibility of meaning without proof. However, no one who must have proof before belief will ever see any extraordinary experience of the bereaved as anything other than an event which must have an explanation congruent with the laws of the physical universe.

> *When our friend Bill was dying of cancer, he told us that the single thing which helped him most was "the people who were loving me from the other side." It is an assurance of connectedness that heals our fear of separation and death. Connectedness not only heals our fear of our own death, but also our fear of the death of those we love.*
> —D. Linn, M. Linn, & S. Fabricant, *The Greatest Hurt.*
> New York: Paulist Press, 1978

Let us now turn to another synchronous event which involved fifty mourners, a third of whom were readily aware of the meaning of the incident. It is presented here from the perspective of a psychologist, a close friend of the deceased and a pallbearer at the funeral. Psychologists are usually quite rigid and biased about the extraordinary. Professor Smith, as we shall call him, is an exception.

"It Profoundly Helped Them in Their Grief Work"

For years before her death from cancer, Mrs. M. had lamented never having encountered a wild turkey despite her attempts to see one. She had lived in a rural area of northern New York, which had an abundant supply of the birds, yet they had eluded her grasp. When the funeral procession arrived at the cemetery and was proceeding to the grave site on foot, a whole flock of turkeys flew into the cemetery and stood a mere 100–150 feet away, not feeding, barely moving, just standing there for several minutes before moving off.

That this was highly unusual is to put it mildly. I interpreted this experience as God's healing—the universe unfolding as it should—the Grace of God ....The message I received was a sense of joyful wonder at the mysteries of God's working in our lives. The message Mrs. M.'s family received was that "Mom's O.K. She got to see her turkey. She couldn't see them when alive so they came to see her when she died. "

I was a friend and pallbearer. I should say that the experience was a warm and moving one for me, and I am not easily moved. For Mrs. M.'s family? My observation is that it profoundly *helped them in their grief work, particularly her two daughters, although at least fifteen other people were directly aware of the significance of those birds and I feel were affected by their behavior.*

It is quite obvious that this psychologist, a college professor who was meticulous in observational techniques and causal explanations, was very much affected by his experience at the burial of his friend. Although he linked the behavior of the flock of wild turkeys to a supernatural cause which benefited a large number of people, he did not believe he was indulging in magical thinking. In his judgment, there was something other than pure coincidence going on here. He, more than most people, is very much aware that emotion can influence perception and belief. And yes, it is true that strong emotion sometimes clouds critical thinking. Nevertheless, in this instance he had no doubt that the incident at the cemetery was somehow meant to be, that it was orchestrated by a power which science is incapable of studying.

Perhaps the timing of the arrival of the wild turkeys is part of the unity and connectedness of all living things. Popular author Wayne Dyer, in *You'll See It When You Believe It*, expresses this sentiment when he says:

In some mysterious, undefinable way, everything seems to be connected, even though we cannot see the connections. In some strange way, the right person or the right series of events crops up just in time to help us over the threshold of some troubling problem. Once we understand that everything is connected in some way, even though we cannot see the connectors, this universal principle of synchronicity becomes more believable, and ultimately more available to us.[5]

The concept of believing before seeing is one which is foreign to our cultural upbringing. Our resistance to it is reinforced over and over by the emphasis on differences and doing our own thing. The prevailing belief in rugged individualism exacerbates a sense of separation rather than affiliation. Interestingly, this does not hold true with most bereaved individuals who have received a gift for coping through a contact experience. They often see the bigger picture, sensing another reality which brings with it new meaning or strengthens already existing beliefs.

In the final illustration of this section, the concept of affiliation and connection is further demonstrated by Ellen. Ellen was a nurse whom I met when I was doing volunteer work as a counselor for a hospice in St. Lawrence county, the largest land-mass county east of the Mississippi. She served a great many dying people and their survivors in the mountains of northern New York with a special kindness and understanding through the years. She had a wonderful disposition and, with thirty-five years of experience under her belt, related well to the dying person. She had a very special way of saying the right thing at the most opportune time. She also had some unusual experiences with her father during his illness and death, which she easily accepted because she had witnessed similar events with the people she had cared for.

"He Was Making Sure I Was Okay"

I loved my father so much and it helped me a great deal to be able to help him in any way possible when he was dying. I was there when he went through his life review and at one time heard him talking as though he were a child. I couldn't believe that voice was coming out of him. I was so taken when I watched him smile and reach out to shake the hand of his good friend who had died previously. Once more, as he was dying—get this—the radio was playing my parents' love song of fifty-one years ago. Not a popular tune. I know most of you academics would chalk that up to coincidence, but that's your problem.

When he died, the funeral and burial were in the Syracuse area. As you well know, Route 81 north in the winter time can be cruel and dangerous to drive. Well, sure enough, the funeral was over and I was about a half an hour into my trip home and it began to snow hard. It was during this bad snowstorm that a raven (Dad was always impressed with these particular birds) came out of nowhere, peered into the car window, flapped its wings and turned around and flew off. The whole scene was just like him. He was making sure I was OK and giving me a final wave of thanks. For me, there was no other reason why that big black bird would be out flying in that snowstorm.

There are many other events in the lives of the bereaved in which animals and birds seem to convey the connection between all things big and small, between the deceased and their loved ones. They can range from beautiful red cardinals appearing in an area where they were never before seen or were clearly out of their normal habitat, to dogs or cats who sense the presence of their deceased owner and make their discovery known to whoever will listen. (You may recall in Chapter 2 when Maria saw an apparition of her father, that the dog recognized the father, went over to the spot where he had appeared, and sniffed for his scent.)

These extraordinary events also include wild animals, as in the following account. Richard and Carole Morsilli's thirteen-year-old son Todd Is one of thousands of Americans who lost his life because of a drunk driver. As with the death of any child, the pain is unbearable at times, but especially so when the cause of death could have been prevented. As Richard tells it, Todd died on a Tuesday. The following Thursday, they were visited by a fox which caused them to believe that their son was giving them a message.

In speaking to an audience of young people some months after the tragedy, he hesitated to tell the story of the fox, but as he left the podium he thought:

I think if I'd told them about the fox, they'd have understood. They'd have appreciated how astonishing it was, when we'd never seen a fox before, to have one come and stand on the patio two days after Todd's death—just come and stand there at the kitchen window before it turned and slowly moved away.

Carole's pregnant sister came to be with her that afternoon. "I've been looking at a book of baby names", she said. "Did you know when you named Todd that it means 'fox'?"

Was Todd trying to tell us he's all right? I think these kids would understand how much we want to believe that.[6]

In my conversations with Richard, he made it clear that they had never seen a fox near their home before or since the lone sighting, although they had been living in the area for fifteen years. The event helped him and his wife to get through the early part of their grief work, but as he emphasized, "We still miss him."

Perhaps what was of equal comfort was what occurred after the account of the fox story was published in *Reader's Digest.* "We heard from people all over the country. It made us feel good at the time, since we later realized that an estimated fifty million people around the world had read the story." Out of the letters and telephone calls from others came similar accounts of unusual occurrences which helped them feel that "it happens for a reason."

Messages and Meanings

As with all extraordinary experiences in which the bereaved are engaged by the deceased loved one, the messages gleaned through the unexpected behavior of birds or animals are very individual and permeated with personal meaning. One may receive a good-bye and a positive feeling that the loved one is now pain-free. Another realizes how much the deceased cared for her or that she will see him again. Significantly, there seems to be a special message which often evolves from nature—intangible hope, a sense of confident expectation about the future.

Unfortunately, hope itself has a very dubious reputation in our culture, because it is always associated with last-ditch efforts to deal with adversity. In actuality, it is the bedrock for meeting every massive change that life presents. Hope is often unconsciously held but always manifests in action taken. While many other types of contact experience may convey the message of hope, there seems to be a special kind of hope which is attached to nature. One finds another reason for living. There is renewed meaning in existence. Nature is considered eternal and most people are reminded through the change of seasons that change is continuous, never-ending, and one can rely on and expect it. Spring will come again. Life will go on.

When a contact experience occurs in a natural outdoor setting it stirs the spiritual essence of the bereaved. There is a sense of unity with a stabilizing force, an assurance that God is still in charge, that nature is indestructible. As part of nature, the birds and animals which dot the landscape seem to be perpetual and enduring; they mirror a great unseen power. Therefore, they often seem to bring a measure of hope by their mere presence, which the bereaved usually find difficult to put into words. Yet it is supportive, and becomes an antidote for fear.

Nature, with its vast array of living creatures, presents a variety of possibilities for transformation. Wherever there are obvious possibilities, there lies hope, always present, and silently working without fanfare to combat our fears. Nature always inspires transcendence.

In the face of loss, there is never accommodation or change for the better unless one can control and eventually eliminate dwelling on the fears associated with worst-case scenarios. "How am I going to bring up the children? How am I going to afford to pay the mortgage? Who will help me with the chores? Will I obtain a decent job? Can I do it all?" Focusing on the worst is not uncommon, but it is a destructive energy drain for those who must cope with the death of a loved one. Hope from any source helps break the worst-case scenario chain and lifts self-esteem in the process. Hope emanates through life within the contact experience with nature and appears to supply the power to help the bereaved invest in the future. For many, nature and its allies take the "less" out of hopeless.

Another Viewpoint

I would be remiss if I did not present another explanation for the events involving birds and animals which take place during bereavement and bring comfort to survivors. Therefore, we shall examine science's rationale for maintaining that these unusual events we have been reading about are merely chance occurrences. I also include the material at this time to help the reader make a more reasoned judgment in deciding how to interpret the synchronistic events in your life.

First, it is commonly assumed by debunkers of any type of unusual experience that people are not accurate observers or eyewitnesses, that what they report as having seen does not necessarily mean that event is what actually took place. From a scientific viewpoint, individuals are basically unsystematic observers. Secondly, people do fabricate stories for various reasons: to draw attention, to make money, to ease pain, to feel better, or to exert influence. As one author stated, some people do "lie unintentionally as well as intentionally because of their misperceptions."[7]

Thirdly, most scientists say that one of the major reasons people mistakenly attribute extraordinary or paranormal characteristics to an event which is normal is due to the "representativeness" fallacy. The fallacy implies that when anyone is confronted with an unusual event, immediate reasoning says that it is probably representative of an unusual cause. In reality, it is argued, ordinary causes are overlooked because they are not normally associated with extraordinary events. In short, ordinary causes could very easily and often do combine to culminate in the extraordinary and the unexpected.[8]

The "representativeness" fallacy, a type of matching apples with oranges, is further supplemented by "magical thinking." While most people believe that magical thinking is exclusively in the domain of children, most skeptics infer that any adult is liable to the same reasoning, which they attribute to the physical architecture of the central nervous system, which they claim produces concepts and beliefs "without any particular respect for what is real and true and what is not." Furthermore, as James Alcock, professor of psychology at York University in

Toronto put it: "We are not always able to distinguish material originating in the brain from material from the outside world, and thus we can falsely attribute to the external world perceptions and experiences that are created within the brain."[9]

Finally, it should be mentioned that we are all notorious for memory lapses. This is especially significant regarding an experience which took place months or years ago. For example, consider the account of the death and appearance of Russell Colt's brother (Chapter 5) which was not officially reported for more than twenty years after it happened. It is argued that many of the details may not only have been forgotten, but new material could have been added to make the story more believable.

I would counter these logical criticisms with a typical remark from someone who has had an experience with a deceased loved one. "I will never forget as long as I live what took place. You know when you hear and feel truth. You feel a warmth, a tingle, another reality. The experience is inherently clear. You feel it in the depths of your being." In other words, in the midst of coincidence or chance, there can always be a moment of grace. In *The Spiritual Frontier*, author William Rauscher adds an especially apt reply:

> *Question No. 1, then, for anybody concerned about whether a particular "psychic" experience is good or bad: Does it help or hinder the individual in living a happier, more fulfilling life? When weighing the spiritual value of psychic happenings, the criterion should be: "By their fruits ye shall know them."*[10]

In the final analysis, nature becomes the instrument through which answers are provided: answers given by faith.

In the following chapter, we move on to examine the importance of the senses of touch and smell in the contact experience. Many individuals have found relief from their anguish and despair through extraordinary experiences involving these two senses.

EIGHT

The Experiences of Touch and Smell

Both truth and communication begin with a simple gesture: touch, the authentic voice of feeling.

—Ashley Montagu in *Touching*

There can be sense-experiences, or something like them, from places not at the moment occupied by sense organs and brains....But, whoever and whatever owns them, they do seem to occur. Nor are they prevented from occurring by the fact that we have at present no language for describing them intelligently.

—H. H. Price, quoted in *Philosophical Dimensions of Parapsychology* by James Wheatley & Hoyt Edge

The following event took place nearly one hundred and fifty years ago and was reported by one Timothy Cooper to the Society for Psychical Research (SPR). It is both ordinary and at the same time possesses a distinct quality. It is ordinary by today's standards by way of the initial method of contact—touching. Its distinct quality is found in the fulfillment of a mother's promise, if, as she said, she could possibly do it. But there is more, for here is another example of contact made before official notification of the death takes place. Thus, we can rule out the possibility that he "needed" to create the event and consequently brought it to consciousness due to anxiety.

"I Am Gone"

My father was a Baptist minister at Soham, Cambridgeshire....Being one of a large family, I went from home to begin the battle of life. There was a great love between my mother and me. When I had been away about a year, I was sent for in a hurry to see my dear mother, who was thought to be dying. I got leave of absence for a

week and went home, and the last day before returning to busi-
ness, while sitting by my mother's side, I said, "Mother, if it is pos-
sible, when you pass away will you come and tell me?" She said, "I
will if I possibly can." On the morning of October 7th, I awoke and
felt like a soft hand touch me, and heard the well-known voice say,
"I am gone," and something seemed to glide away from my side. I
awoke the young man who was sleeping with me, and said, "My
mother is gone. She has just been here and told me so;" and just as
I said it the clock standing on the stairs struck three. The news
came to hand that my mother had died at five minutes to three.[1]

Being touched by a deceased loved one is one of the most common ways that a
survivor appears to be awakened from sleep at the beginning of a contact experience. In the anecdote just given, twenty-one-year-old Tim did not indicate specifically where he was touched by his mother. Usually the touch is felt on the arm or
the hand and occasionally on the head or face. Recall in a preceding chapter how
Lynn was awakened for the long conversation with her mother by the familiar
touch on the nose (which she had so often experienced as a child) when her
mother wanted her to get up. On rare occasions, as with a grandmother and her
grandchild, it may be a kiss on the forehead. When a person experiences the
physical sensation of touch during normal waking hours, it is usually in the form
of a hand on the shoulder or a feeling of being embraced. In any event, "both
truth and communication begin" for the recipient of touch.

The description of the sensation of touch experienced is very real to survivors. They leave no room for doubt. "It was as real as real can be. It was as warm
as any embrace I have ever had," are not uncommon responses. The same contact
experience of touch also occurs frequently in dreams or dream-like states, as we
shall see shortly. They provide equally convincing communication to the
bereaved to gently let go of the deceased. The tactile experience leaves an indeli-
ble and unforgettable mark on the psyche of the survivor; it is often what is first
recalled and dwelt on initially by a survivor in describing a contact which
involves more than one of the senses. Here is an illustration from Melissa who
was very close to her grandmother.

"I Knew She Was There"

We all loved Grandma so much, and it was especially difficult for
my father who had faithfully taken care of her for so long before
she had to go into the hospital. Toward the end she couldn't speak
and the sores on her face bothered her. I remember one evening

being at the hospital and my father said not to kiss her, just shake her hand.

She died on a Saturday. The following Wednesday evening I awoke to my grandmother clasping my hand. I was startled and I could feel the hair on the back of my neck stand up. I still feel it when I tell someone about it, like now. I didn't see her in the dark but I knew she was there. She had to be okay, I thought.

In talking to Melissa about her tactile experience, I was preoccupied by her non-verbal behavior as she was speaking. Although her transformative experience had taken place many months prior to our conversation, she was visibly moved in describing what had occurred. It was obvious that the impact of her grand-mother's touch would never be forgotten and the experience had convinced her that there was another reality that had touched her as well.

Although they lived several generations apart, young Melissa and Timothy share a common bond that is potentially present for any bereaved person who has a contact experience—their personal world became larger and more inclusive. Through their contact experience, Melissa and Timothy had the opportunity to change the way they looked at themselves, their loved ones, and their futures. They became more capable of loving, having been touched by the love of a mother and grandmother. Nonphysical reality manifested itself in a literal way.

But the love will have been enough; all those impulses of love return to the love that made them. Even memory is not neces-sary for love. There is a land of the living and a land of the dead, and the bridge is love, the only survival, the only meaning.
—Thornton Wilder, *The Bridge of San Luis Rey.*
New York: Grosset & Dunlap, 1927

The deceased who are able to communicate with the living—whether through the enablement of a Supreme Being, the unconscious, or their own volition—demonstrate the quality of love that many of us only talk about. There are few gifts which one could give that are greater than to help assuage the grief of a loved one. Thus, the experience of touch is in itself a message of love as much as it is transforming and liberating; it highlights our spiritual nature, and as Ashley Mon-tagu suggested in the opening quote of the chapter, it is the beginning of truth and communication. Touch is a force which challenges conventional wisdom causing one to rethink the eternal cosmic questions: Who am I? Why am I here? Touch suggests that the answer is to learn to love and become wiser.

The Most Common Touch Experience

What is arguably the most common touch experience involves a person who is grieving alone and receives comfort from the deceased. Such is the story of twenty-eight-year-old Barbara Ann. She was alone in her room, deeply distressed over the death of her beloved grandfather.

"Then I Realized . . . It Was My Grandfather"

My relationship with my grandfather was a very strong one. The last several years of his life he had lived in Norwood, where I was living, so I had spent a great deal of time with him. My grandmother was also there until she died several years before. So we had become closer.

He had died in August, so this happening was three or four days later, maybe even five. I was in my bedroom and this overwhelming sorrow occurred and I was crying. I had backed up against the wall and had sunk down and was, I guess you would say, in a ball with my knees up to my chest. You know, I was thinking about him and weeping and all of a sudden I felt this hand on my left shoulder. And it was such a strong feeling that I turned to see who was there. Then I realized, without anyone saying anything that it was my grandfather.

When that happened, and I realized what it was, I had a feeling of warmth and relief. It is difficult to explain because it was so real and truthful. The quality of what happened defies words. Also, in some strange way, right after I left the room the thought came to me to give him permission to go. So I said to him: "It's okay to go. It's okay to go."

The typical situation preceding the common touch experience (one is alone, in distress, and deeply saddened) highlights the realization by the mourner that the touch has come from the deceased loved one. There is no hesitancy on the part of the mourner to declare the authenticity of the touch ("I could clearly feel the fingers and the warmth of his hand"). In the case of Barbara Ann, it is notable, though not unusual, that her experience began with her deep expression of sorrow and yearning, yet it concluded with her thoughts of telling her grandfather that it was all right to go on. She was going to be okay.

Another comforting experience of being touched by a deceased loved one occurred to Evelyn Smith of Midland, North Carolina. Her husband Harvey battled kidney cancer for nineteen months and died on August 1, 1994. On September 25, 1994, the following contact experience took place.

"I Felt Warm and Secure and Was Not Scared"

I woke up around 3:00 or 4:00 A.M. I was cold as I really missed Harvey's body heat which at times was like a furnace. I said, "Harvey, I need you here to keep me warm. I'm cold." I turned over to my left side and pulled the covers over me. At that moment, I felt something mold to the back of my body and an arm come over my shoulders (not a human flesh arm, but a dark mist or fog-like arm). The arm had a gold watch on and it was Harvey's. Harvey had not worn his watch for six months, but it seemed to glow in the night. I know that was an additional sign to assure me that it was him and for me not to be afraid. I felt warm and secure and was not scared. I fell into a deep sleep, the best I had in a long time. I knew that it was Harvey and this brought me great peace.

I asked Evelyn if it was possible that her experience had been a dream. Her response was that she had clearly awakened. There was no doubt in her mind that she had been awake during the entire experience and the sight of her husband's gold watch was of special significance. As she stated: "I know that this event was not a dream. I saw it with my own eyes." This account also demonstrates a combination of three ADCs.

Dreams and the Experience of Touch

The sense of touch occurring when one is dreaming about the deceased is just as meaningful as when it happens in the waking state. In the dream scenario, however, some young mourners experience great difficulty in accepting the reality of the contact if they are dealing with their first death of a loved one of their age. Also, if they have had extreme anxiety and emotional pain over the death, lasting for weeks or months, the spontaneous quality of the contact experience may at first be frightening and pose an additional threat to their equilibrium. They may even have to do battle with a long-held illusion that they should always be in control. Few of us want to surrender to the mysteries of life or the self, for to believe in the unexplained is to challenge the predominant world view and the cultural teaching that we are limited. Corrine is an example of this dilemma.

"Meg Came to Me and Put Her Arms around Me"

In 1990 I lost my best friend Meg to a brain aneurysm. She was twenty-nine years old. Meg left behind a husband and two small children. Up to that point I had been fortunate enough not to have lost a loved one. Meg's death was a terrible shock to me. Soon I began having nightmares every night of her sitting up in her casket and saying that she wasn't ready to die and telling her children that they couldn't run in the funeral parlor. I found myself crying throughout the day and trying to make sense out of why God would take such a wonderful person. I even received help from a priest and a psychic.

About two months after her death I had what I thought may have been a dream. Meg came to me and put her arms around me and told me she was okay and happy and that I had to stop grieving for her. We hugged each other. It was as clear and convincing as anything that has ever happened to me. Her touch, her presence, was as real as if I were awake, even as I thought, "Doesn't she know she's dead?"

I turned to my husband in bed and woke him because the experience frightened me. I tried to make sense of what had happened that night, and the only explanations I could come up with were that my subconscious mind was trying to help me heal from this terrible tragedy—or that Meg did actually come to me but felt she had to do so in a way so I wouldn't be too frightened.

I still think about her every day and sometimes I still have a hard time believing she is gone. But I do feel this experience helped me in my grieving process.

In her attempts to process her experience and determine how best to interpret it, Corrine said that she first sought the guidance of the priest and psychic. In my interview with her, she said that the priest suggested that Meg may have come, knowing how emotionally distraught she was. The psychic told her that there was no question about it—Meg came to ease her anguish and help her in her sorrow. In any event, Meg's hug was the convincing factor in her acceptance and belief in the contact. Both of these discussions, however, led to a validation of her experience and a change in the course of her grief.

Corrine gave me permission to interview her husband regarding the hug experience. He corroborated her account and thought that the constant nightmares preceding the experience with Meg had added to her fear. She had never awakened him before, and he felt she did so because she needed to share the reality of the experience right away. In reflecting on her experience he said tersely, "It was heaven sent. No more bad dreams. It's been great ever since then." He concluded that since that night she has been a different person, adjusting to her loss and under less duress and he offered, "I was never a believer in this (that people get messages) but now I am. It's definitely changed my view on things."

It is interesting that Corrine considered that the experience may have been the work of her subconscious mind. If we follow Jungian theory, the unconscious is more than capable of providing a dream-type experience to help the bereaved cope with any loss. Because the unconscious is of a totally different nature than the conscious, and little is known about it, it shows "qualities of the trickster in that it always escapes our intentions to catch it."[2] The collective unconscious, a psychic structure common to and connected to all mankind where there is no such thing as space or time, possesses the creative ability to heal through the type of experience Corrine had. As Jungians are wont to say: "Parapsychological events belong to the very nature of the collective unconscious; they are synchronistic events....We are not aware how much we are connected with each other when it comes to the unconscious."[3]

To this day, Corrine is not sure whether her experience was a dream, an apparition of her best friend, or a combination of both. She only knows that the hug had a vivid impact, that Meg's words were encouraging, and that the contact has begun the healing process. Corrine had met the challenge of the most devastating loss of her young life. The cathartic nature of her experience was perhaps its most significant aspect.

To further emphasize the importance of touch in the dream contact experience, I would like to present a dream with some similarity to the experience of Corrine and her best friend. However, in the following situation a husband and wife play out the drama of letting go and beginning a new life. Again, an embrace plays the key role in the meaning and impact of the event on the survivor, a thirty-three-year-old widow I will call Sara, whose husband died unexpectedly at age thirty.

"Nor Will I Ever Forget the Feeling"

We had only been married for four months when my husband Sean died of a brain aneurysm. It happened at night in the new house we had been in for four weeks. I was with him. It was a terrible scene, especially the noise he made just before he died.

Six months later I had a very vivid dream where he appeared. We spoke about his death. I was very concerned for him, that he was okay where he was. He and the dream felt very, very real. He told me in the dream that he was there with me. I said, "Hug me so I know you're really there." It was an incredible hug. I've never felt anything so real. It was a weird feeling; I could actually feel the sensation. He held me for a very long time to prove it. I have never felt the sense of touch in other dreams; nor will I ever forget the feeling and I've had many dreams of him since.

The message it gave me was that he was at peace and not angry at dying so young and so suddenly. I needed that peace to know he was okay. I also don't have that dreadful scene and the noise like I used to . It seems to have faded. No. It wasn't my imagination. It meant too much to me. Do you know what I'm saying? Having this experience did help me through the grieving process, as painful as that process is. I finally felt it was okay to let go and stop living in the past.

One other thing happened. As I said, I still had dreams of Sean even after the hug dream, although they were not like that one. However, when I started dating again, about a year later, and then had a regular dream of him, it would mess me up the next day. I would be upset. Finally, I had a dream of him and was able to say, "Sean, please don't come to me anymore in my dreams." From that time until now, I have not had another dream of him. He has honored my request.

Sara had no fear associated with her contact and accepted it with a sense of wonder and joy. She attached very personal meaning to being held by her husband, proof that he had come and sincerely intended to help her in her grief. Her recognition that she should not live in the past was influential in the course of her grief work, as it took great courage for her to tell Sean not to come to her in her dreams.

Let's conclude our examination of the experience of touch by considering two cases which occurred during the daytime and one which took place in the middle of the night. The first involves a middle-aged woman who was attending the funeral of her husband. Here is her account.

"I Felt Someone Put Their Arms around Me"

I was deeply distressed over my husband's death even though the doctor had told me well in advance that he was losing his liver function and it would only be a matter of days before the end would come. My older son had helped with all of the funeral arrangements and the eulogy he gave was something Roger would have loved.

We were all led out of our local church after the services and were standing in the vestibule waiting for the funeral director to bring the casket out containing Roger's body. I cannot explain how I felt. There are no words to express my sorrow. Then, as I was standing there, I felt someone put their arms around me even though nobody was in front of me. My son was standing on my left and my sister on my right. I was not imagining this hug, which came totally unexpected. It was as clear to me now as it was then and I felt comforted. I don't think it was my husband. I think it was the Lord. He knew how much I needed His comforting touch and it gave me the strength to go out to the cemetery for the burial and then have friends back to the house.

In the next tactile experience, a woman I'll call Eva was touched on the shoulder by her father several months after his death, and a family joke was repeated as his smiling face flashed before her.

"I Never Felt Grief as Much Again"

It was Christmas time, about six months after Dad had died. I was standing in the kitchen, having gone there to get my Mom a glass of wine. I was facing the kitchen counter when I felt him touch my shoulder, spin me around, smile with love, and say a private family joke. All of this took place in a split instant. I know that in that split instant he was there. The love that filled the room in that instant was so great that I never felt grief as much again.

The sense of touch is a powerful communicator. In both of these daytime experiences, survivors were strengthened in their resolve to deal with the crises they faced. On the one hand, it meant getting through that one day of the funeral. On the other, the effect was a change in the intensity of grief because Eva and her mother were dealing with the first Christmas without her father. To be spun around, as Eva described, would take a rather forceful maneuver from her point of view, so that it is not something that she easily misinterpreted. She was sixty-one years of age at the time of her experience and had no reservations whatsoever that the event was real. Having shared the experience with her mother, they were both treated to an early and loving Christmas gift.

*It is only in the last hundred years, perhaps, that fewer and
fewer people truly know that life exists after the physical body
dies.... Spirituality is an awareness that there is something far
greater than we are, something that created this universe, created life, and that we are an authentic, important, significant
part of it, and can contribute to its evolution.*

—Elisabeth Kubler-Ross, *On Life After Death.*
Berkeley, CA: Celestial Arts, 1991

In this last case, I interviewed a woman we'll call Greta, who was in her late sev-
enties. She was in good spirits and excellent health both at the time of our meeting as well as when she had her tactile experience. It occurred in the middle of
the night, about eighteen months after her husband's death.

"I Thought I Was Going to See Him"

*My husband died after a relatively short illness and I felt bad that
I was not there at the hospital at the moment of death. Maybe he
died when he did so I would be spared the added pain. He would
have done that if he thought it would help me.*

*Anyway, I knew for sure he was with me one night a year and
a half later when he patted me on the side of the leg as he always
used to. All during our marriage, whenever we decided we were
going to do something or go someplace, he had a habit of saying,
"Come on kid, let's go," and he would pat me on the leg. On this
particular night, I had gotten up to go to the bathroom. I still sleep
in the same bed as we used to. When I came back, I got into bed,
fixed the covers and got comfortable. Now I was under the covers
and he patted me on the leg. I felt it through the blanket. I said,
"Ned!" and I sat straight up and felt my leg. I said to myself that
there couldn't be anyone else in the house. Then I got out of bed,
turned on all the lights and went through the house. I thought I
was going to see him but I didn't see him. I know he was there
because I didn't imagine what I know I felt.*

*It was clear to me he was there as he was when he was alive. I
have always felt that he has been around to watch over me, like I
used to watch over him.*

As I listened to Greta I couldn't help but realize that she and her husband
had a mutually satisfying relationship during their long marriage. They were

devoted to each other. To her, the pat on the leg was a reassuring sign that Ned was still there for her.

The Contact Experience of Smell

The sense of smell is intimately bound up in human behavior. The aroma of a favorite food or beverage, for example, is enough to send us scurrying to order a delicacy or enough to compel us to stop and enter a restaurant or delicatessen. Who hasn't made a choice to purchase or not to purchase a product based on smelling it first? Communication, social interaction, influence on others, relaxation, and the expression of our emotions are a few of the many forms of human behavior that are significantly linked to our amazing ability to smell—although we have a relatively small number of olfactory-sensory cells (about five million) compared with other animals. Dogs, for example, possess a sense of smell "one million times more acute than a human's."[4]

It is also significant for our discussion of smells associated with the deceased to recognize that everyone sends smell messages. We all have our particular body odors or smell signals, although it is common today to mask or overpower these with various hygienic or cosmetic products. Our ability to detect and respond to these smell signals is more powerful than we realize.

However, according to some authorities, we are not proud of our sense of smell even though it is an ever vigilant sense which is fully operative long after sight, hearing, and touch have been dimmed at the close of the day. It is said that this is the result of smell reminding us that we are animals and the learned dislike of "anything associated with waste products."[5] This lack of recognition may be reflected in a smaller number of olfactory experiences being reported by the bereaved in comparison to other contact experiences.

Perhaps one of the most significant aspects of the sense of smell is its ability to evoke memories and stimulate emotions. Here is an example from Jack, a thirty-five-year-old teacher.

"It Was a Wonderful and Specific Reminder"

My neighbor had a fire in his silo earlier in the spring. For many months the silage slowly smoldered (a sixty-foot-tall silo filled to the brim smolders for a long time). On a couple of occasions, when the wind was blowing in the right direction and I was outdoors working, the smell of the smoldering silage would remind me of my father (who died in January of 1985). The key was his cigar smoke. The burning silage smelled like a White Owl cigar.

The first time it happened I was somewhat taken aback. In the moment I looked around for him, fully knowing he had died years before, but searching anyway. I stood there inhaling and "feeling" him. I enjoyed it immensely. Before the silo burned out completely I had this pleasurable experience a number of times. On a rational level I understood the specific chain of physical events (fire, smolder, smoke). On an emotional level, it was a wonderful and specific reminder, completely out of the blue, of a person I love.

While this was a happy and emotional experience for Jack, I have begun with his story for two reasons—to show the meaning derived from smells which evoke vivid memories (he remembered the cigars they enjoyed together) and most importantly, to demonstrate the clear cause for the memories that surfaced—the burning silage. This type of experience is not what we are referring to when we speak of the olfactory or sense of smell experience. In the latter, there is no origin for the odor which triggers memories. It is critical to understand the difference for the following reason.

Although we all have an extraordinary memory of smells, there must be soluble molecules of the scent in the air in order for sensory cells in the nose to be stimulated. Once this occurs, then the chain of events resulting in messages to the brain which evoke memories ensues. Strikingly, in the contact experience involving the sense of smell, no odor source is found. As author Ruth Winter states:

Every thing has an odor to some degree but particles for either taste or smell must be soluble.... In order to be smelled, molecules also have to be volatile. They must leave their source and float around in the air, even if the air is still. When you smell an after-shave lotion or the perfume someone is wearing, you smell the molecules of the scent which have drifted to your nose.[6]

The key concepts for our consideration are these: there must be a source for what one smells and the odor has to be airborne. In the sense of smell contact experienced by the bereaved, both of these factors are absent, yet the smell associated with the deceased presents itself. Here is a typical example from a man we'll call Jess, who at age seventy is grieving the loss of his wife and best friend.

"It Was as Though We Were Going out for Dinner"

In our later years Sylvia and I used to eat out frequently. We both loved a little French restaurant which was only a few blocks from where we lived. If we went there once in the past three years, I'll bet we went there a hundred times. Each time she would dress up and wear the pink wide-brimmed hat we had bought when we took our last trip abroad a year ago. Each time she would put on her trademark perfume, Dove. I always said the same thing to her, "Syl, you smell so nice."

Well, anyway, this was about three months after she died. I was in our bedroom in the late afternoon and decided I was going to go out for a short walk. I had just finished tying my sneakers and stood up and I smelled Dove. I looked around and called out, "Syl." There was no answer but the scent persisted. I knew I had cleaned out all of her cosmetics and clothes about six weeks after she had died, after putting it off because I couldn't handle doing it. My belongings were strewn all over the place. What a contrast to how neat the room used to look.

I started looking around thinking I may have overlooked something of hers but I knew everything was gone as far as her perfume was concerned. Her clothes were gone also, so it couldn't have been any left on her clothing.

I'll bet her perfume smell stayed with me for at least five minutes. I think it was her way of saying that she knows it's hard for me and she's looking after me.

This type of contact experience is common. It may include a variety of different scents that were directly associated with the deceased, including their own personal body scent. The smell of a scent associated with the deceased may be a precursor to the sense of presence contact. For example, a survivor might say, "First, I could smell the scent of those candles she used to burn in the evenings; then I could sense her presence in the room."

Here is another example of a widow, Evelyn Smith, whom we met earlier in this chapter, and the last contact experience she had involving the cologne her husband used to wear.

"Some Would Say I Was Dreaming or Hallucinating"

On September 24, 1995, I woke up feeling good having had a good night's sleep. I turned to my husband's side of the bed and smelled his cologne just like he was beside me. I turned back to my side of the bed and lay there for a while and could not smell the cologne on my side of the bed. When I turned back to his side, the smell had disappeared. This was one day short of a year after the first time I experienced Harvey's presence, when he had put his arm around me. Some would say I was dreaming or hallucinating but the strange thing was that the cologne I smelled was not one of my favorites that he wore. It would seem to me, that if I was imagining things, I would have imagined what I liked best.

"I was not hallucinating or dreaming," she said. "You can't believe it unless you have had it happen to you. He was always a comfort. That was the way he was." Today Evelyn is visiting hospitals to help others in need and is going into the clowning ministry as a volunteer.

Sometimes what one smells may reflect the scent from flowers and the special interest the deceased had in a particular type of flower. Becky had this sort of experience after the death of her father.

"I Felt He Was Trying to Tell Me that He Could See Me"

I was thirty-two when my father died, and it was the biggest shock of my life. I thought he would live forever. He was an outdoors-type if there ever was one and loved to work in his rose garden. He also cultivated other flowers and some vegetables, although everyone knew roses were his favorites. Part of this I think was due to my mother who also loved them. So Dad always had roses to give her on special days, or he went out and bought them.

Months after my Dad died I was cleaning in my upstairs hallway when this beautiful fragrance passed through. It was roses. It was Dad. At the same time "something" brushed by my shoulder. A vision of my father's smiling face passed in front of me. I felt that he was trying to tell me he could see me every day and was looking in on me from his resting place in heaven. I have no explanation for what caused the experience but it made me feel happy and positive about my Dad's death.

As with the tactile experience, the sense of smell often precipitates a flood of emotions and additional indicators of the sense of presence of the deceased, i.e. a momentary vision or a touch. Some survivors place greater emphasis on one aspect of the combination of contacts in relation to the personal characteristics that they remember of the deceased.

We have acknowledged in earlier chapters that more than one living person may be involved in a contact experience. The same holds true in terms of the sense of smell experience. I came across one incident which included three survivors. Let Pat tell of the event as she experienced it:

"We Were Speechless"

My grandmother died after a long illness and I was away at college at the time. Ours was a close-knit family and it was my mother's mother. She stayed in a little house near my parents for the last four years so we could help her live alone and maintain her independence as much as possible. She still loved to bake cakes and cookies.

She had told my parents that when she died she wanted to be buried with my grandfather back in her hometown, about seventy-five miles south of us. So we all took the trip back and had to stay overnight with my Aunt Marge. After the funeral we drove home and decided that we would go over to her house the next day to start going through her things and get the house ready for sale. It had been closed up for several days and we wanted to air it out and start cleaning.

When we arrived early the next morning, my parents and I were greeted with an unexpected surprise. My father unlocked the door, we all walked in, and immediately smelled a fresh batch of cookies, as though they had just come out of the oven. Now my grandmother had not baked a thing in that oven for a long time and still the aroma of cookies in the house was as clear and as strong as if they had just popped out of the oven. We were speechless. Nobody, not even my father, could account for it. We looked at it as a reminder of her love for us.

Our rational, logical thought processes will not allow too many of us to believe that the contact experience of smell is anything other than a memory flashback triggered by a similar aroma (most of us cannot tell the difference between the smell of roses and lilacs, for example) or an actual aroma from an undiscovered source. We are faced once again with the same question which shadows all contact experiences: where is the proof?

You may not agree that minimal circumstantial evidence is enough to build hope, assurance, and faith in the future unless you have had the experience. So we are back again to considering whether or not the unseen and the seen interact in ways that scientific conservatism does not understand. The hidden realities that exist between the survivor and the deceased today are as hidden as they have always been from the scrutiny of science. So the important question really is, "Do the contact experiences of smell and touch result in benefits for the bereaved?" The response has to be an overwhelming "yes." And there is no reason friends or family members should not grasp the opportunity to support the bereaved in a positive assessment of the experience.

Joan Wester Anderson, author of *Where Miracles Happen*, believes that unexplained aromas are simply another way that Divine Providence gives comfort and reassurance:

> *Lights and music are not the only means by which God sends comfort to us at a time of sorrow. Several people shared stories of unexplained aromas, usually flowers but also fragrant perfume, as Chris Costello experienced. "I thought the scent of lilac powder suddenly flooding the car's interior must be coming through the vent, from something on the expressway," a teenager wrote, describing the drive home from her grandmother's wake. "But when I rolled down the windows, I just smelled diesel fumes. Grandma always loved lilacs, so I knew it was her saying good-bye."*[7]

Not infrequently, the sense of smell experience is interpreted as a farewell, depending on the circumstances in which it occurs. Common to all of these situations is the inherent belief that the deceased is absent in body but not in spirit.

Our next classification of contact experiences deals with significant signs and symbols which provide excitement and awe, as well as major changes in beliefs for some survivors.

NINE

Symbols and Symbolic Thinking

Symbolism is an instrument of knowledge and the most ancient and fundamental method of expression, one which reveals aspects of reality which escape other modes of expression.
—J. C. Cooper in *An Illustrated Encyclopedia of Traditional Symbols*

We know the truth not only through our reason but also through our heart. It is through the latter that we know first principles ....
—Blaise Pascal in *Pascal Pensees*

A symbol is commonly defined as "something used or regarded as standing for or representing something else." Symbols are the "stuff" of symbolic thinking. They are everywhere and in everything we do. In fact, much of what we have discussed in earlier chapters may be considered symbolic. I have chosen to use the theme of symbol in this chapter to illustrate another aspect of ADC: Non-living objects that are sources of comforting messages to many bereaved people.

To begin with, everyone thinks in symbolic terms to some extent because symbols help us make sense out of life and death and give meaning to existence. There is no more important use of symbols than in language. Butterflies and rainbows, for example, are universal signs of hope; the Bald Eagle symbolizes freedom; artists portray peace by painting the lion and the lamb lying side by side, while the skull and crossbones has long symbolized death and destruction. Symbols, therefore, send messages that give a sense of connection to others, help reduce fear, or camouflage ideas to minimize their harshness. Furthermore, and most important to our discussion, symbols are links between physical and nonphysical reality.

One of the most important symbols for everyone is something we dealt with in the previous chapter—touching. Touching often symbolizes caring, and it illustrates the perennial philosophical question regarding the significance of a symbol.

The meaning of touch, like beauty, is in the eye of the beholder. Although some symbols are accepted by most people, others tend to be interpreted according to individual experience and preference. Touch sends powerful messages of love, power, control, challenge, or caring depending on who does the touching and under what circumstances. As with many symbols, and particularly with symbolic communication in the contact experience, meanings vary immensely.

There are numerous symbols which may be meaningful to the bereaved and give them reason to consider various implications of their experience. Symbols range from objects such as toys, pictures, decorations, and clothing, which appear in unexpected locations, to beautiful outdoor scenes, to favorite objects of the deceased loved one. Any of these symbols, while being highly meaningful to the bereaved, are often dismissed by others as insignificant. Here is an example from a young woman who wrote me the following note:

> *After reading about paranormal experiences I was reminded of when my grandmother died. The clock in her room stopped at the exact minute she died. It was as though there was a greater recognition of her life as well as her death. She died at home and 10–15 minutes later we were standing by the front door with our pastor when the doorbell rang. We immediately answered the door. No one was there. Our pastor said, matter-of-factly, "Things like this happen." It was like God came to take her away and wanted everyone to know that everything is under control.*

Wisdom from the young: "God came to take her away and wanted everyone to know that everything was under control." The concept of recognition and control in the face of disorganization is an insight we can apply to many unusual events as a way of putting them in a context of purpose. Her interpretation of the symbolic meaning of a clock stopping and a doorbell ringing, which she associated with her grandmother's death, held deep purpose in her frame of reference. It helped her find meaning in the death of someone she loved; a sense of immortality was reinforced.

Generally, such happenings are judged totally insignificant by those far removed from the experience because such experiences defy rational explanation other than "coincidence." Unless one is directly involved in the unfolding event, it is mind-boggling to try to figure out the reason or the timing and what the message, if any, could be. Although the bereaved obviously have less difficulty in this regard and are able to use the event to their benefit, sometimes even medical professionals are deeply moved by the unexplainable. Here is an example of a typical response.

The physician who told this story to a well-known newspaper columnist wished to remain anonymous. He was strictly oriented toward science and brack-eted most unexplainable phenomena as chance occurrence.

As a resident at a large medical center, he was on duty when an elderly woman died of cardiac arrest. It was 2:30 A.M. and he was thinking of calling the deceased's daughter, who was her only survivor. However, he reasoned that "it seemed unkind to call her at that hour, given that there was absolutely nothing she or anybody else could do. I would wake her up, she would hear the awful news and be unable to go back to sleep." So he put off calling until 4:30 A.M. when he finally called and told her. The daughter did not act surprised but quickly asked the doctor if he had called earlier. He replied, "No, why?" She said she had received a call at 2:30 A.M., having checked the time by the digital clock on her night stand. When she answered the phone, no one was on the line.

The doctor's reaction to the daughter's remarks were immediate: "I got chills. I actually shuddered, and the hairs stood up on the back of my neck. . . . I said that we were sorry this had happened. I think I was just trying to avoid the subject, because it was so creepy. It never came up again, but I never forgot it."[1]

How does one explain clocks stopping at the moment of death, doorbells ringing when no one is there, or phantom telephone calls that signal time of death? These sound like plots for grade-B thriller movies. Perhaps the "happen-ings" are part of the interface between physical and nonphysical reality—like the unusual behavior of birds and animals—so often associated with the deaths of loved ones. Could they not be symbols of structure in unstructured circumstances which say there is something greater here than mere death? Might they be sym-bols of hope, trust, or reliance which are helpful to the bereaved?

In other after-death circumstances, people have indicated to me that a vari-ety of hard-to-explain events have occurred. In one instance, a music box which had been inoperative for a period of time began to play immediately after the grandmother died. It was as though this action were a celebration that the deceased had lived a good life and was now on her way to a much happier place. Family members accepted it as an important sign concerning the destination of their loved one. It held great meaning in view of the fact that shortly thereafter the music box again became inoperative. This time it was considered beyond repair by a technician at a local store which sold the same model.

Obviously, stories like these are not only prime candidates for the "coinci-dence bin," but they often cast doubt on the veracity of those who tell the story. Nonetheless, time and time again, as I speak to those who have witnessed such unusual phenomena, I cannot deny their sincerity and convictions. The events are looked at through spiritual eyes with a sense of interconnectedness. The survivors strongly believe these events to be associated with the deceased—and that is what counts. Utilizing symbols is a liberating gift.

Perhaps one of the most significant experiences I have come across which speaks of the interconnectedness of symbolic contacts occurred several years ago to Dennis McCarthy of Wausau, Wisconsin. Here is his meaningful story.

"We Had Both Received an Angel"

When the deputy sheriff arrived at my door late that evening, I was not concerned. Being a deputy also, I assumed he had just stopped by for a visit and perhaps a cup of coffee.

"Do you know where your Joe is?" he asked. Certainly I knew, for he had left the house only two hours earlier with a good friend of his.

My son Joseph had just completed his first year at the University of Notre Dame. He was at home for a few weeks awaiting his Marine Corps ROTC summer training cruise.

"What is the name of the friend your son went out with?" inquired the deputy. When I told him the name of Joe's friend, he became very quiet and looked solemnly at the floor. "What's wrong?" I demanded. He told me that my son's friend was killed in an automobile earlier that evening and that an unidentified passenger was also killed.

No! That passenger can't be Joe! Joe is only 18—so full of life, so loving, and so talented. It just can't be him.

The deputy drove my wife and me to the funeral home. We would view the other body and confirm that it wasn't our son Joe. He was surely safe somewhere else. When the attendant brought us into the viewing room our worst nightmare unfolded. There in death lay our son, the child we had so often referred to as a very special gift from God.

The loss of our son sent us reeling. We prayed for assurance that he was going to God. The prayers and consolation of family, friends, and church added great comfort, but the nagging question still remained.

Three days after his death I was walking through the basement when I saw the angel that tops our Christmas tree lying in the middle of the floor. A bit strange, since Joe died on June 10 and the

Christmas ornaments had long been stored away in an upstairs closet. There was no logical explanation for how this angel had gotten there.

Later that day I mentioned the incident to my wife. She looked at me, tears welling up in her eyes, and asked me if I remembered the four little angels, each inscribed with our children's names, that hang on the Christmas tree each year. Of course I remembered them; they were very special. "Well today," she said, "while vacuuming the family room carpet, I saw one of the gold angels lying on the floor. Not quite understanding how it got there, I picked it up and set it aside. Later I decided to go back and see which one of the kids' angels it was. There inscribed on that little angel was the name Joseph."

We had both received an angel that day and the consolation that our son was going to God.[2]

When I spoke to Dennis about his experience, which happened several years ago, I asked him if in the intervening years he had any idea how the angels may have been placed where they were found. He immediately responded: "I can't tell you how many times I have been asked that question. Those angels had been stored away for months. You decide." It was unthinkable, under those circumstances, that finding the two angels on the same day could not be interpreted as anything but a sign that Joe was okay. To this day, Joe's angel is framed and hangs on the wall in the living room of the McCarthy residence as a symbol that he's gone home.

We have been brought up with the absurd prejudice that only what we can reduce to a rational and conscious formula is really understood and experienced in our life. When we can say what a thing is, or what we are doing, we think we fully grasp and experience it. In point of fact this verbalization . . . tends to cut us off from genuine experience and to obscure our understanding instead of increasing it.

—Thomas Merton, *New Seeds of Contemplation.*
Norfolk, CT: New Directions, 1972

A similar experience of finding a symbolic object, this time a pillbox, occurred to John Bramblett, the author of *When Goodbye Is Forever: Learning to*

Live Again after the Loss of a Child. His two-year-old son Christopher was killed in an accident in their driveway. Several weeks earlier, John himself had been diagnosed with melanoma, a potentially deadly cancer which easily spreads once it goes through the skin and gets into the bloodstream. His world had turned upside-down. Clutching each other, he and his wife had to deal with the long hard road to acceptance of their son's tragic death as well as his own personal nightmare. Along the way, they were assisted by several unusual experiences which were extremely helpful in meeting the necessary challenges imposed by the massive changes to be faced.

The first, which occurred the day after his son's death and relates to the main subject of the pillbox story, involved a discussion in the bedroom of their home with their ministers (the bedroom was one of the few quiet spots in their home on that day). John was responding to a request for something that could be mentioned in the service being planned. As he was telling the ministers how much Christopher had enjoyed the cuckoo bird in the clock which hung in his bedroom, "there was a soft tapping sound at the window behind me." He turned and saw a small bird maintaining a mid-air position as it gently swept its wings against the window. The synchronistic timing could not have been more perfect.

On returning to their home in Vermont, after the funeral for their son, the family had to settle into their home for the first time without Christopher. Shortly after arriving, John found himself at the big bay window in the dining room looking out on the lawn where Christopher had been playing the day before his death. What happened next is best described in John's own words:

"A Small Gold-Filigree Pillbox"

Tears welled up in my eyes as I remembered how happy he had been that day. Through the blur of tears I saw an object lying in the grass. I didn't know what it was, but I sensed that it did not belong outside.

Quietly I walked out into the yard and around the house. There on the lawn, underneath the same window where the bird had appeared, was a small gold-filigree pillbox that had been passed down through several generations in my wife's family. It had been her mother's and her grandmother's before her.

While I had seen the pillbox many times before I had really never taken the time to look at it carefully. Now, as I picked it up from the grass, I saw the porcelain inlay on the lid for the first time. Etched into the porcelain was a beautiful picture of a small

bird with a note held tightly in its beak flying to the outstretched
hand of a tiny blond cherub angel.

When we had left for Ohio two weeks earlier the pillbox was in
our bedroom. How did it get from our house to the yard? I asked
everyone in my family, but no one had any idea how it happened.
For my family and me, the connection between the etching and
the previous incident involving the bird at our window carried a
message that we simply could not credit to coincidence.[3]

When I asked John what meaning came from his experience in finding the pillbox, he said, "I felt it was a sign that there was something better. I felt it was God's
way of making me aware that there were things I didn't fully understand but eventually I would." John and his family continued to experience a series of events like
the pillbox and the bird which buoyed their spirits in those difficult days of adjusting to the absence of their beloved family member. Later he would write: "If you
have experienced the awareness of God's presence of which I speak, you know full
well that I haven't lost my mind. If you haven't had this experience, let me assure
you that my mental health is far better than it has ever been. As difficult as it may
be for the rational mind to accept, I now believe God works in supernatural ways
and is more than able to interact directly with us in our natural world. All of us
are exposed to "little miracles" day after day, but in our rush of activity we often
don't have the presence of mind to see them."[4]

How have both the McCarthy and Bramblett families explained the cause of
their supportive experiences? John sums it up this way: "The fact that these things
we sometimes label and casually tuck away occur so perfectly in space and time,
that they so often come to us when we truly need them, that they are so obviously
reassuring, leads me to the conclusion that they come from a powerful and loving
source." Perhaps these are God's footprints in all of our lives when we are confronted with the agony of massive change and need a gentle reminder that we are
not alone after all.

In the conclusion of my conversation with John, he said, "Without exception, I have not met a parent whose child has died who has not had some type of
unusual contact." (I should add that both of these experiences involving the
angel symbol occurred long before the current angel craze.)

Putting aside for the moment the extraordinary or paranormal dimensions
of experiences involving objects, it is important to recognize that objects like
the gold angels and the pillbox may become useful long-term connections to
the deceased. John, whose cancer treatment was successful, found solace through

his experience with the pillbox. Symbolic representations of the dead child (or adult) are healthy ways to establish a new relationship, a different relationship in which there is integration of the irreparable loss into life. Any object or event may become a connection to the dead and can be used to recall special memories and to invoke a sense of peace. It is only when used as a linking object to promote an illusory external relationship that this connection is unhealthy.[5] One may also find something other than an inanimate object which becomes the connecting link to the deceased. A memory or a family pet, for example, could provide similar links. Birds and animals (Chapter 7) fulfill the same function.

Through these symbolic connections, solace (that which gives comfort, pleasure or relief in time of sorrow) and belief in immortality is maintained.[6] Here is an example of a woman whose child used to look for sand dollars when she was with him at the beach. This memory was an important one in developing her new relationship with him after his death.

"A Small but Perfect Sand Dollar"

In February I went to Padre Island and one lonely evening I walked the beach alone—just the sand , the sea, a beautiful setting sun, the screeching gulls, God and me. It was there I begged Him to show me a sign that E. lives—to "please send me a sand dollar." I knew it was not the season for sand dollars. Even the local people had told me that they had not seen sand dollars since last summer. But I only wanted just one sand dollar—just one! Watching the fading sunset and listening to the roar of the waves, darkness began to fall, so I turned to go back when there by my feet, the waves pushed up one lone sand dollar—a small but perfect sand dollar!

That is exactly the way it happened and I cannot begin to tell you the feelings I had. My prayer had been answered.[7]

This experience was instrumental in the mother's belief that the child still lives, something all mothers and fathers wish for after the death of a child. Equally significant to her healthy adjustment is the recollection of an answered prayer. "Now that she has had the intense experience of finding the sand dollar, the memory of this experience can be invoked and the memory itself can serve as a linking object."[8] Unquestionably, her experience at the beach was especially helpful in the course of her grief work. Symbolic links and other phenomena are often important grieving tools for those coping with the deaths of adults as well as children.

But what happens when a wish for a sign is not answered? Does one keep looking? The answer is yes. Most people continue the search. Sometimes their faith is rewarded, but the timetable, of course, is not under their control. As we have seen, most contact experiences are spontaneous and unsought.

An object associated with the deceased need not be found a short time after the death for it to provide the impetus for the feeling of connection. In the following experience involving a young woman I'll call Nina and her grandmother, a period of nineteen months had elapsed between the time of death and the event which brought the focus of attention on how the grandmother still cared.

"I Felt Her Still Caring about Me"

I had always been close to my grandmother and when she died in January of 1990 it was a very sad time in my life. She had given me so much and she had a way of making me feel so important when I was around her.

In August of 1991 my husband and I moved into the first home that we were able to purchase. During our first week there I saw a card lying on the floor by the front door. When I opened it I was shocked because it was a card saying, "Best wishes in your new home. Love as ever, G.G. (my grandmother's name). I was not mistaken; it was in her handwriting. The date on it was August 1988, which is when we first moved to Glenville.

I have no recollection of ever saving the card and I know I never unpacked it. How could it have gotten there? I have no idea. Rationally, I tried to explain it away by realizing that maybe my four-year-old daughter, who likes to save things, could have kept it and may have dropped it. Perhaps she had put it in her desk and it fell out when we were moving. Even so, it was hard to believe that the card appeared right at a place where I would find it. She (my daughter) also would have been two and a half when I had originally received the card.

Regardless of how it got there, I felt extremely happy because although I thought it was a very strange coincidence, I also felt as if she was still involved in my life. I had missed her tremendously, even though she had died over a year and a half ago. I felt her still caring about me. Despite the fact that the card was from the past, her concern could be carried over to our present move.

Ominous sign? Genuine phenomena? Who can say for sure? This is an extremely interesting case, even if the mother or the child had saved the card. The fact that it fell out near the door—not in the moving van or outside of the house and was taken by the wind—is a source of much comfort. The card invoked memories of deep caring and became a symbol reinforcing the bond between grandmother and granddaughter.

This is not a rare occurrence. Postcards or letters written by deceased loved ones have turned up elsewhere in the lives of other bereaved individuals, some quite famous. For example, Bishop Pike had an experience similar to Nina's involving his son.[9]

There are also objects which are lost and never found that may help the bereaved reevaluate their relationships with the deceased or even alter their lifestyles. This is what happened to Elaine, whose mother died after a long illness. Elaine's unusual experience brought a mixture of happiness and sadness.

"I Had to Experience Her Death in a Different Way"

I had been grieving for a year over the death of my mother. She had been so good to me all her life and at times after her death I had felt that perhaps I should be grieving more than I was.

Among other things, she had given me her engagement and wedding rings and I had them re-set into diamond earrings, although I had not worn them. On the first anniversary of her death I decided to wear them as a way to be closer to her. They were beautiful and had a special meaning for me. On the exact hour and date of her death, I reached up to touch the earring— and one was missing. I was frantic and looked all over for it. I searched for many hours and never found it.

There are several interpretations of this event. Two are most important. First, on the positive side, I know it was her way of telling me that she was with me. But she also knew I was a little extravagant at times and probably spent too much on myself. Actually, having been in a generation in which money was tight, she was reminding me all the time that I was spending more than I should. Losing the diamond earring was a sign of her disapproval of my remembering her with material "things." She probably would have wanted me to remember her more in loving ways, with pictures and going to visit at her grave. The message was that I had not taken her death to heart (I don't know why I didn't grieve as I should have the first time. I was too accepting and I also felt guilty that I wasn't with her when she died. My sister was with her and I had stepped out to go get my hair done), and now with a second loss I was to experience the death again in a different way. That I did. My grief was stronger and much more outgoing, expressive.

Although I experienced a more "traumatic" second time "death" experience that day, in retrospect it may have been necessary for me to go through it in order to move on in the grieving process. That I have done. I have changed. The result is that I think less about finances. I have re-focused on love and the family. I came away from it having grown and I have a better relationship with my mother.

When I spoke to Elaine about this second loss, she felt very loving toward her mother, realized that her lifestyle had been a bit lavish, and that she should be more judicious in the management of her finances. Losing the diamond was a reminder which she said was needed. She now feels she is much better for having had the experience as difficult as it was.

A final note: Between the first and second time that I spoke with Elaine she and her daughter had a second experience. Elaine had taken some of the diamonds from her mother's rings and had a bracelet made for her daughter. She gave it to her when she graduated from college. Because it was an expensive piece of jewelry ($5,000) she asked her not to wear it right away. She complied. However, the first time she wore it, she lost it and it has never been found. Her daughter had worn the bracelet with another one on the same wrist. Yet the expensive bracelet was lost; the inexpensive bracelet stayed on her wrist. There is only one person who can answer the question of what the experience means: Elaine. Her understanding of her mother's wisdom and guidance has motivated her to change priorities, and in doing so alter her lifestyle for the better.

The Symbol of Light

A universal symbol that typifies a transcendent reality, a dimension beyond death, is light. Often one will report experiencing images of a beautiful land filled with an indescribable light during a dream. Some who have had an encounter with apparitional figures refer to them as beings of light or as surrounded by light. Many who have had out-of-body experiences have said that they have been drawn to a light which human words cannot describe, or that they encountered a master Being of Light. Going to the light is also part of the prayer of some believers who are praying for the dying or the deceased.

Light is also symbolic of prayers answered or messages received. Consider the unusual experience recounted to me by twenty-six-year-old Carol Ann whose two-year-old daughter died unexpectedly:

"I Feel It Was a Sign for Me"

Even now when I talk about it the pain is still there. How can I forget that dreadful day when Leah, my two-year-old daughter, ran out into the street and was hit by a car with a drunken driver behind the wheel. I can see every detail as though it happened yesterday.

I had so much trouble accepting her death, which I later came to learn, through meetings of The Compassionate Friends, was really quite normal. At the time though, I thought I was crazy.

For a long time I prayed for some type of sign that she was all right, wherever she might be. When I would be in the company of others and they would be talking I would always be thinking about her.

About two years after her death, we were visiting some friends and as usual I was thinking about her and hurting. Out of nowhere, about five or six feet away, I saw a large blinding flash of light. The flash was white, not yellow, and it was warm. I could feel the heat from it. I looked at the others who were with me but no one saw what I saw. There was no visible cause like lightning or an electrical short. I not only saw it; I felt it. It was a sign for me; it made me feel that she was okay.

I never told anyone about it for a long time, not even my husband. He doesn't believe in those kinds of things and it would just upset him. When I told my closest girlfriend, she was sympathetic and agreed with me that my prayer had been answered. I always prayed to see it again but I never did.

For Carol Ann, the white light was a personal message of hope that Leah was in good hands. Her first step forward since the experience with the light has been her ability to talk more about her daughter and the feelings she still fights regarding the senselessness of her death. The white light was the beginning of renewal. The wisdom of Carol Ann's friend in providing support and agreement is an excellent example of how important it is to share one's contact experience at the proper time.

Next we examine one of the most impressive contact experiences which has a unique impact on the mourner's beliefs: The third-party contact.

TEN

Third-Party Contacts

God knows the depths of our heartache and loneliness, how much we long to be reassured that our loved ones are in his care. As we remain open to his will and timing, He may send comfort just when we most need it, from those who live on the other side of the veil, in the Eternal Light.
—Joan Wester Anderson in *Where Miracles Happen*

There exists in our cosmos a dynamic element, imponderable and invisible, diffused through all parts of the universe, independent of matter visible and ponderable, and acting upon it; and in that dynamic element there is an intelligence superior to our own.
—Camille Flammarion in *The Unknown*

There exist a number of instances in which a grief-stricken person is the recipient of an unusual contact with a deceased loved one which is initiated through another person. Often, the third party is a child, although adults may be the bearers as well. These third-party contacts are among the most dramatic and believable of all contacts which the bereaved are subject to experiencing. They provide strong evidence that love transcends all barriers, including the physical laws of the universe. For the recipient of a third-party contact they are proof positive for him that there is another existence, a dimension of reality of infinite possibilities.

I would like to emphasize here that the third-party experience does not refer to any type of contact with a deceased person which purportedly is the result of a commercial medium. The third-party contact is as spontaneously made as any of the other experiences, with the exception that it comes through someone else and not directly to the survivor. However, the major impact of the contact is on the primary mourner and the assuaging of grief. Because of the nature and quality

127

of the contact I have never heard of a survivor who has not been helped by the experience. Few of the bereaved's contact experiences are as filled with the trappings of the miraculous as are apparitions, but what is arguably the most impressive and comforting are third-party contacts involving apparitions that are seen by children. Whether it is due to their psychic sensitivity or greater spiritual awareness is a moot question. The following is an example of this experience.

In the early 1980s, I was teaching at a state university and also had a small private practice. One day a woman in her late fifties came to me in great turmoil. One of her daughters was dying of cancer. But at that moment, she was especially distraught because of the relationship she had with her estranged husband. We talked for about an hour, mostly about her husband, and when the session was finished she left without making another appointment. I thought that perhaps she was not happy with the way our first meeting had gone, and I reluctantly dismissed the session as being the result of my inability to establish a friendly therapeutic environment.

Several months later, I was going through the serving line in the campus cafeteria when Mrs. Jones, as we shall call her, stopped me and asked if she could come to my office again. We met the next day. After informing me that her daughter had died, she began to take me on an incredible journey which—well, I'll let her tell it.

"And She Was Smiling"

I became very close to my daughter toward the end of her life and I knew that when she died she would be taken to heaven. I was sure of it. So I asked Carla that if she could, to send me a message that she was all right; and equally important, to watch over Kenny, her sister Irene's little boy, who was being abused by the father. Irene's marriage was in deep trouble and the little four-year-old was in great need.

About three months later, I was over at Irene's house helping out. This time, I was giving Kenny a bath in the big bathtub. He was having a good time and I left him for a moment to go into his bedroom to get his pajamas. No sooner had I gone through the doorway into his bedroom when I heard him in an alarming voice call, "Grandma!!" I immediately returned to the bathroom to see him climbing out of the tub. He was obviously frightened and I said, "Kenny, what are you doing?" With a strained voice he said, "I saw a picture of Aunt Carla and she was smiling."[1]

Kenny had seen an apparition of the face of his Aunt Carla and didn't know what to make of it. His grandmother was as surprised as Kenny was frightened. But she needed validation, someone to share the experience with and help her to sort out the many confusing thoughts and feelings she had about the event. So she asked me the most important question on her mind: "Do you think this could have happened?" I paused for a moment, fumbling for words, looked at her and intuitively said, "Yes, this could have happened." A look of relief came over her face. Through her grandson, her wish had been granted, for she wanted to believe this was the message that she had asked Carla to send. Yet she wondered if she were losing her sanity; she had been through so much that she could hardly trust her senses. Sometimes we delude ourselves or find that our state of mind is such that we don't know what to believe. Not only had Carla sent her an "I'm okay" message, but Kenny was no longer being abused. Her daughter and son-in-law had separated. She marveled that the message would come through a four-year old. She left my office immediately and I never saw her again.

I thought a long time about Mrs. Jones' experience. Had she concocted this story? For what reason? What did she have to gain? I had no reason to believe she had fabricated the story. In fact, her sincerity had fortified my conviction that her experience was clearly authentic. I could find no reason to doubt the genuine manner in which she had related her story to me. Later, whenever I told someone about this event I would get that uneasy feeling, which I can best describe as a faint chill running through me. But that was not the end of my connection with the story. Unexpected corroboration of Mrs. Jones' experience was to come ten years later.

It was during the summer session at the same university where I had first met Mrs. Jones. I was teaching a course on bereavement and death which included a lecture on the extraordinary experiences of the bereaved. In changing the story enough to protect confidentiality, I proceeded to tell the class about the third-party experience Mrs. Jones had with her grandson. After the class ended I was approached by an older student who, without hesitation, stepped up and said, "That was my son you were talking about."

The first thought that came to my mind was to ask Irene if what I had said in my lecture was essentially what had happened. She nodded in the affirmative and was very willing to talk about it, although I must confess I was stunned. Well, almost. Her son was now a teenager, was doing well, and remembered the evening in question in every detail. I asked her how he felt about what happened that evening. She smiled and said, "He doesn't like to talk about it."

I was happy that Mrs. Jones' daughter corroborated her story even though it had occurred so long ago. She had reinforced my own belief in her mother's credibility and had obviously not forgotten its significance in her own life.

There are, indeed, some rare contacts in which the third party does not know the deceased or the primary mourners. Take, for example, the incident which was reported in the December 1974 issue of *The Spiritual Frontiers Fellowship Newsletter*. It involved a graduate student at Loyola University who was working late one evening at a suburban gift shop. She had been directing her attention to the laborious job of taking inventory when, with a suddenness which was almost electric, she glanced up to see a young boy standing a short distance in front of her:

"The Yellow Doctor Denton Pajamas"

He was looking at me with a direct and solemn expression. I judged him to be four or five years old, with red hair and a strong little chin. The fact that he seemed to have a blue light around him and that I could "see through" the edges of his body seemed to be nothing unusual while he stood there. Neither did his yellow Doctor Denton pajamas appear odd, until he literally melted into nothingness a few seconds later. It was then that I realized that my little visitor was not of mortal flesh.

Why had he come? I felt no fear, only a surprising naturalness at his visitation . . . . Relating the event to the shop owner, she told me some rather startling news. Until his death the previous June, the four-year-old red-haired Tommy had been a frequent, chatty visitor at the gift store with his mother and older sister Susie. Since his death, his bereaved parents had desired communication with their child and the confirmation of an afterlife and the power of love over death.

When I met his parents and described the apparition in detail, I felt rather silly describing the yellow Doctor Denton pajamas . . . . When I had finished, there was silence for a minute. Then Tommy's mother said, "He died in those pajamas. And he came back to us by way of a stranger who would have no way of knowing him or the details surrounding his death."[2]

Opposing Explanations

For many people, both of these stories are remarkable examples of how a loving God works through others to ease the pain of loss and separation, and to strengthen loved ones who are struggling to find some meaning in their cata-strophic losses. In both examples, by their requests, survivors had set in motion the initial chain of events and a Perfect Intelligence took the ball and ran with it for them. While it can be argued that third-party experiences are evidence of supernatural intervention to assist the living in their transition, it assumes that we live in a spiritual universe, not a physical one. For the empiricist, because we can make images anytime we want to, this is unacceptable. It can readily be argued that seeing Aunt Carla and Tommy in the Doctor Denton pajamas was simply a function of our image-making capability. As has often been said, don't look for a remote or distant cause when an obvious one will do.

Not infrequently, I am met with incredulity by those who cannot entertain the possibility of a world of immortality. Since the progressive secularization of Western culture has all but ended the notion of supernatural causes for the unex-plainable, dismissing third-party events out of hand is not uncommon. Logic is said to be the only basis for discerning truth. Spiritual experiences are not logical in the scientific model of cause and effect. Let me illustrate this point.

During the writing of this book I began asking people in various fields of sci-ence if it is possible to prove when someone has a hallucination. Then I would proceed to tell them Mrs. Jones' story. I had finished telling of her experience to a geologist at a local community college and he responded in the following man-ner: "You know, Lou, some four-year-olds are very perceptive and sensitive to the feelings of adults. I can see where this little fellow realized how sad it was for his grandmother to deal with the loss of her daughter and decided he would do some-thing about it." In essence, he implied that Kenny had staged the experience of seeing his Aunt in order to help his grandmother and make her feel better. His immediate counter-response is indicative of the relentlessly closed minds of many scientists who have begun to formulate an alternative explanation before one fin-ishes describing the experience.

My geologist colleague could not accept the possibility that Kenny had actu-ally seen an apparition or an image of his aunt. Furthermore, his response reflects a fact of life regarding contact experiences of the bereaved—there is always an alternative explanation if you look hard enough for one. Someone can always counter one explanation with another. That's a given. No one can prove an apparition or an image. But one thing is clear—for Kenny and the graduate stu-dent, what was experienced was real.

Although the most widely accepted current explanation is that apparitions represent illusions or hallucinations on the part of the survivor, there are many other theories as to their cause. An early theory which persists to this day suggests that they are telepathically caused by the dying or deceased person who first sends a cue from which the survivor is able to project the image of the deceased.[3] Others believe they are engendered as a function of the unconscious mind. It is the unconscious mind which is said to be the great well of knowledge and experience which has been the source of inventions (Elias Howe received the final idea for the lock-stitch sewing machine through a dream). Many poets and musicians credit the unconscious with some of their best works as they report they were not consciously aware of what they were writing. Thus, the unconscious is considered to be "the medium through which we get the messages from the psychic and the material world."[4] Through an apparition, the unconscious mind is at its creative best in communicating to the individual.

A third explanation for apparitions, supported by the many reports of out-of-body experiences, is that we all have an energy body or etheric body. This invisible body is said to disengage from the physical body; sometimes when we least expect it during life, and when death finally occurs.[5] What is clear in my examination of the literature on the subject is that there is no agreement among parapsychologists regarding what causes apparitions. At the risk of oversimplification, I would suggest that your theory, if you have one, is as good as any other one. It would seem that we (and apparitions) are much more than energy, projections of the unconscious or conscious mind, or a form of telepathic communication.

As an aside, I should tell you that in my research I have also come across individuals who insist that they have seen apparitions of dead pets. They are as sincere in the telling of their experiences as any bereaved person who is grieving the death of a loved one. Once more, the emotional investment in the dead pet is as deep and complex as it is when a loved one dies and the ensuing grief is as intense as in any loss experience. If you wish to pursue the topic, I have included resources to consult in the bibliography in the back of the book.

Back to the problem of explaining apparitions. The major question still persists: How does one prove that a hallucinatory image formed by the unconscious, a telepathic message from the deceased, or an energy body which each person possesses, is the reason an individual sees an apparition of the deceased? There is no more scientific proof for these explanations than there is to say that the apparition is a spiritual experience formed by the hand of God. That apparitions occur is not questioned; it is a certifiable phenomena. How it comes about and whether it is an internally generated process or the result of an independent outside agent will be the subject of eternal debate.

The debate must lose intensity when we consider the third-party experience, however, since the individual seeing the deceased often has little knowledge of the deep innermost thoughts of the primary mourner. In some cases, there is no knowledge whatsoever concerning the mourner. Moreover, in some situations, the third party has no prior knowledge of the death of the loved one. An example of such a case was given to me by a nun in an eastern city.

I had just finished speaking to a group of hospice volunteers and nurses on a wintry evening and was packing up materials to leave when a nun, who was a volunteer, asked if I had read the newspaper account of the seventeen-year-old boy who had been killed in an automobile accident earlier in the week. I vaguely remembered it, but could not recall the details. She then proceeded with the following account of the experience of a child that the seventeen-year old had often taken care of. As so often happens, the babysitter and the child had become very close friends.

"Eddie Was Here Yesterday and Told Me"

Little Mike was a typical four-year old: full of energy and always looking for someone to play with. Since Eddie liked athletics and was himself very active they both hit it off very well from the first time he was asked to come over and watch Mike. Their mutual admiration grew over several months and Mike's mother always said that it was a draw when it came to deciding which one tired the other one out.

The fatal accident was tragic. Mike's mother was at a loss to decide how she was going to break the news to her young son. It was two days since Eddie had died and he had been scheduled to come the next afternoon, as soon as school got out, for his weekly babysitting duties. After talking it over with her husband, Mrs. S. decided that she would sit down with Mike early that evening before she and her husband went to the wake. She was especially concerned that he did not find out about the death from someone else or on the radio or television. It was also necessary to tell him that someone else would be coming to take care of him tomorrow.

When the time arrived, Mrs. S. began with, "Honey, I have something very sad to tell you about Eddie. He won't be coming to take care of you anymore." Before she could say another word, Mike interrupted and replied, "I already know that, Mommy. Eddie was here yesterday and told me he wouldn't be seeing me any more. I know where he's gone."

His mother was speechless. Finally, she began to ask questions about Mike's visitor. He had very little to add to what he had said and his mother decided for the time being to let the startling revelation rest.

Because little Mike had no knowledge of the automobile accident or that a death had occurred, most likely Eddie's appearance and conversation was not generated by anticipation, anxiety, or imagination. On the other hand, was it possible that Mike sensed changes in his mother's behavior and made up the story? In either case, the experience was extremely helpful for the four-year old, not to mention the effect on Eddie's parents.

The Death Bed Vision as a Third-Party Contact

Another type of third-party contact which may occur involves a death bed vision. One of the most common near-death experiences (NDEs) that have been recorded throughout history is the death bed vision. A typical NDE of this sort involves the dying person seeing or having a conversation with a deceased loved one. The conversation may take place minutes or days before the person actually dies. Usually the dying person feels happy seeing deceased loved ones and is often welcomed by them. While this scenario is taking place and the dying person is responding in an overt, positive manner, family and medical personnel in attendance do not see the deceased relatives. They do witness patient responses and are moved by them.

Based on a Gallup poll, Kenneth Ring (author of *Heading Toward Omega*, an eye-opening and intensive study of the NDE) suggests that some eight million people have had at least one type of the experience when near death. (Incidentally, this is about one-fifth of the number of ADCs experienced.)That the NDE occurs is beyond question. As Ring states: "From all the work in near death studies, we now can say with assurance that the NDE has been established as a certifiable phenomenon that occurs in many people who come close to or experience clinical death."[6]

In the third-party contact involving an NDE, the deceased relative is the intermediary whose presence eventually has a comforting effect on survivors, like the three children had on the survivors in our previous examples. The survivor who is helped by the exchange between the dying person and the deceased relative is a family member or sometimes a caregiver.

The general public often forgets that caregivers grieve the deaths of their patients. Even though caregivers meet with each other to discuss their relationship with the patient (sometimes referred to as evaluation therapy for the caregiver) after a patient dies, there may be considerable grief work for them to do. The third-party contact, which takes place before the actual death of the patient, reduces and in some instances has the potential to virtually eliminate the caregiver's grief.

In the following account, a forty-five-year-old nurse I'll call Olivia had just such an experience which was instrumental in how she was able to deal with the death of her patient.

"I'm Coming, Bernadette!"

I have been working at the general hospital in our town for many years and it doesn't take me long to become attached to my patients. Part of the reason for this is the fact that in our community everyone seems to know everyone else long before they ever become ill.

For several weeks I had been taking care of an elderly nun and we talked very openly most of the time. Gradually she became weaker and weaker and it was obvious that the end was near. One afternoon when I had a few minutes to spare, I sat with her after giving her some ice chips. She had not moved much when all of a sudden she picked her head off the pillow and in a clear distinct voice said, "I'm coming, Bernadette! I'm coming, Bernadette!" I knew she had a sister named Bernadette who was also a nun and had died several years ago. She lay back down and went back off to sleep.

The next day when I came in, my patient was awake and able to talk. We talked about what I had heard her say. At first I was amazed. I don't know what caused it but I know it happened. We both knew that she had really seen her sister and soon she would be with her in death. There was a great sense of peace about it all. It helped me very much a couple of days later when she died. For some reason I knew she was happy now and I did not feel bad about her passing.

Having the opportunity to discuss the death bed vision with her patient after it occurred was an unusual gift for Olivia. Not infrequently after seeing a vision, the dying person either dies or is unable to respond coherently. In this case, the discussion between Olivia and her patient was of great significance. Both caregiver and patient were assisted in their grieving. The dying are grieving the loss of all of their relationships with the world. Seeing and responding to her deceased sister was extremely important to the dying nun as it was to her caregiver when death finally came. Perhaps the ADC and the NDE are opposite sides of the same coin.

A final example of a third-party contact involving an adult as the intermediary is an account which comes from Edmund Gurney's *Phantasms of the Living*. It concerns the Reverend Arthur Bellamy whose wife had made a pact with a friend at school. Both had agreed that whoever died first, if divinely permitted, would appear to the other. It was many years later that his wife, who had not been in touch with her friend, received word of her death. She was reminded of their agreement of years past, was a bit nervous over the prospect, and decided to tell her husband about it. He accepted her story but had no idea what her friend looked like. Nor had he ever seen a picture of her.

The significant event occurred a couple of nights later. Reverend Bellamy tells the story:

"I Doubted not that I Had Really Seen an Apparition"

. . . I suddenly awoke, and saw a lady sitting at the side of the bed where my wife was sleeping soundly. At once I sat up in the bed, and gazed so intently that even now I can recall her form and features. Had I the pencils and the brush of Millias, I could transfer to canvas an exact likeness of the ghostly visitant. I remember that I was much struck, as I looked intently at her, with the careful arrangement of her coiffure, every single hair being most carefully brushed down. How long I sat and gazed I cannot say, but directly the apparition ceased to be, I got out of bed to see if any of my wife's garments had by any means optically deluded me. I found nothing in the line of vision but a bare wall. Hallucination on my part I rejected as out of the question, and I doubted not that I had really seen an apparition. Returning to bed, I lay till my wife some hours after awoke and then I gave her an account of her friend's appearance. I described her color, form, all of which exactly tallied with my wife's recollection of Miss W. Finally I asked, "But is there any special point to strike one in her appearance?" "Yes," my wife promptly replied; "we girls used to tease her at school for devoting so much time to the arrangement of her hair." This was the very thing which I have said so much struck me. Such are the simple facts.[7]

Whatever your religious attitudes or beliefs, we can be sure that Reverend Bellamy used common sense in checking out what he had seen and was convinced he was not hallucinating. All too frequently, those who hear the description of an apparition from a person with a religious vocation are tempted to assume that the individual would necessarily be more prone to "create" such a scenario, even in good faith. We can only speculate why the apparition did not awaken the minister's wife. As is usually the case, an apparition or voice which is experienced by a third party is especially powerful in bringing convincing authenticity to the message being conveyed.

And sometimes only a voice is heard. I am reminded of an incident which occurred following the violent death of a young man whose sister was in great need of solace and support. The woman had a long-time friend who, in the middle of the afternoon at her place of work, felt the presence of her friend's brother and heard his voice say, "Vicki, tell Celeste I'm okay." The reality of this event was overwhelming for her, and as much as she wanted to deny it she realized it was real, not an illusion. Again, common sense won out.

I have used the phrase "common sense" to emphasize the need to allow our own faculties to guide us in decision-making when unexpected events take place in our lives. Because most contact experiences defy the laws of physics and what we understand about the universe, it is important that we not allow our rigid cultural training to deny the presence of our spiritual side. In many instances common sense must overrule the scientific model or we impugn human nature and our spiritual heritage. This is exactly what Reverend Bellamy did—check first for possible physical explanations, use reason to determine whether the event can be explained by acknowledging another reality, and then accept the experience as a very real gift.

At this point, I should also remind you that there are a number of people who may have a potentially positive experience—just as moving as Reverend Bellamy's—yet interpret it in a negative way. Thus, it is never recognized for what it was intended to be—an inspiration to embrace life. One such possibility is the subject of the next chapter: Dreams of the deceased.

ELEVEN

Dreams of the Deceased

We are somewhat more than ourselves in sleep and the Slumber of the Body seems to be but the Waking of the Soul.
—Sir Thomas Browne

What if you slept? And what if, in your sleep you dreamed? And what if, in your dream, you went to heaven and there plucked a strange and beautiful flower? And what if, when you awoke, you had the flower in your hand?
—Samuel Taylor Coleridge

Dreams are a mystery.

Dreams are a source of wisdom and self-knowledge.

Dreams are a normal and healthy part of grieving.

These three observations are common in the literature on dreams. While accurate and descriptive, they cannot begin to mirror the manner in which dreams bring respite for survivors from the overwhelming feeling that life is suffocating, and meaningless after a loved one dies. Dreams carry one into realms fully accessible to those with childlike trust and openness, and convincingly demonstrate access to another reality; a reality leading to greater self-understanding and a wealth of knowledge that has benefited all of humanity. Despite the fact that dreams are not a high priority in our culture, paying attention to our dreams often leads us to the realization that there is an enormous intelligence behind them.

There is no lack of theories on why we dream, but one thing is clear: no one has a universal answer for the question of why everyone dreams each evening— some 150,000 dreams in a lifetime. And unless we make a concerted effort, we forget most of them. Arguably, not all dreams are important; nevertheless, they possess several features which can lead to happiness and peace of mind. Dreams, then, can do many things, as dream analysts and researchers have found.

One of the most significant contributions of dreams about the deceased is that they bring comfort and support in times of duress. As we shall show in this chapter, many dreams have brought life-changing results by reassuring survivors that they are capable of dealing with whatever life has to offer following the death of a loved one. The bereaved's feelings toward their plight can change drastically after a single dream.

On the other hand, dreams can also bring sadness. I remember a recurring dream that my father shared with me in the months after the sudden death of my mother. He would dream of her wearing a favorite dress. She looked beautiful, alive, and well, in seemingly good health. It was very meaningful to him, but when he would wake up and realize that it was a dream and she was gone it would devastate him. "You don't understand how it feels," he would say. "To see her looking so alive and then realize she is dead is very hard for me." He could not interpret the dream as saying, "I know it's hard on you but I'm okay. I'm whole again. Someday we'll be together. Continue to help others." His persistent inter-pretation of the dream as a taunt instead of a positive message was a major source of emotional pain for many months. Someone was providing help that he could not accept.

Dreams have also provided advice and guidance for the dreamer. Dreamers may be "told" to reconsider their present behavior in light of what has happened to them and how they are presently responding. Some individuals are given a lit-tle nudge to change direction. This may come through a nightmare or a peaceful vision in accordance with personal needs. Nightmares are not enemies; they are another way your unconscious—your inner wisdom—is trying to get your atten-tion, to get you to think about an imbalance in your life.

One of the most interesting guidance dreams in history concerns parts of the manuscript for Dante's *The Divine Comedy*. For months after his death his sons searched the house and his papers to no avail—until Jacopo had a dream of his father dressed in white. He asked his father if he had completed the poem. Answering with a nod of his head, Dante proceeded to show his son a secret place in his room which contained the rest of the manuscript. The next day, with a lawyer friend of his father's in tow, he went to the room in the dream, and behind a small window, covered with mold, were the missing papers. His father's visit in a dream resulted in the eventual publication of *The Divine Comedy*.

Thirty-eight-year-old Brenda's contact experience is another typical example of the guidance dream, one which occurred after the death of her husband. It brought her the message that she would be able deal with life again.

"I Should Continue My Life"

I remember asking my husband to come to me in a dream after he died. I really didn't expect him to remember, but he did. He came to me very affectionately and held me in his arms, making me feel comfortable, self-assured, and confident.

My husband or my mind was trying to help me realize that I would be OK and would be able to continue with my life. I received a message of peace, tranquillity, and wholeness. It made me feel that my husband was all right and that I should continue with my life.

From the dawn of civilization, dreams have been the source of creative solutions to tens of millions of personal problems. Current theory has it that symbols in our dreams are guides to truths about ourselves and our inner conditions. Dreams and the unconscious mind work to expand our conscious world and make us whole. By heeding our dreams, we can make giant strides in uncovering and combating fears as well as in healing deep emotional hurts. Because many mourners are emotionally handcuffed to the past and unable to accommodate life without their loved ones, dreams often provide solutions to their resistance to inevitable change. Not infrequently, a dream can be a means of saying good-bye when loved ones were unable to be at the death bed or attend the funeral of the deceased. The following example of the peaceful death of Adele's father-in-law fits perfectly.

"I Was Really Able to Say Good-bye"

When my father-in-law had his heart attack, family members were immediately called to the hospital, including my husband. I had to stay at home with our children because it was in the middle of the night. Unfortunately, he died in the early morning hours.

My husband told me what time he had died and, at that time, I had been half-asleep waiting for a phone call. It was during that time that I dreamed that my father-in-law summoned me to the hospital, and it was there that I was able to say good-bye. In my dream he waved good-bye and nodded. In my perspective I was floating up over him, and, as he died , he floated up past me. I loved my father-in-law a great deal and I feel he communicated to me so he could say good-bye too.

I remember how peaceful his death was and that his children and wife were there to say good-bye. It's as if he deliberately waited until they were all present before he allowed himself to die.

My dream helped me because I believe he was really able to say good-bye to me, just like he did to the rest of the family.

In all of the instances in which dreams help the dreamer, one must interpret the dream in reference to what is going on, or should be going on, in his or her life. Be wary of anyone who tells you what your dreams mean. Any counselor can suggest possible interpretations, but in the final analysis, it is the dreamer who must decide the meaning of any dream in relation to his or her current waking thoughts and behavior. Examine all possible interpretations, and then decide what feels right.

Accordingly, books that give blanket interpretations of all types of dreams should be regarded as suspect. What applies to one person who has a dream about life, death, or coping may not be at all applicable to someone else. Some dreams are confounding and mysterious, and we may need expert guidance in obtaining useful information from them, preferably from a counselor who is a dream analyst. The unconscious speaks in symbolic language through dreams, and some symbols possess universal meanings. Still, they do not fit the same way into everyone's dreams, and the individual context, what is going on in a person's own life, must be the guiding light of interpretation. What the dream means to you must take precedence over what it means to members of your dream-sharing group, a friend, or an analyst. The eminently sane words of Dr. Ann Faraday, one of the leading dream therapists in the country, are appropriate here. When conducting dream-sharing groups, she encourages alternative viewpoints and interpretations. However, in the final analysis she makes it clear that "the dream is the property of the dreamer, a unique production arising out of his own vast network of memories and associations, and, in the end of the day, is meaningful in whatever way he himself finds most useful."[1]

Where Do Dreams Originate?

Brenda's explanation of her guidance dream has already given us clues to partially answer this question. She said that she wasn't sure if it was her husband or her mind that was trying to help her. Her observation is based on a very significant concept in dream interpretation: that dreams are trustworthy, honest representations of our inner life at any given time. This is rooted in the fundamental assumption that the layer of the unconscious from which dreams evolve is essentially interested in the welfare of the dreamer. Thus the prevailing wisdom says that dreams are a product of the inner self: the subconscious mind (Freud's term) or the unconscious mind (Jung's term). It was Freud whose early writings emphasized that dreams are impor-

tant communications from the inner self, supplanting the belief that they are supernatural in origin. One of his most frequently quoted remarks states that dreams "are
the royal road to the unconscious." This should not negate the alternative explanation that many dreams may well have a supernatural origin, as history attests.

Dr. Clyde H. Reid, author and psychotherapist at the Colorado Institute for
Transpersonal Psychology, has his own answer to the question of dream origins
when he states "It is my conviction that the inner world, the world of the
unconscious, does not belong to psychologists alone. It is the realm of the spirit,
the place of healing energy, the abode of God's spirit within us. When I work
with people as a pastoral psychotherapist, I am helping them to be in touch
with their soul."[2]

Recently I heard contemporary singer and songwriter Billy Joel say "All of
the music I have composed has come from a dream. I even dream arrangements
and solos." Because the land of dreams has been a fertile ground for all of humanity, especially poets, writers, inventors, scientists, and musicians, the Supreme
Spirit Reid refers to may well be what psychologists call the unconscious.

There is no doubt that dreams have been a spiritual resource for millions of
people. Here is example: This contact experience came to my attention through
a mother who had attended one of my lectures. Her four-year-old daughter had
what her mother could only believe was a dream of her own grandmother. She
described it in the following way.

"I Spoke to 'Nagy Mama'"

*One morning my four-year-old daughter came downstairs for
breakfast and told me she had spoken to "Nagy Mama" during the
night. She said it so naturally but it caused me to stop in my tracks.
I was speechless because "Nagy Mama"—Hungarian for grandmother—was what I called my grandmother. But my daughter did
not know this nor had we ever talked about her using that name.
More convincing than anything else was that she mentioned several things that "Nagy Mama" had said to her (personal things
which I would rather not discuss here) that only someone knowing
my grandmother would know.*

*While I have no idea what caused this, in some part of myself
I believe my grandmother actually did communicate with my
daughter. I believe that love exists even beyond this world as we
know it. My grandmother and I were very close and I can imagine
that she would want to see my daughter.*

My grandmother died many years ago and it helps me to
believe she is still close to us. Also, only after this happened, was I
able to share my memories with my daughter. I was helped so
much. "Nagy Mama" continues to be very special.

It is noteworthy that this dream, which occurred many years after the death of
the grandmother, was the event which allowed the mother to share her inner
feelings with her daughter and the family. She had held it all within for a very
long time. This type of dream could also be considered as a indirect or third-
party contact, since the four-year-old had no apparent knowledge of the grandmother or her mother's grief. It was the mother's belief that Nagy Mama had
indeed visited her granddaughter.

Interpreting Dreams About Death

Many people report dreams about their own deaths or deaths of loved ones
before they have died. This is not at all unusual. I once had a young woman
come to see me whose father had died unexpectedly in a tragic accident. Shortly
after his death, she began to have dreams of her own death which were very
upsetting to her. Most dream analysts suggest that dreams about your own death
represent the death of a part of your old self or a part of your life that you are
changing. It could also represent the death of a relationship with another person
or an outmoded way of thinking. In short, a dream of our own death "indicates
the death of some obsolete self-image, from which comes rebirth into a higher
state of consciousness and authentic self-being."[3] The dream that Adele had
about the death of her father-in-law could have possibly represented a deep-
seated fear of her own death, as death was now something very real in her own
life for the first time.

What may be happening when we dream of the death of someone who is currently alive, particularly if it is a family member? Again, there is more than one
possible answer. Because the metaphorical language of dreams usually points to
our needs, feelings, and potential changes to make in our conscious life, death
dreams of others often indicate relationship needs which are dying and should be
looked at more closely. Succinctly stated, it may mean that whatever the dying
person or persons in the dream represents to you is also dying.

What about dreams that seem to hold a premonition of death? Most often,
one dreams of the death of another, and such dreams usually turn out to have no
predictive quality whatsoever. Such dreams, however, are considered to have
more to do with the behavior of the person who dies in the dream than of the

dreamer. Psychological causes such as resentment toward the person who dies or withdrawal from an intimate relationship have been suggested. But in instances where one dreams of a person dying, and shortly afterward the dream comes true, most authorities believe that "...it can almost always be traced to signs of sickness or imminent death which have been picked up by the dreamer's waking mind though he may not be fully conscious of it."[4]

All of the previous is based on belief in a model which suggests that dreams come exclusively from the inner self. What each of us have to decide is whether all dreams of loved ones dying are visual metaphors or telepathic communications to a part of the brain capable of receiving such information from an outside source. As we all know, some dreamers have received predictive dreams of the death of a loved one. This happened to my wife the night before our infant daughter Karen died. She saw that Karen had stopped breathing and I was giving her mouth-to-mouth resuscitation—which is exactly what took place the following afternoon. There may well be a whole side of us that operates outside of space and time.

Science would argue that since millions of people throughout the world occasionally dream about the death of a loved one, the laws of probability alone would predict that some few would actually die. Physician and researcher Melvin Morse believes there is something else other than probability at work, and from his studies of precognitive dreams he is convinced that each of us possesses an area of the brain which both creates visionary (dream) experiences and detects them. In his words: "Just as we have a region of our brain that helps us regain our balance when we trip and almost fall, we have an area which is devoted to communication with the mystical. It functions as a sort of sixth sense. In short it is the 'God sensor.'"[5] Again, the agnostic would counter with the thesis that we are by nature image-making creatures.

How does one tell the difference between a death dream that is a metaphor and one which may carry significance beyond the usual? Most often predictive dreams, as well as dreams of visitation from deceased loved ones, are what some therapists call "big dreams." They stand out by themselves as possessing qualities unlike any dream you normally recall. Such "big dreams" stay with you, are easily remembered in great detail, often providing clear messages or directions; they often reduce and/or replace fear with beautiful memories. In any event, if you are unsure of the precognitive death dream by all means say something to the person involved if you sense deep within that it is the thing to do. Otherwise, let it go.

*The secret of understanding dreams is to recognize that there
is something within us which is connected to a greater store of
wisdom and perception than we normally think of ourselves as
having. If we are able, through whatever means, to access this
"something" we will be able to move deeply into areas of
understanding which otherwise might seem impossible.*
—Alexander Lukeman, *What Your Dreams can Teach You.*
St. Paul, MN: Llewellyn Publications, 1990

Let us turn now to looking at other "big dreams" which bring healing, comfort, and a sense of completion when the dreamer feels that the relationship with the deceased was incomplete. These dreams not only bring wholeness to the new relationship between the survivor and the deceased, but provide a healthy sense of closure. In this context, closure does not mean the past is locked out or forgotten. Rather, one is now free to recall the deceased with joyful memories whenever necessary. This first dream occurred several weeks after twenty-eight-year-old Lori's father died.

"I Felt Tremendous Joy and Relief"

*My Dad's death was very painful because he was very alive and
vital and a "fighter." He died of leukemia when he was fifty-seven.
He always gave us (my sisters and I) big bear hugs. Due to his condition he was unable to do this. Many times when I spoke of my
grief I'd state that what I missed were Dad's hugs. I spent the last
few days with him and was the last to see him alive. Before I left
the hospital the last night I washed his hands and feet in preparation for his passing. It was a way for me to give him unspoken permission to go. After his death I had the following dream.*

*It was morning in the house I grew up in. I was in the living
room. My Dad came in the room. I'm surprised and I wonder if
I'm clothed enough—I notice that I'm wearing a nightgown and a
yellow terrycloth robe I had when I was seventeen. I figure I'm seventeen but does my Dad know he's dead? I decide not to tell him
because I want to see him.*

*We go into the kitchen for breakfast. He wants to go get the
mail. I don't want him to leave, because once he goes out the door
he won't come back, because he's dead. He hugs me (I felt this—it
was very real) and asks, "Do you want to come with me?" I say no*

because I am afraid. I don't want to die too. He says, "Okay, the next time I go you can come with me." The dream ends.

I felt tremendous joy and relief that the one thing I missed was given. I feel that once again my father felt good and strong and wanted to comfort me in a loving way. Later, sharing my dream with friends, I made the connection of my Dad being able to assist me through a life crisis or my own death—helping me bridge the change. This dream helped me so much because I could feel that the time with my Dad was complete. I saw him strong and happy and vital again, the way he enjoyed life. I could let go of the pain and fear he felt that made such an impact on me. I could once again cry and yet have a powerful, joyous memory/gift to really boost my healing.

The hug Lori received was not only an act of love, but a critical symbol of completion for her. What had been left undone had suddenly become whole since it reflected her acceptance of his death, his release from pain, the return of her father's health, and new-found joy that her wish had been granted. Who granted that hug? Was it her unconscious mind? A Supreme Being? Her father? Or were all parts of the dream merely symbols to be interpreted in an altogether different way? Only Lori knows.

Jana is likewise convinced that her two dream experiences were unlike any other dreams she had ever had in her life. They were about her daughter who died of SIDS at the age of five months. The suddenness of baby Angie's death left Jana racked with guilt and despair. Furthermore, she was obsessed with two critical thoughts: never seeing her daughter as a grown woman, and believing that her daughter did not know how much she loved her. Both of these issues were resolved in two dreams, the first occurring a few months after her death.

"She Showed Me the Power, the Infinity of Love"

This dream occurred in the early months following my daughter's death. I was feeling like she had "left" me. I felt rejected and abandoned and I was convinced she never knew how much I loved her, and I thought she did not love me. This was exacerbated by several shows I had seen on television regarding near-death experiences. These individuals who had had an NDE spoke of not wanting to leave their new world and return here after a kind of confrontation with a God force, a light. I was convinced my daughter never even missed me. I was in agony.

I dreamed of her . She was an infant, a beautiful infant as she was when alive, not the horror of her body in rigor mortis when we found her dead, her face in a horrible frozen grimace. Now she was smiling at me. She was bathed in a kind of light that was more than the light we know of. This light was a presence of a universal kind of knowledge. It was a light of peace, of wisdom, and of love. These words do not, even in the tiniest way, describe what that light was in its entirety. But I felt it in my soul. It calmed me and uplifted me and reassured me.

She started to laugh, sort of. It was a noise I will never be able to describe; it was like the notes of a harp, the gurgling of a brook, the cooing of an infant, all together somehow. She was speaking to me in this language and I understood her. She said, "Mommy, I love you." She was bathed in this light, kind of floating in a soft blue sky. I awoke peacefully and quietly.

I call these dreams "visitation dreams." They feel to me that they come not from within me, not from my psychology or my trauma or memory or anything else from my life. They have the feeling of being "put" there. They are an externally placed experience, conscious and generated by something outside, instilling in me a kind of joy and peace that is infinite.

Explicitly, my daughter answered a question and soothed my suffering immensely. Symbolically, she showed me the power, the infinity of love. It is never broken by death; death is only a gateway. She helped me to get "unstuck" from that negativity and self-destruction, to move on towards acceptance and peace.

Although Jana was well on her way to healing, she was still deeply distressed by her "loss of the future," which for her meant never seeing her daughter grow up to become a woman. One and a half years after her daughter's death, she had another powerful dream which was the solution to this obstacle to healing.

"That Dream Was an Answer, an Answer of Love"

I saw my daughter as a twenty-eight-year-old woman in my dream. She had black, thick, wavy hair and large blue eyes with full lips shaped like my husband's. She was in a white long flowing robe and there was that same indescribable light that I had experienced previously—of peace, wisdom, and love.

This dream had a very specific quality to it that is consistent with the other "paranormal" experiences I have had since my daughter died in 1990 from Sudden Infant Death Syndrome. Again, this dream had the quality of being put into my consciousness, not a part of my mind, experience, or psyche. It was a visit, a gift. I felt profound peace. For a moment there was no end to myself and no beginning of anything else. I was a part of a cosmic whole. Time was a silly construct, meaningless and patently absurd.

I feel a Oneness and I no longer miss my daughter. We are not apart. It, of course, is fleeting. This particular "visit" dream was an answer to the agony of a bereaved parent who loses a baby and loses a future. I was especially grieving weeks before that dream, crying alone, often wondering what she would have looked like as a woman. She was a beautiful baby. That dream was an answer, an answer of love.

Seeing a glimpse of my daughter as a mature young woman I received a message that her life was meant to be brief; that was her path. It was not a waste and she was smiling, reassuring me of the eternity of peace she existed in, her waiting for me to join her, and a kind of patience with the suffering of my world. She showed me it was a part of a bigger whole.

The experience was healing because it presented to me, in a loving way, a peacefulness and meaning following the acute pain of her unexpected traumatic death. Somehow it made sense: the suffering was a part of a larger dynamic I was not privy to—but still, I was given a glimpse of by her love for me. Life was part of a continuum followed by death, a passage, and another life.

These two dreams, over a year apart, gave Jana the basis for resolving the two key questions which had haunted her since the death of her daughter. She has also had occasion to sense the presence of her daughter when her other children have been at home with her. This has further supported her belief that her child lives on and the family will someday be together again.

While Jana's dreams were critical tools for defusing guilt and correcting the false assumption that her daughter did not love her, some dreams give directions and forewarning from the deceased. In doing so, the survivor is often able to deal with immediate problems and find strength in the bond forged by the dream. Such is the account of fifty-four-year-old Annette who received two visits from her father-in-law after his death.

"He Reassured Me that All would Be Well"

My father-in-law was a good person who I admired and who always gave me wise counsel. When he died I felt I had not only lost a good friend but also a confidant. He was so interested in our family and their welfare.

I had two dreams of him which occurred seven years apart. Both dreams were very clear and distinct. The first dream concerned my daughter who was going through some very difficult times. In her early twenties, and hanging out with a rough crowd, she was a major cause of stress in my life. When he appeared in my dream he looked fit and began to give me very clear instructions about my daughter, which I made every effort to carry out. He reassured me that all would be well. Five years later all came to pass. It did work out well.

Seven years later he came again in a very clear dream. This time it was one week prior to the death of my father. He knew my father was not doing well and he wanted to let me know that Dad would be leaving. He left me with the impression that he would be coming to greet my Dad. He would be there at the time of death. I have never had another dream like those two again.

The result of his coming in the second dream was that I was given in a sense some preparation time. With my Dad's death I was not surprised when it occurred. I was totally at peace with Dad moving on. I knew he was safe.

As with so many of the other contact experiences, dreams usually provide the bereaved with the explicit or symbolic message that there is a life after death, and that deceased loved ones are still near. However, they also provide much more. Often, as we saw with Jana, the dream allows the dreamer to finish unfinished business with the deceased; it gives others a chance to say good-bye and express feelings. Some people believe a deceased loved one may appear in one's dreams for the sole purpose of having fun, as when a deceased child visits his mother.[6]

For many individuals, a dream contact is an excellent time to reexamine one's worldview; including beliefs about God, the hereafter, and the meaning of life. After all, through your dream, the collective unconscious or God (in whatever form you choose to believe) is talking to you. Perhaps you are keeping divine appointments.

Widows often have a number of dreams which play important roles in their grief work. These dreams have very special meaning since they are often marked with clear messages of love and encouragement, helping the survivor in dealing with the reality of the loss. Here are three dreams shared with me by Maita Floyd (widow and author of *Platitudes: You Are Not Me*, and *Caretakers, the Forgotten People*) which brought comfort and understanding in her difficult transition.

"It Was Not My Time or My Airplane to Catch"

One of the first dreams I had after Bill died in 1985 made me realize that I had to accept the fact that it was not my time to die. I worked for thirty years for TWA as an airport ticket agent and many of my dreams were located at the airport. This made sense to me as most of my waking hours were spent there.

In my dream Bill and I were going on a trip. Of course, as the employee I always took care of the passes. When we arrived at the counter Bill said, "I will go ahead to the gate." As he went away I watched him getting smaller and smaller. I ran after him. When I reached the gate the agent said, "You are too late." I brushed past him and ran to the jetway. The airplane door was closed. I pounded on the door. . . and woke up.

I wanted to go with Bill. During our marriage we used to wish that if we had to die we would both die in a plane crash. But the message was clear to me: It was not my time or my airplane to catch. It was Bill's time. I had no choice. I would be on the ground until my time was up. Very symbolic.

"I Love You"

We had moved four months before Bill died. He was told in March that he had two to six months to live and died in September. When I didn't dream about the airport the scene would always be at the other house where we had lived for fifteen years.

In this dream I came home and walked through the back door into the kitchen. From there I saw a light in the living room and asked, "Is anyone home?" I walked into the living room and Bill was sitting in his favorite chair. He was smiling. I went over to him, bent down with my face next to his, and he kissed me and said, "I love you." When I woke up, I felt that he was somewhere around, sending me a message, sending me his love. It was comforting.

"Don't Give Up, Don't Ever Give Up"

You should know that Bill was very active. He ran every day and also lifted weights. He took good care of himself.

In this third dream, Bill was lying on the living room carpet, exercising. There was a bandage on his left side where his cancerous kidney had been removed. He looked up saying, "Don't give up, don't ever give up."

The message was clear to me since Bill was always concerned about my future alone. He was giving me encouragement and that was good. I always feel "up" when I think of this dream.

Maita is an excellent example of utilizing her dreams to deal with her life without her beloved husband. She realized she was still loved, that she had to accept Bill's death, and was encouraged to continue on with her life. And what a supportive admonition from someone she loved so dearly—to be told to persist and not to give up!

The Recurrent Dream

On some occasions, mourners experience the same dream over a period of days or weeks. It may occur shortly after the death or years later. The following dream was shared with me by Ronnie Petersen, former professional liaison with the National Organization of Compassionate Friends, a self-help group for parents who are grieving the death of a child. Her son had died in an automobile accident at age seventeen.

"Ma, You Knew I Was All Right"

I don't remember when this dream started. I think it was quite a long time after Tony died. It may have been as long as a year. At the time, I was a substitute teacher up at the high school and I was there teaching several days a week. So I was in school quite regularly. I had this dream perhaps five or six times.

I would be substituting and I would have a free period. During that time I was walking down the hall past the door to the cafeteria. Now it was not lunch time; it was mid-morning. But the door of the cafeteria was open, and as I walked past, I glanced in and there was a group of five or six boys sitting at the table just inside the door. And Tony was among them and seemed to be the center of attention. I don't mean abnormally. It wasn't "Oh my goodness, he's here." It was just that, as usual, he was the leader of the group. Well, I stormed into the cafeteria and screamed at him "We thought you were dead , how dare you scare us, why did you do this to us. We thought you were dead and here you are goofing off with your friends." And he would just look up at me in the most

*casual way and say "Ma, you knew I was all right." And that
would be the end of the dream.*

*Originally, I was very upset about this because I thought,
"How could I be so angry at him? There I had a chance to see him
again and all I did was yell at him. What's the matter with me?
Why didn't I go in and give him a big hug? Instead, I'm screaming
at the poor child." I thought about it a whole lot and went over the
details again and again. Finally, after I had the dream five or six
times, I thought, "Oh, my reprimand is not the important part. The
important part is what he said to me. 'You know I'm all right.'"
(Now I'm going to have tears come into my eyes as I say this.) And
I think, of course, "He's all right. What am I fighting against? I'm
the one who is in trouble. He's all right." Of course, I never had the
dream again once I came to this conclusion.*

Once Ronnie focused on her son's message in the dream, she realized why it had
been repeated. She had allowed her anger to continue to be expressed and overlooked the essential meaning of the encounter with her son. As she later said, "I
had to learn from the dream that he was okay. Once that happened, I didn't have
to have it anymore. Now as I think of it, it doesn't bother me that I was angry at
him." Perhaps she needed to express some form of anger in her dream, if she was
unable to do so in the waking state. Eventually, the persistence of her unconscious
won out and she was happy about it.

A Special Kind of Dream

There is another type of dream that has very special meaning to the dreamer who
has a life-threatening illness. This is not to be confused with the deathbed vision,
a type of near-death experience commonly reported by the dying shortly before
death. The contact dream experienced by the dying person involves a loved one
who has already died.

The illustration I am giving here involves a gay man and his partner who
died two months previously. He was forced to deal with his grief over the loss of
his partner as well as the grief over his own impending death.

"We Were Going on a Journey"

*Several nights ago I had a dream of Dan that has been very help-
ful to me in many respects. I was fully clothed lying in bed with my
backpack on and my hiking boots, ready to go on a hike. At the
time I was using the backpack as a support like a second pillow.*

Then as I looked down at the foot of my bed there was a slight mist and I was surprised to see Dan standing in the mist waiting for me. He too was dressed for the hike. He was greeting me and together we were going on a journey.

The experience brought considerable peace to this dying man. He had felt lonely since the death of his partner, and to meet him in this dream gave him a new sense of assurance that he would not be alone in death. This is an example where reassurance came not in being able to deal with beginning a new life, but in being able to live one's dying.

Dr. Dennis Ryan at the College of New Rochelle has studied the death dreams of 472 people, ages eight to eighty-eight. His key research question was: What do you think the dream is trying to tell you? Based on interviews with respondents, he found four major results of dreams of deceased loved ones:[7]

- They helped the dreamer accept the reality of the loss—to accept that the person is dead, and life is different.

- They assisted in experiencing the grief, anger, and/or guilt associated with the death.

- They provided a way to review the relationship with the deceased, whether the relationship was a positive or negative one.

- They were a means to come to closure and get on with one's life.

These are all healthy, life-affirming results. I have seen these same results expressed in a variety of personal ways through dreams, some of which we have reviewed in this book. Be confident in using your dreams in these or other ways to help you cope with the changes accompanying your loved one's death. If you have a dream regarding your deceased loved one, whether you deem it a "big dream" or not, write it down as soon as you awaken. Include all details you can remember. Then seek someone you trust to share it with. That alone may be enough to begin the healing process and help you deal with your loss. If possible, find someone who has had some training in dream analysis for additional input. Then you can make use of the experience in a healthy way and gain insight into your feelings based on discussion and what your heart tells you.

The process of using your dreams to manage grief work will help you determine how you would like to relate to the deceased. We all have to establish new relationships with our deceased loved ones as part of reconciling our losses. This is one reason grieving the death of a loved one is a longer process than most people recognize. Establishing "newness" is a major task of grieving.

Failure to tap into the wisdom of your dreams is to abandon a part of your spiritual self that has been utilized for great comfort by many in dealing with all kinds of losses. Before you go to sleep, ask God, your subconscious, or the collective unconscious to talk to you in this way and to help you remember your dreams. Your unconscious is incredibly wise and loving and wants you to work through your grief, cope with the changes imposed by the death of your loved one, and become whole again. Remember, you possess a huge pool of wisdom, a limitless computer within. Most importantly, dreams can be a guide to assessing your place in the grief process and to determining where to make changes to assist the transition. As the research suggests, being "open to aspects of life beyond the physical-materialistic realm can be conducive to health and well-being."[8] In particular, a single dream may provide lasting rituals for coping, assist in preserving memories, help you affirm the reality of the death, clarify thoughts, express emotions, and become a linking object of great value.

We will examine the subject of skepticism in our next chapter, since we all harbor a healthy touch of this cultural arbiter. It is part of the human condition. If by some chance at this point in your journey you are not quite sure where you stand on the issue of the credibility of the contact experience, here is an opportunity to come to grips with your dilemma.

TWELVE

Skeptics All

In spite of its reputation as the most powerful arbiter of reality, it is nowhere written down that science is the only or the best gateway to what is real. We invented the scientific method; it did not descend from on high.
—Larry Dossey, M.D. in *Healing Words*

We tend to delegate the spiritual to others who are more interested in it, or who we feel are perhaps better equipped to deal with it. In reality, of course, the spiritual can't be delegated. We all participate in it. It is our very nature, the core of our humanity.
—Rachel Naomi Remen, M.D. in "Spirit: Resource of Healing," *Noetic Sciences Review*, Autumn 1988

One day when my wife and I were on our way to visit friends, the topic of the extraordinary came up in our conversation. I proceeded to tell her about the "visit" that the world-renowned psychiatrist Elisabeth Kubler-Ross had from a patient who had died ten months earlier. As Kubler-Ross tells the story, she was about to quit her work of giving seminars on dying and death for caregivers at the University of Chicago, and possibly discontinue this phase of her work permanently when she had this experience. Her former patient "visited" her for two reasons—to thank her for all she had done for the deceased person when she was alive, and to implore Kubler-Ross not to stop the vital work she was doing in the field of death and dying. Kubler-Ross at first wondered if the experience was the result of working too hard or having seen too many schizophrenic patients. However, realizing that nobody would believe her about what was happening, she asked her "visitor" to write a note to a mutual friend. She obliged, wrote, and signed the note.

On concluding the story my wife looked at me and said, "Do you expect me to believe that a deceased woman came back and wrote a note as proof of her existence for this psychiatrist?" "Well," I said, "that's up to you."

We are all skeptics by nature. At times, we all question the validity or authenticity of something which has been presented as truth. Some people are skeptical of anything that is presented to them as "the real truth." Certainly, we all have our doubts about a variety of topics in many fields of study—philosophy, sociology or psychology, to name a few. And within each of those disciplines we may doubt specific theories or doctrines and embrace others. Some of us may be skeptical of the infallibility of the Pope in Church matters, the sincerity of owners of professional athletic teams, or the reality of the id, ego, and superego. Others of us may be skeptical of the near-death experience, the validity of aptitude or IQ measurements or the existence of the Bermuda Triangle. Skeptical opposition to the supposedly unscientific field of parapsychology abounds, even though in 1969 the Parapsychological Association was granted affiliate membership in the American Association for Advancement of Science. Of course, the same natural skepticism is quite obvious among scientists themselves when they do not agree with a new theoretical model introduced in their specialty field.

The Making of a Hard-Core Skeptic

No one is immune to skepticism. It is a natural product of our deductive reasoning abilities. However, some skeptics become excessively rigid and unbending. The point of concern is this: How do we become skeptics about a subject, particularly one as controversial as the spontaneous contact by a deceased loved one, and how can we balance our skepticism? In a single word, the answer is our perceptions—the way we grasp a given subject. It is our world view, our paradigm. Interestingly, once we change our paradigm or worldview, we change our attitudes and beliefs about a given subject.

What are perceptions and how do we come by them? Perceptions are the *personal meaning* we give to an observation or an experience. And perceptions are highly variable because, although we all see with our eyes, we perceive with our brains. That is why two individuals can look at the same object or experience and perceive it quite differently. Recently, for example, a dear friend of mine was about to make a telephone call to a prospective employer to follow up on an earlier inquiry her son had made for a part-time job. As she was looking up the number, the telephone rang. It was the potential employer wanting to speak to her son. Her immediate response was: "How about that for telepathic communication?" Her son countered with the view that it was just plain coincidence. They had both shared a common event but they had perceived it differently. No two people perceive the same event in exactly the same way. We all see the world through our own lenses.

There are several factors which play prominent roles in the development of the way we perceive an event or an experience, including the length of time a person has lived (age usually affects the meaning one attaches to an event), the self-concept (how one feels about the self, good or bad, positive or negative), immediate needs (whether or not what you are perceiving fills a present need), past experiences (all of the opportunities one has had to perceive as part of his/her cultural heritage), the nature of the physical organism (we see things quite differently when we are sick than when we are well, and we are all very different at the cellular level), and finally, the experience of threat.[1] All of these factors help shape how one gives personal meaning to an extraordinary or paranormal event. Because threat (fear) most dramatically influences perception, let's examine how threatening circumstances aid in the development of hard-core skepticism.

Threat hinders perception; it narrows the focus of observation, creating a tunnel vision of sorts. Thus, we consciously (and sometimes unconsciously) refuse to be open to alternative explanations. We limit awareness. For example, if you fear water and are told you must take a swimming course, your fear will reduce your awareness of the mechanics of any swimming stroke that the instructor is trying to teach you. The result is predictable: you will find many excuses not to attend class—you have a cold, you forgot your bathing suit, or (if you are a female), you are having your period. In all of this, the focus is switched from learning to swim to doing everything to stay out of the dreaded water. Because fear is the major catalyst of threat, it too is consciously or unconsciously the center of attention. In either case, it is damaging to growth and the development of new awareness and knowledge about any topic. Most importantly, fear eliminates openness to the new.

Science is sometimes threatened by that which it cannot explain or does not understand. Furthermore, there is a genuine fear among some medical professionals, scientists, and even counselors that their closely guarded view of reality might crumble. Yet, the likes of Pasteur, Salk, Einstein, and thousands of others have had to deal with their fears associated with forging into uncharted waters and were able to manage their dilemmas. The unexplainable was not shut out; it was given careful consideration.

We all have our fears which distort the way we perceive certain life events. In many instances, threats to deeply held beliefs cause people on both sides of an issue to become dogmatic and demanding—a defense against the possibility of change and the apprehension which is so often inherent in giving up the old for the new. Author and physician Melvin Morse suggests that the insensitivity of some physicians to death-related visions is the result of their fear of criticism and loss of control. That is, they cannot control the arrival or departure of death-related phenomena.[2]

Probably the most influential factor of all in the way we perceive any event is our belief system. What we believe to be true affects everything we do, and there are many unconscious beliefs we are not aware of that affect our behavior. In fact, there is much evidence to suggest that more of our daily mental activity takes place on an unconscious level than on a conscious one.[3] These unconscious beliefs are ingrained early in life and heavily influence perceptions and our actions. Consider the following unconscious beliefs associated with grieving:

- Grief should be brief.
- Controlling the expression of sorrow is essential.
- Crying is a sign of weakness.
- Women are expected to be emotional.
- Men must "be strong."

Medicine and psychology have shown over and over again that beliefs also strongly affect our biology. Gerontologists, for example, have changed the beliefs of many elderly people, encouraging them to refrain from sedentary lifestyles and remain active. The result is a reduction in the loss of skeletal and muscle tissue. Further evidence of the reality that belief affects biology is a study of cancer patients in Birmingham, England, who were informed that the chemotherapy they were to receive would cause loss of hair. Unknowingly, a number of patients were given a placebo of no medicinal value, yet all suffered hair loss.[4] In fact, the field of psychoneuroimmunology—the study of the relationship between the brain, the endocrine system, and the immune system—shows that what we think affects the viability of the immune system as well as every cell in the body.

Culture and the Skeptic

Especially when it comes to examining extraordinary phenomena, beliefs which the culture imprints below the level of conscious awareness—like seeing is believing—play a leading role in how we perceive and ultimately judge an event. For example, even though our senses do play tricks on us at times, most people are still led to believe, sometimes erroneously, that reality is that which can be seen.

It is commonly accepted that Western civilization is particularly oriented toward scientism and naturalism. Indeed, we have made huge strides forward in all fields of endeavor because of the scientific method. Belief in it is thoroughly ingrained in each of us. How did that come about?

A major player in the thrust of transforming society from the strict authoritarianism of the Middle Ages to the equally strict scientific method we know today was the canon and lawyer Nicolaus Copernicus. The Copernican Revolution (not to minimize the contributions of Galileo and Kepler) challenged the old belief that the earth was the center of the universe, and ultimately showed that the earth revolved around the sun. More important to our discussion, this discovery, among others, was the beginning of the rapid swing of the pendulum away from ancient authority and the old way of looking at the universe. This swing also brought about a change in critical beliefs about the role of Providence in the creation of the universe, the occurrence of miracles, and the possibility of supernatural or unseen phenomena.

In the past, contact experiences—visions, voices, apparitions, unexplained happenings—were quite normally accepted. For example, in the tradition of the prophets in both the Old and New Testaments, what we now call the extraordinary or the paranormal was considered quite normal in communicating with Divine Providence. In this vein, consider when Paul was about to be shipwrecked on his voyage to Rome. With the Adriatic Sea erupting in tumultuous waves an angel appeared and told him that God granted safety to him and all who sailed with him. The ship was destroyed, but not one of the 276 people on board perished. Then there is the account of Joseph and Mary fleeing to Egypt, having been warned in a dream that Herod wanted to kill the Christ child. Spontaneous appearances of angels, prophetic dreams, unusual signs, or voices heard were constant forms of communication. For some, mystical experiences of various kinds were actively sought after.

However, as the scientific pendulum picked up speed with the publication of Descartes' *Discourse on Method,* it also picked up and strengthened the belief that truth and authority are only found in direct systematic observation and experimentation. Assumptions, anecdotal data, and the spiritual nature of people and the universe did not fit the scientific view of reality. A new theme was gradually adopted, one that asserted we are not spiritual beings; we are physical beings with anomalies science has yet to explain. In the late sixteenth and early seventeenth centuries, the new belief structure fashioned by the scientific method took on additional potency by branding all which could not be systematically observed and categorized as either nonexistent or the work of devious men trying to trick a gullible public.

The swing of any pendulum commonly goes to extremes. And the swing from church authority to scientific authority was bound to bring abuses. One of the most serious was the loss of the importance of mystery, faith, and the acceptance of the extraordinary. There has been no place for that which cannot be systematically observed, such as a vision or an apparition. Because science would not allow for any phenomena which would transcend space and time, miracles were now forbidden to exist. One historian says bluntly that the scientific revolution was "the most momentous mutation in human affairs since the advent of agriculture or the dawn of civilization."[5] Whenever the collective belief is that an event is fictitious, it is very difficult for an individual not to conform and go along with the prevailing winds of disbelief. In our society, science has a monopolistic claim to knowledge.

Why the Unseen is So Hard to Believe

Is there only one reality? As a society we have minimized, indeed forgotten and expunged, the huge untapped resource of the unseen for healing and renewal in daily life. The beliefs accompanying this loss have been passed down from generation to generation, affecting the way we perceive any unproven or unproveable event. Consider for a moment a common response to the following: Telepathy, clairvoyance, psychokinesis, and precognition. What is your initial reaction to reading these words? Do they strike you as being unscientific, occult, mysterious, or strange? Do you immediately feel a less-than-open attitude toward the processes they represent? Not infrequently, such attitudes are a product of the subconscious resistance toward the unseen inherent in the beliefs of Western society. And I would be one of the first to admit that it is no easy task to change those ingrained resistances.

Some of those resistances are reinforced by the media, which has sensationalized the extraordinary for entertainment and profit. Credibility is strained as contact experiences are portrayed in grossly distorted fashion. At the time I am writing this, even one of the popular daytime soap opera shows is featuring a story line in which one of the characters is regularly visited by his deceased wife, who is upset by his new romantic interest.

Every society has its way of programming its members, which is why each country possesses very strong beliefs about what is important and valuable. It is the cultural programming of values, beliefs, and traditions which causes conflict among countries. Generally, the citizens of each country believe that what they have been taught is the way it should be everywhere. We often forget we are wearing these cultural lenses, and our way becomes, to us, the only way of looking at life. In short, it can be argued that we are all in a cultural trance of sorts and it takes concerted effort to break the trance. Consequently, the cultural ethic in the mind of Americans that regards extraordinary phenomena as being nonexistent is strong. Indeed, it is just as strong as our beliefs in individual freedom and due process under the law. We have learned our lessons well in many ways, and are closed off to the possibility that nonphysical reality may be as genuine as physical reality.

> *Extensive clinical and experimental research and anthropological observations have provided further support for the hypothesis that to some degree we only see what our culture tells us we can see, only know what our society tells us we can know.*
> —Willis Harman & Howard Rheingold, *Higher Creativity.*
> Los Angeles: Jeremy P. Tarcher, 1984

The negative image of the unseen has been reinforced through the years by the uncovering of fraudulent behavior by unscrupulous pretenders. It is important to recognize at the outset that the field of the extraordinary (or the paranormal, if you prefer the term) has been riddled with trickery, deceit, misrepresentation, and misunderstanding. And, as in most fields of study, it has its share of incompetence, overgeneralization, and self-deception.

You will not have to search far to find chicanery. Many books on parapsychology give ample coverage to the fact that fraud in this area has been a fact of life, especially in the early history of the study of unusual phenomena.[6] Many Society for Psychical Research (SPR) investigators exposed the fraud and deception of those who purported to have had extraordinary experiences. The SPR's mission has always been to investigate the extraordinary within a strictly scientific framework. At times, it seems the SPR's research designs have been too rigid as they try to appease the skeptics. (For example, many high-quality experiences submitted for research purposes have been discarded because of time lapses between the time they occurred and they were reported.) However, in recent times, there are a number of organized groups (like the Committee for the Scientific Investigation of Claims of the Paranormal, a not-for-profit scientific and educational organization) which zealously point out the faults in some reports—sometimes by means which are themselves suspect.

As a result of this fraudulent history and the demand for evidence far exceeding standards required of other disciplines, the likelihood of the scientific community demeaning any type of extraordinary phenomena—as well as those reporting it—is naturally increased. However, as with most controversial issues, there are various degrees of truth, half-truths, and lies to be dealt with, not the least of which are the host of statistics and evidence purportedly showing proof for or against the validity of the phenomena. Of course, scientists are not immune from supporting their pet hypotheses with less-than-quality work either. They have to deal with the occupational hazards of ambition, greed, and jealousy just like those in other lines of work. Both science and parapsychology are only as reliable as those who apply their methods. It is clear that either side can sometimes be found sacrificing truth on the altar of notoriety.

What I am getting at is that it may well be impossible to obtain scientific evidence to say unequivocally that the contact experience is, beyond a shadow of a doubt, true. Unfortunately, but undeniably, the evasiveness of the contact experience is another reason mainstream scientists have shunned investigation of the phenomena. Who is ever going to pull off an apparition in a laboratory setting? Who will be able to obtain the cooperation of a deceased husband to talk to his widow with researchers standing by in white coats with pencils poised? As they say in Missouri—show me. I regret to say at this time that such a demand cannot be met, and probably never will be. So some individuals will always look at those reporting extraordinary events with a jaundiced eye, and view the events as simply captivating tales. It is a prejudice deeply based in cultural consensus.

Balancing Your Skepticism

But what about those who are on the fringes of believing, who are unsure, who are open to the possibility that some of the bereaved may be experiencing something that is real, that maybe they "know" something that we can't yet fathom? The decision to be open about those possibilities is the most important single step you can take toward understanding such experiences. Keep in mind that the attitudes and beliefs of the people you live and work with have a major impact on your own beliefs when it comes to subjects that cannot be easily explained. The power of suggestion is a potent force. So we have to counter those influences and introduce alternative explanations.

Even if you are a full-blown skeptic, who insists that there is no evidence to support the existence of the unexplainable, let me recommend where you can start to make progress on coming to a more reasoned judgment about the unusual experiences of the bereaved. It all begins by being open to the possibility that the phenomena can be explained. As Goethe, Germany's gifted man of letters, put it: "Man must cling to his faith that the incomprehensible is comprehensible, else he would cease to investigate."[7] It is good to be skeptical, but not to be overcome by skepticism.

In the opposite vein, the same over-identification happens to some people who think they have had a contact experience when they have not, or who believe that all unusual experiences are supernatural in origin. For example, some people have reported apparitions which on investigation have turned out to be nothing more than shadows or reflections off of shiny surfaces. They build on their biases and close off any reasonable discussions to the contrary, and their reasoning becomes heavily biased without their being fully aware of it.

So to avoid both traps, you need to start from the bottom and build. How? First and foremost, do your homework. Become as fully informed about the content and meaning of the contact experience as you can. Once we become fully aware of perceptions other than our own, we often find some things we can agree on. Read a number of research reports on the subject. You will be surprised that although there is some questionable data bandied about, a number of studies are reputable and deserve serious consideration. The American and British Societies for Psychical Research have several thousand cases of every description in their archives, many well documented, and they will provide some of the most interesting reading in this regard. Make it a point to read *Human Personality and Its Survival of Bodily Death* by F. W. H. Myers, *Hauntings and Apparitions* by Andrew Mackenzie, and *Parting Visions* by Melvin Morse. These books will provide material that will suggest lots of new questions for you to consider. See the suggested readings section at the end of the book for additional information. Then you will be in a much better position to make a decision about the authenticity of contact experiences from a new frame of reference.

Next, make every attempt to locate and speak with someone who has reported a contact experience. Start first within your own family and with your relatives. You may be surprised that someone in your family has had an experience but has been afraid to share it within the family, since there is always the fear of being branded too far out or too imaginative.

In my own family, my twin sisters finally told me after fifteen years that a day or two before my mother died, they both saw a dark cloud over her head as they saw her working at a crafts fair in our town. It was, to say the least, a strange premonition of her death, since the cloud was not seen by anyone else and was there only momentarily before suddenly disappearing. Was it a premonition, a sign? Did it occur so that they would later be able to deal with her death in a more healthy manner, because they were very close to her? (Some people who receive a premonition of this type believe it to be a privileged sign which reinforces their belief in an afterlife and a Supreme Intelligence.) Or was it simply their imaginations working overtime—and at the same time? And why did only the two of them see whatever it was? It is well known that twins often possess psychic ability. However, neither of them offered to tell me about their experiences until I told one of them that I was gathering data on unusual experiences of the bereaved. Then they knew I was safe to talk to. To say the least, I felt bad I was not told of this when it happened, yet I could understand their motivation for maintaining their silence.

After checking in your own social circle, try finding a counselor or clergyperson you may know. Ask if they have had people who have reported extraordinary events when grieving. Try to obtain their opinions about what they believe they have seen. The more you can become informed, the more you may be able to partially balance the one-sided view which we all so easily pick up, and which closes the mind to the possibility that the unseen is a viable reality.

You can ask if someone who works in or is a volunteer for a hospice has heard any unusual stories about the bereaved. Hospices provide follow-up care for the families of people who die in their care by way of ongoing bereavement support groups. Open discussion of unusual events is encouraged. Of course, your efforts in this regard will only provide anecdotal data, which is not considered as evidence of anything. Nonetheless, you will at least get an idea of the variety of experiences reported, which will raise more questions in your mind than provide answers. That's good, because additional questions will spur you on to seek more data upon which reasoned decisions can be made.

Also consider this: A huge data base has been generated (see Chapter 2) through the millions of people who report a variety of extraordinary experiences concerning deceased loved ones. Isn't that enough to say, "Let's take a closer look at what's going on out there?" There is no question that people have extraordinary contact experiences, and other not-easy-to-explain experiences as well. Let's not close our eyes and say that the phenomena is impossible to experience. Use the scientific method to acknowledge there is something going on that science can't pinpoint, but which is, to use their language, a major anomaly to be studied.

The Seen vs. The Unseen

One of the most critical factors in denying the existence of any type of difficult-to-explain activity, whether it be psychic ability or contact experiences, is the overvaluation of material or physical phenomena. From birth to old age we are ceaselessly subjected to a constant barrage of visual imagery from the environment in which we live. The abundance of movies, television, billboard advertisements, pictures, video games, and the glittering decor of the cities is both attractive and eye-catching. This persistent one-dimensional view of reality becomes an integral part of our lifestyles, highlighting the importance of physical reality while minimizing the possibility of other realities. We are engulfed with media hype from all sides. As mentioned earlier, it is that same media which, as part of its entertainment goals, has distorted extraordinary phenomena, adding a fairy tale dimension.

This exclusive focus of our society on physical reality is self-reinforcing. The need to see, measure, weigh, and touch that which one thinks is real becomes the sole criteria for deciding what to believe. Our orientation to physical reality significantly limits our awareness of, and participation in, the spiritual development of our humanity. Let's illustrate this in the following way. For comparison purposes, consider the two lists below:

Physical Reality	Nonphysical Reality
Conscious Mind	Unconscious or Subconscious Mind
Reason	Imagination
Logic	Faith, Hope, Love
Scientific Method	Extraordinary Experiences
Cause and Effect	Miracle Healings
Conversations	Autosuggestion
Physical Senses	Visualization Techniques
Space/Time Barriers	Visions
Research	Intuition
Objective	Subjective
Experimental	Spiritual

Obviously, the lists are abbreviated. Nonetheless, the topics in the left-hand column are very much a part of our physical orientation, while those on the right cannot be accurately measured. I dare say that many people utilize some of the items in the right-hand column on a daily basis, or turn to nonphysical reality when dealing with persistent problems and to enrich their lives. For example, millions of people successfully use visualization techniques in coping with stress, or as motivation to achieve a specific goal. In fact, we often utilize that which is invisible and difficult to measure and receive tangible and visible rewards for our efforts. Consider the many scientific studies on the efficacy of prayer found in the highly regarded book *Healing Words*, written by a physician who has observed that, simply put, prayer works. Yet some scientists still scoff at the possibility that prayer could affect the healing of someone miles away.

Nonphysical factors, among others, lead to the development of our often-neglected spiritual side. Surely, the reassuring presence of nonphysical reality bolsters faith and the motivation to go on in the face of loss. Actually, both of the columns are simply a beginning description of the totality of each person—we are not merely physical beings, but rather both physical and spiritual. French philosopher and mystic Teilhard de Chardin put it this way: "We are not human beings having a spiritual experience we are spiritual beings having a human experience." Indeed, the nature and quality of physical reality is a direct reflection of the degree to which the nonphysical is embraced.

There is a question of profound significance to ask ourselves: Is the materialistic scientific worldview an adequate view of reality? A second and related question of consequence is: Does gender play a part in the overemphasis on physical reality? Let's begin with the second question which will lead us back to the first. It may be of more than passing significance that the most vociferous of skeptics happen to be males (who are also seldom seen at support groups for the bereaved). Men have lost a great deal of their feminine side, that sense of mystery and awe in the presence of the unknown, and there is too much mystery in each of us that is not fully understood to calmly accept the thesis that the materialistic worldview is the only answer to the question of our nature. We possess what appears to be a variety of puzzling abilities, yet at the present time I am inclined to believe that there are far fewer contact experiences reported by men because they are less willing to recognize and share their experiences for fear of damaging the false image of strength imposed by society. There are few males willing to say, "Yes, I've had a spiritual experience."

Regrettably, we are very uneasy about mystery; we have trouble accepting or dealing with it due to our orientation toward clear-cut matter-of-fact answers. That is why labeling contact phenomena an illusion, a hallucination, or a chance occurrence gives a sense of security and control; we have a formula to explain the unknown. But mystery is part of the richness of life, and labeling limits the awareness of mystery: it narrows our vision. The perennial problem of language is that by labeling we prejudge and assume. What is becoming clear to many people is that the conventional model of reality does not fully address actual experience.

The dilemma of mystery and our spiritual malnutrition is exacerbated by pre-occupation with the material world. In *A Return to Love*, author Marianne Williamson put it another way when she wrote, "We overvalue what we perceive with our physical senses, and we undervalue what we know to be true in our hearts."[8] What we know to be true in our hearts is often not amenable to scientific study, but that does not necessarily make it less valid in our experiential world. In fact, knowledge of the heart is more embracing and inescapable than scientific knowledge.

Ask members of the medical profession what happens when you cover one eye for a period of time, and they will respond that the remaining eye becomes stronger and dominates the scene. The subject also loses their depth perception. That is exactly what has happened with our covering of the subjective and spiritual side of our being—we are dominated by physical imagery and have lost touch with the depths of our beings, our spiritual selves—greatly diminishing the true nature of our humanity. We have two selves which naturally coalesce unless they are purposely kept separated. If we are to attempt to reduce our dogmatic skepticism and open ourselves to explanations that cannot fully carry the scientific seal of approval, it is necessary to surrender some of our personal resistance and let our defenses down. Robert Jahn and Brenda Dunne, in *Margins of Reality*, have rightly suggested that extraordinary claims demand extraordinary proof, but they follow this suggestion with an important admonition:

> *Nonetheless, that same science, and that same psyche, must have the openness of mind, the humility in the face of empirical evidence, and the flexibility of spirit to accommodate to new information when such is incontrovertibly presented, for therein lies the only route for their vital growth and maturation.*[9]

If transformation occurs in the lives of many of the bereaved who have a contact experience—and it obviously does, as we have witnessed in the preceding chapters—then regardless of our preconceived notions about cause, let's muster that "humility in the face of empirical evidence" and begin the search for the how and why.

To sum up, there are five key points to be restated in view of the firmly entrenched skepticism that engulfs the extraordinary in general and the contact experience in particular, and thereby eliminates the healthful effects for the bereaved. First, the personal meaning we give to an experience is based on several factors, not the least of which is the dominant scientific orientation of the culture, particularly when it comes to addressing the topic of the extraordinary. Second, fear and the perception of threat reduce awareness and the ability of many hard-core skeptics to entertain an openness to the possibility that the contact experience is something other than the product of overactive imaginations or people "in need." Again, the consequences for the bereaved can be damaging when the significant people in their lives trivialize such a meaningful event. Third, just because the contact experience cannot be systematically observed and authenticated, it should not be categorically ignored nor should it automatically imply that many of these experiences are not real. Fourth, each of us can develop a healthy questioning attitude about the contact experience by first doing our homework and finding out all we can from the most reliable sources. And finally, the overemphasis on and the overvaluing of physical reality puts us at a disadvantage by minimizing the spiritual dimension and the mystery which is an integral part of every individual.

If only for the potential healing benefits to the bereaved, let us take that first step of exploring the wide range of their extraordinary experiences with a pragmatic view. In so doing, we will be gathering data which may break the logjam between believers and unbelievers. After all, as Dr. Larry Dossey stated in the opening quote of this chapter, "It is nowhere written down that science is the only or best gateway to what is real."

We turn now to our final chapter to discover what we can do to assist those who think they have had a contact experience.

THIRTEEN

Helping a Person Who Experiences a Deceased Loved One

Real vision is the ability to see the invisible.
—Jonathan Swift

Grief is ultimately about making new discoveries.
—Bob Deitz in *Life after Loss*

Whenever those who are grieving accept your offer to walk with them through their intense emotional pain—or reach out to you for assistance—you have been honored. Someone in the throes of traumatic change will most often turn to those they have confidence in and can be vulnerable in front of without fear of humiliation. In a word, you are looked upon as a trusted friend. Of course, that is only the beginning of what often turns out to be a much longer journey than you had anticipated; but you should never forget that you have the opportunity to help someone heal, to serve them in their darkest hour.

If this is a first time for you helping a friend or relative, it certainly will not be the last. You will have many opportunities to step forward and provide the most important service one human being can give to another—to be there when another is in excruciating emotional pain. This is no easy task. Yet being there on a consistent basis, often in silence, without offering clichés or platitudes, is perhaps the most demanding service one is called upon to give throughout life. I emphasize the word "silence" because there are many times when your presence alone will be a great comforting force and all that is necessary for the moment. The silence will be difficult for you. You will be anxious, thinking you have to come up with comforting words. But maintain the silence and let the mourner be in charge.

During your silent vigil, you will eventually be called upon to offer an opinion. You will be confronted with direct questions: "What do you think I should do? What will be the best thing to say? Who should I consult for advice with this problem? What do you make of this dilemma? Do you agree with me?"

You will be tempted to want to give immediate helpful answers in the hope that they will take away the pain that surrounds you and your friend. However, you must be cautious not to take over and reinforce the feeling that the survivor is also a victim as well as a survivor. Victims by definition are helpless. Survivors need people willing to listen to them repeat and repeat what has happened and how their loss is affecting their lives. Still, there is a fine line between providing support and creating total dependence on that support. You will sense when you must answer a question with a question and ask how the survivor wishes to deal with the issue. Then, when appropriate, alternative possibilities can be offered. At other times, you must learn when to summarize the core of the related experience and reflect it back in concise terms in order to show that you are trying to understand the experience and the dilemma.

You may also have a special advantage in helping a friend or loved one if you are also grieving the same loss, because in giving of yourself you will benefit from being able to share your honest feelings and hurts. You can do both: provide support and share your sorrow. This will often be an invitation for your grieving friend or relative to be more open and honest in the relationship. However, this does not mean to imply that you must be grieving the same loss in order to provide the best comfort and care. You can be a major support for anyone—if you are willing to be around pain. We all need to train ourselves to be around pain. That commitment alone means that your healing presence can be helpful. You are there and you care.

One other point: Confidentiality is a must. You will be hearing and seeing the deepest emotions and feelings another person can express. Some of these feelings may move you to tears, cause surprise, or even alarm. When a friend who is grieving tells you he has heard, seen, or somehow felt the presence of the deceased, you will be especially pressed not to divulge this information. Honor the intimate relationship that is being formed, and resist the temptation to relay any part of what has been entrusted to you to another family member, unless the mourner gives specific permission to do so.

Basic Guidelines

Here are three very basic guidelines for helping your friend without creating total dependency. These are applicable in most loss situations involving major change, and they will facilitate the mourning process, which in part I defined in Chapter

3 as "sharing one's grief with another." At the same time, they will provide a framework within which the mourner will feel more comfortable in talking about a contact experience, if one has occurred.

First, review the relationship with the deceased. Whenever you are committed to helping another who is mourning, the first thought which may come to mind is: How can I reduce the pain? What you really want to do is to help your friend squarely face that pain. That is the only way one can deal with it and then gradually let it go. So your overall goal in helping a friend or relative is to review the relationship the person had with the deceased loved one. Doing so will usually bring more tears as poignant memories, or even a few unhappy ones, will surface. Be assured, this is a time-consuming task; it will challenge your endurance and may take days, weeks, or months. I say weeks and months because, as I said earlier, it is important for mourners to repeat what they have already told you (and they will); and as holidays and birthdays roll around, there will be more memories to talk about. But remember, by helping the mourner experience the pain and face the changes you are helping him or her grasp the reality of the loss.

Not infrequently, it is during this review that you may find the mourner sharing any contact experience with you. If you feel comfortable, it is even appropriate to ask whether or not the mourner has experienced one. Let the story unfold and accept it as you would any other part of the relationship with the deceased.

How do you facilitate the review of the relationship? By a simple question or two at the appropriate time. To begin with, something like: "Please tell me about your Dad," is all that may be needed. Later, you can ask questions based on what you have been told. "Where did you always go fishing? Did he give you your first fishing pole? What did he say when you dropped your pole in the water that day?" These are all appropriate questions, and part of the review.

The second approach in your caregiving is to normalize the feelings associated with the loss of a loved one. This means saying it's all right to cry, to feel sad, experience loneliness, to regress, or to feel any number of other emotions. That is all part of the grief process, and is nothing to be ashamed about. Furthermore, several months later, when the person thought he was beginning to feel better but suddenly has a day which was like the first week after the death, be there to normalize, to say that the experience is not unusual. One of the big misconceptions about grief is that it is a two-week job, and people should be their old selves in a very short time. For many, grief is much longer than anticipated. You can reassure your friend or loved one that there is nothing wrong with them when they are moved by a special memory or reminder of the loved one even years later.

Third and last, remember that grieving is hard work. As I said in Chapter 3 grieving is ongoing hard work because the "year of the firsts" entails all sorts of adjustments and reminders of previous years when the loved one was alive. They are painful, but it is necessary pain which leads ultimately to letting go of (but not forgetting) the deceased. And sometimes adjustments and reminders will be problematic for years, depending on the personal characteristics of the mourner, the nature of the loss, and the quality of the mourner's support system. Nevertheless, new routines have to be fashioned, and your friend or relative will have to work at refusing to anticipate what used to be done with the deceased on a daily basis. That was life in the past. Now the present has to be structured, and new routines laid down, routines which do not include the lively presence of the loved one. Of course, this is easy to say but difficult to carry out, and you will have to be infinitely patient in supporting the mourner and providing comfort during the long period of transition.

As the support person, you not only have to be aware of the work of grief (and read about it), but you must let the mourner know you can only imagine how he or she must feel. Grieving is a long and arduous road at times; an endurance race, if you will. You will be there, walking hand in hand, when needed; but it is the mourner that must choose to see the race to the finish.

What to Do when the Contact Experience Is Shared

Somewhere along the way the mourner may have a contact experience and decide to share it with you. The first question that you must deal with is: How should I respond? Remember that if you say nothing, your silence will still make a statement. Also, your body language will make a statement. It could be a positive statement or a negative one, depending on the content of the experience as you hear it and the degree of your awareness of the normalcy of these events. Body language doesn't lie. That's why it is so important for you to understand that an extraordinary or paranormal contact may seem real to the mourner, no matter what your own beliefs might be. If you dismiss the possibility of a contact experience, you hurt your friend and risk damaging the relationship and the precious support he is depending on.

Step 1: Validate and Explore. Your first step is to validate the possibility of the experience by calmly seeking additional information. As an example, consider the opening paragraph in Chapter 1 involving Mrs. Lucas, who told me she saw her deceased son standing by the stairs. When she told me that had happened the previous night, I immediately asked her, "What was he wearing?" She then proceeded in a calm and relieved voice to describe the blue jeans, shirt and hat that he had on. I was normalizing the experience.

By asking a question, honestly seeking further information, you not only begin to obtain a better picture of the incident, but at the same time you legit-imize the event and the possibility that it could have taken place. Most impor-tant, you convey the idea to the mourner that he or she is not suspect, is not in need of special treatment, and that this experience does not indicate a problem. Your initial reaction, then, is crucial to maintaining the trusting relationship. In addition, it is vital to the survivor's use of the experience as a potential source of reconciling grief and the death. An immediate negative response, one which denies the possibility that an extraordinary experience occurred, adds to the already-existing anxiety of having decided to share the experience, and may result in reduced dialogue on other matters as well. It goes without saying that many support persons have lost the trust of the mourner at this point because their non-verbal response (often their facial expressions) implied to the mourner that he was just not thinking coherently.

Keep in mind that the contact experience is an excellent way for the mourner to establish a healthy relationship with the deceased, even use it as a rit-ual to eventually say good-bye. All too often, people think that when a loved one dies, a survivor gets well again when he or she is able to forget about the deceased. In reality, a new relationship has to be established in which it is clear that the loved one has died but can be remembered in healthy ways. Many people have healthy relationships with deceased loved ones by still observing traditions they started, talking about them at appropriate times, recalling memories (particularly on specific holidays), or completing works of interest they enjoyed. For example, some survivors have completed unfinished paintings, carpentry work, volunteer jobs, or charitable endeavors begun by the deceased before death occurred. Recently, I was having dinner with my wife and her mother. My father-in-law had died five years earlier. In talking about the dinner, my mother-in-law casually remarked to my wife that "Your father always loved to have fresh bread or rolls at dinner." This was a very healthy reference to a man she had been married to for forty-nine years. My wife replied, "Oh, yes. I remember how he especially liked French bread." These references to the deceased were reflective of the healthy new relationships both my mother-in-law and my wife had established with some-one they will always love. Often, I have heard someone say about their contact experience that "It was just like Ted to do something like this." Or, "Mary was always concerned about my being able to go on without her. That's why I've had this experience. She's telling me I can do it." They recognize the person is dead, yet they relate to the deceased in a different context. Love continues even though the loved one is physically absent.

There are innumerable healthy ways to relate to the deceased loved one that will not keep the survivor living in the past. The healthy contact experience happens to be one of them, so there is no reason to discourage the mourner from recalling the contact experience if it brings comfort. Of course, as with any type of behavior, it can be a source of stagnation if the experience is the sole source for building a new identity. Achieving balance between reality and fantasy can be a constant struggle during one's grief work. Living in the past must be abandoned; memories of the past must be carefully chosen and nurtured.

> *Help the griever to understand that a healthy new relationship with the deceased must be formed. Although death has separated the mourner from the deceased, it has not ended the relationship. It simply means that the relationship has changed from one based on the deceased's presence to one relating to memories of the past.*
>
> —Therese A. Rando, *Grief, Dying, and Death*

Step 2: Check for Personal Meaning. Once you have validated the possibility of the experience (this does not mean you necessarily believe it is a paranormal or spiritual experience), find out what it means to the mourner. Provide the opportunity to discuss whether the person feels it is "just part of my crazy thinking" or whether the event was clearly a contact that can't be summarily dismissed. A simple "What do you think about this?" or "How do you feel about what happened?" is enough to give the mourner a sign to go on and talk about interpretation; it shows that you are ready to listen and are not afraid of what you have heard. Your openness will allow you, in part, to assess whether or not the person has made up the story, believes the experience was real, or has replaced reality with pure fantasy.

Deciding on what fantasy is and what may be a plausible contact is not as difficult as it may seem. Obviously, if someone tells you that he or she has seen his loved one for the past six months every time he looks up at a cloud in the sky, or he has spoken to every deceased person he knows, you certainly have every right to be suspect. However, your suspicions do not necessarily give you the liberty to confront the mourner. Ask yourself if this type of behavior is hindering the mourner's ability to accept the loss, or if it is negatively affecting current relationships with others. If the answer is yes, then it may be appropriate to seek professional advice. If the answer is no, and he or she is progressing in the work of grief, you should be observant, give it time, and wait to see what transpires.

On the other hand, you may hear of some experiences that seem miraculous and yet could have easily occurred. Take, for example, the experience of Jane Nichols, Coordinator of Bereavement Services at Children's Hospital Medical Center in Akron, Ohio.

She was called in by maternity staff nurses after a young teenage mother was acting very relaxed with no signs of sadness after the death of her newborn infant. In Jane's own words:

> *I made a post-death follow-up visit to a still-hospitalized young mother whose newborn infant had died in the delivery room after an unsuccessful resuscitation. The consultation was made at the request of maternity staff nurses who were concerned that the mother "was in denial" about the actual death of her baby. The nurses reported that the mom was behaving in a "normal" way, thought to be incongruent with the fact of her child's death. In short, she was behaving as if nothing had happened.*
>
> *I asked the mother what happened. She recounted, apparently accurately, the events which had occurred in the delivery room, including the death of her baby and the fact that she had not seen the baby. (That was the custom at the time of this incident: mothers were kept separate from their dying/dead babies.) The mother did not appear to be saddened or grief-stricken while telling her story. Her telling of the story was rather matter-of-fact. It neither denied the death nor expressed distress.*
>
> *When I asked how she was feeling, this young woman beamed and answered that she knew her baby was okay. How did she know? She said she knew because Jesus had come to her bedside the night before carrying the babe. He had shown the mom the baby's sweet face, dark hair, blue eyes (just like hers), and perfect little body. (Later I verified the accuracy of the description with the nursing staff.) The mother also stated that Jesus reassured her that the baby would be with Him. The mother appeared to be at peace with that knowledge. Her face and body were relaxed and her manner was easy. She stated that she was ready to go home and get on with her life.*

How would you respond to such an experience if it was presented to you by a friend or relative? As Jane did in her conversation with the mother, it would be essential to obtain the entire story without prejudice. She not only listened intently, but observed the mother's nonverbal signs which indicated unusual calm and acceptance. Next, she checked for meaning and found out that the mother was very comfortable with her interpretation of what had transpired. As Jane put it: "This mother was clear that she was not dreaming. Who am I to doubt that Jesus appeared carrying her baby? I believe the specific message this mother received was that her baby was OK. I am comfortable with the notion that this mother was comforted and released from the sadness of her baby's death by this experience." This Christ encounter is not unusual, although contemporary Christ encounter phenomena receive scant attention.[1]

Step 3: Consider Alternative Explanations. Once you have validated and explored the nature of the experience, it is natural for you to consider other explanations, even if the mourner is convinced otherwise. For example, if the experience involves seeing a deceased loved one, you might wish to consider if the apparition could have actually been someone who is alive and mistaken for the deceased. It would also be prudent to consider if the apparition could have been a reflection off a shiny object or the result of medication being used by the mourner. There are three reasons for examining alternative explanations:

- To rule out possibilities which, when later realized by the mourner as mistakes in judgment, would cause added anxiety or the feeling that "I'm losing my mind."

- To assist the mourner who is unsure of how to interpret the experience and cannot decide if he should dismiss it or use it.

- To assist the person who feels he is losing his sanity because of the experience.

Exploring alternative explanations may help the support person who is trying to understand the nature of the event. But remember, we are not trying to prove anything, nor are we trying to convince the mourner he or she has misinterpreted the event. A contact experience cannot be proved, it can only be believed or disbelieved. Furthermore, in many instances you will not have to seek explanations because the description of the event by the mourner is sufficient to either use the event in a positive way, discount it, or simply let it be an inconsequential happening. In the final analysis, of course, the decision rests with the mourner.

In Jane's assessment of the young mother whose baby died, she was able to rule out medication, and she was convinced the apparition was not a dream after speaking to her client. She also concluded that it was quite possible the young mother had indeed been visited by Jesus. Most importantly, she was impressed with the behavior of the mother based on available evidence.

It should be stressed right away that although you may be trying to decide on the authenticity of the message and the messenger, from the mourner's perspective the contact experience most often brings new meaning and insight, moves the mourner towards acceptance of the death and reinvestment in life, and focuses the attention of the survivor on the mystery of love.

In summary, here are the questions to ask the mourner in order to help him or her bring normalcy to the experience. How do you feel about it? What do you think is the message or messages, whether explicit or symbolic? What does it mean for you? How does it help? What can I do? Give assurance that millions of others have had similar experiences.

Before we turn to the question of whether it is wise to routinely ask survivors if they have had an extraordinary experience, let me touch on one other concern: Can all three steps we have discussed be used in the same conversation or visit with the mourner? The answer depends on how you read the mourner after he or she has told you about the alleged contact with the deceased loved one. You have to decide how the mourner has reacted to your responses (both verbal and non-verbal). Here, your intuitive instincts have to be your guide. Only you can decide whether to pursue Step 3, at the risk of alienating the mourner. It may be best to wait until a later date, or the conversation may very naturally turn in the direction of alternatives. In my experience, it is often best to wait to bring the subject up at another time, although on occasion the mourner may want to pursue the topic in order to confirm his own thoughts. In most situations, when the mourner enthusiastically embraces the event, Step 3 is not necessary.

Helping the Child with the Contact Experience

Perhaps more than any other age group, children who say they have seen or talked to the deceased are often not considered credible. Imagine for a moment that your child comes to the breakfast table one morning and says, "I talked with Grandma last night." Now, Grandma died a year ago. Many parents would dispatch the remark with a "this is my son's highly active imagination acting up again." Certainly, many children have imaginary friends; they also have contact experiences just like adults, like the "Nagy Mama" account in an earlier chapter.

It is all too easy to dismiss what a child has to say, especially if that child is grieving the death of a family member. At that time more than ever, we need to tune into the feelings associated with the child's confession and give the child an open forum in which to express what is happening inside. So the first reaction to an announcement by a child that he has seen or heard the deceased is to get in touch with the flow of feelings that such a pronouncement represents: I miss Daddy or Mommy or Grandma or Uncle Bill. This is an important first step so that you do not cut off essential dialogue. Of equal importance, if you invalidate the experience at the outset, you lose the opportunity to help the child with her anxiety and ability to understand.

Give the child the benefit of the doubt. Express no disbelief. Then, as with anyone who has had a contact experience, find out the circumstances in which the "visit" took place. Again, ask questions like: What was it like? What did your Mommy say? You are simply asking the child to express his or her feelings in an atmosphere of acceptance. You have not made an irreversible judgment. You are simply open to wherever the conversation may lead.

Begin then to look for meaning. How does the child size up what took place? Is it healthy? Are there good memories to encourage? Are there foreboding indicators? Does the experience bring peace?

When After-Death Communication occurs, whether with an adult or a child, if a sense of peace prevails, follow that feeling; it is highly significant and may well be from a spiritual source. Or if you are dealing with an ADC of your own and are in the process of deciding on an interpretation, go with the decision that brings peace of mind. You personally may credit the Absolute or the Holy Spirit for your communication, or you may not. Whatever the case, the vast majority of these experiences cause people to slow down and begin to expand their awareness. This shifts the focus away from the self toward other people. Thinking of others (and their ADC) ultimately causes them to look at life in a wider perspective, and even change their worldview. Whether child or adult, when we are at peace we see things differently. Look for the quiet resolve and new-found happiness which often accompanies the experience, and support the mourner in affirming life through the contact experience.

To Ask or Not to Ask?

Now back to the question of whether or not to routinely ask the bereaved about paranormal or contact experiences at an appropriate time. Given the current negative perspective on the credibility of contact experiences, most people tend to shy away from inquiring about the phenomena. Some counselors concur (unless they themselves have had the experience), although a main reason given is they do not want to risk putting ideas in the minds of the bereaved which may cause additional anxiety. Others are well aware of the positive results which can derive from such inquiries, and commonly ask questions like "Have you felt you have had any communication with him/her since he/she died?" "Have you had any unusual experiences regarding Jim/Jane since he/she died?" "Have you ever sensed the presence of Jim/Jane?" Such questions can easily be answered in the negative if the mourner is not ready to talk about such an event.

There is little solid evidence to dictate against a tactful inquiry by a relative, friend, or counselor as long as it takes place at the right time, in the right place, and by the right person. The right time means that this is not a subject which is to be introduced early in your support efforts, unless the mourner brings up the topic. Usually, this suggests that some time has passed since the death, and you have already provided comfort and support on several occasions. The right place simply means that there is privacy and a comfortable setting for conversation. And, of course, you must feel confident that the relationship between you and the mourner is strong and that trust is evident.

At some point, however, the question should be routinely asked just as you would ask if the bereaved has been eating, getting any sleep, or needing assistance with children or household chores. By asking, you are likely to harvest a wealth of information which becomes fertile ground for furthering the progress of one's grief work. Use whatever format you feel comfortable with. I usually preface my question with something like, "There are some people who, when mourning, sense the presence of their deceased loved one. Others have vivid dreams, which are quite normal." Then I will ask a straight question: "Have you had anything like this happen since Joe died?" You may want to ask the question in an indirect manner, saying something like "You must feel he is far away. Do you ever feel he is particularly close?" Again, use what is most comfortable to you and present it in a gentle, matter-of-fact way. And use the name of the deceased person when you ask.

If the mourner's answer is in the affirmative, listen attentively without interrupting, and then begin the three-step procedure previously outlined. To stimulate further input and gauge feelings, you might ask, "What do you think Joe (the deceased) would say about this?" Then use the response to further clarify meaning and possible action that can be taken based on the experience.

Should You Encourage Praying for a Sign?

One of the most searching and anxiety-producing thoughts of many bereaved people concerns whether deceased loved ones are safe and in good hands, wherever they may be. Clearly, one of the most satisfying aspects of any type of contact experience is the relief offered in regard to this disquieting concern. Counselor Ken Czillinger, who for many years has been involved in a special ministry to the bereaved, provides a positive answer to the question of asking for a sign when he says: "Hope for some type of comforting presence of your loved one. Many parents/siblings need reassurance their child/brother/sister is okay after death. They long for some type of communication, i.e., a dream or vision. I've listened to many bereaved persons share either the joy of experiencing such a vision or dream or the agony of waiting for some kind of reassuring presence of their dead child." [2]

Hope may involve praying for such a sign. Many religions teach that the deceased are in a place where they can now be prayed to for comfort and assurance. In the Christian tradition, there is the communion of saints, an interrelationship between all of the living and the dead where intervention can occur on behalf of the living. The living pray for and to the dead and there is no reason to believe that the dead cannot intercede for the living. Czillinger gives the following rationale in praying for or looking for a sign that a deceased loved one is in good hands: "I believe God can give Gift of Recognition experiences which provide comfort, peace, meaning, and hope. These experiences involve gift and mystery. They can't be self-created, manipulated, or guaranteed. Pray/be open to these signs/recognition events."[3]

There is a potential problem you should be aware of that is related to seeking a sign that a loved one is okay and receiving a sign. It concerns a family or a group of friends, one of whom is the recipient of a contact. Although not altogether common, some family members or friends who do not receive what could be interpreted as a sign may feel as though they have been rejected or passed by. They question, and rightly so, "Why did someone else receive the gift and I did not?" Here we are confronted with a universal question I will address later in this chapter; namely, why everyone who grieves does not have a contact experience. There is no definitive answer, only possible explanations. You may want to review those possibilities should the dilemma present itself in your family.

In any event, it is possible that a single sign may be applicable to all involved as we saw in Chapters 7 and 9 with the gold angels and the wild turkeys. And this should be emphasized whenever possible. At the very least, the message received from the deceased should be emphasized, whatever it may be. It is the message and the relief it brings which should be the main focal point to dwell on with anyone who feels he has been slighted.

And What about Angels?

What can you do if a friend or relative confides that "I was visited by an angel" or "My friend came to me and looked like an angel?" One of the most common explanations for ADCs or the direct contact experience is the work of angels. No doubt, some contact experiences do involve angelic features. Here is an example from a woman I'll call Liz whose best friend died in an automobile accident.

"An Angel Floating over the Stairwell"

When I was eighteen years old my closest friend was killed in a car accident. One night after her death she appeared to me as an angel. When it all began I was in a deep sleep. When I realized what was happening I was sitting up in bed with an angel floating over the stairwell. She was beautiful (in a pink dress) and it was Sherry. She was asking me questions about her boyfriend Brian and telling me to talk to him. It all felt so real. I was awake enough to go downstairs and tell my mother. Thank goodness she was supportive and told me it very much could be real. I felt so peaceful when I was talking to her. To this day (I'm thirty-four) it feels like a true experience.

In reality, I feel it was a spiritual experience. I was struggling and grieving so intensely on my own. Sherry's loss for me was just devastating. She was a friend I phoned daily and sat with on the bus and stayed at her house on weekends. I needed to know that she was okay. I felt confused about death. I felt it was her spirit that came to reassure me.

The message I received was that she was OK. She looked beautiful. She had been injured horribly in the accident. Now there were no visible scars on her face. She had looked horrid in the casket and that was so frightening for me. Her angel appearance reassured me that she was okay. I also wanted to talk to her boyfriend but wasn't able to. I was not on good terms with him because he was abusive to her before her death and I didn't like him. Sherry had encouraged me to talk to him. I knew he would understand what I was going through too. That experience gave me permission to reach out for help. I cannot recall who I shared the experience with besides my mother—but I did reach out and talk to friends. It was a great help to me.

There are several interesting aspects of this account. First of all, Liz's mother was intuitively correct in telling her daughter that what had taken place could have been real. It was obviously a major reason Liz eventually was able to speak to others about what had happened. And such conversations with friends and family are what the mourning process is all about. Sharing her pain was a critical action in assimilating the tragic aftermath into her life. Of course, the suggestion by Sherry for Liz to speak with her boyfriend was also a form of giving Liz permission to grieve, since Liz used the suggestion to reach out to others. That Liz has interpreted the experience as a spiritual gift, one which brought the spirit of her friend to her, brings us to the question of whether or not it was Liz's imagination or possibly an angel.

To begin with, angels in religious literature have a long history of helping people in a variety of ways, not to mention the fact that in the Bible alone they are mentioned over 300 times. That they guard and guide is clearly spelled out in both the Old and New Testaments, while it has long been taught that God works many wonders through these spiritual intermediaries. Despite the commercial New Age fad of angels, there are numerous legitimate accounts of angels of various descriptions who have appeared purportedly as unseen hands pulling someone from a sinking boat or car, or as a voice, vision, or in the traditional white-robed version. Often, there are reports in which someone is saved from imminent death, and the rescuer suddenly vanishes without a trace. The implication here is that angels do have the ability to assume different, even material, forms. This may stretch your imagination. Nonetheless, Pagans as well as Christians, Jews, and Muslims all believe in angels.

However, those who have had a direct experience or contact with an angelic being do not confuse it with a ghost or write off the experience as a coincidence (although many so-called coincidences could be the work of angels). In the words of Sophy Burnam, who wrote *A Book of Angels,* "But angels are different, and no one who has seen an angel ever mistakes it for a ghost. Angels are remarkable for their warmth and light, and all who see them speak in awe of their iridescent and refulgent light, of brilliant colors, or else of the unbearable whiteness of their being. You are flooded with laughter, happiness."[4] If you are not inclined to believe in the existence of angels, consider them the work of the creative unconscious or Jung's collective unconscious.

What is important for you to know in helping someone who shares an angelic experience with you is that the encounter may very well be real to that person. There is a wealth of tradition behind their existence, and literally thousands of people in this day and age who will testify to an experience involving one. Angels are considered to be messengers of God's will, reminders of His love for humanity, and deserve your attention for no other reason than they (or someone) have been the reason that motivated many of the bereaved to deal with their losses in a healthy manner. In today's world of computers and high-tech wizardry, it is easy to dismiss the explanation that angels are behind some of the contact experiences of the bereaved. I urge you to be open to the possibility when helping a friend or loved one who reports such an experience: it could mean the difference in pro-tracted anguish and pain or a sudden new lease on life. So regardless of the spin you put on "Angelology," at the very least they are messengers of hope.

As we come to a close to our excursion into the world beyond the cultural norm it is important to address two commonly asked questions.

Why Don't All Mourners Have a Contact Experience?

One of the most frequent questions I have heard goes something like this: If so many contact experiences are considered "real" —and apparently helpful—why is it that all bereaved individuals do not experience them? This is a fair question, as well as a an important observation. Although no amount of theoretical specula-tion or argument will answer the question to everyone's satisfaction, there are sev-eral helpful possibilities.

- To begin with, it is evident that all survivors do not need a contact expe-rience in order to deal with the death of a loved one. As I mentioned in Chapter 3, there is a wide range of normalcy in coping. Some individu-als are able to integrate a death into their ongoing lives with relatively minor complications. Often, they perceive death as a door, not as a wall, and the door opens to a richer existence. For others, the acceptance of death has been a part of family education; death was not a taboo topic and was considered a stimulus for living a quality life. And there are still others who, like Benjamin Franklin, feel that death is like that well-deserved sleep after a good day's work. For all of these, the contact expe-rience may not be necessary in their adjustment to massive change.
- Some individuals do not have a contact experience because they find it impossible to believe that such events could occur. Their beliefs are

encapsulated by the laws of materialistic science in a space-time framework which excludes the paranormal or spiritual experience. I am not implying that some of these individuals do not experience the extraordinary. However, they are prone to overlooking or dismissing the experience as a function of their anxiety-filled state of mind or a product of fear and refuse to consider the experience altogether. Put another way, in some instances, one must believe in order to see. Little miracles, especially when grieving, seem to be abundant in the lives of all of us—but we are too busy to see them. Disbelief may be a powerful reason some survivors do not experience the extraordinary. Faith may have as much to do with some forms of physical healing as it does with having a contact experience.

- Fear of the unknown. Repressing the experience is also possible with some individuals. Repression (unconsciously burying or forgetting the experience) may occur out of fear that one is losing his sanity, or because one does not wish to deal with the meaning of the event at the present time. On the other hand, suppressing the experience (one consciously chooses not to deal with it for whatever reason) may also occur. One may be literally scared of having sensed the presence of the deceased or experienced some other form of contact. I am inclined to believe, for instance, that some males choose not to examine the contact experience because it clashes with their cultural expectations of maleness.

- Certainly, one's frame of mind is also involved in whether or not a contact experience takes place. Anger at the deceased, pessimism, or other negative energy drains may negate receptivity to any contact experience. Such negative states may preclude any positive experience, including an extraordinary one.

- Finally, for some contact experiences, such as apparitions or hearing the voice of the deceased, a given individual may not possess the ability to see or hear what others have been allowed to experience. In this vein, the reception of the extraordinary in general, and the contact experience in particular, may be a gift given to some but not to all. St. Paul, in his first letter to the Corinthians, recognized this possibility when he said, "The particular way in which the Spirit is given to each person is for a good purpose. One may have the gift of preaching . . . another prophecy, another the gift of recognizing spirits." In short, many of us may simply not be able to recognize in our midst the spirits of our loved ones or the signs they are permitted to convey.

What if the Contact Experience Is Negative?

On rare occasions, the contact experience may initially be frightening to a survivor as it was with Corrine (who kept having nightmares of her best friend Meg who had died of a brain aneurysm) due to her questionable interpretation. Or worse, it may strike deep fear into the hearts of the bereaved. In my work, the negative contact experience has been associated mostly, but not exclusively, with dreams or dream-like states just before one falls off to sleep. The half-awake state is called hypnagogia, and for some people it is also a highly creative state during which they may find solutions to problems.

It is also possible that some touch experiences may include an apparition or dream, and the survivor becomes upset because the deceased does not appear in complete form. In one instance, for example, only the upper part of the body of the deceased was seen and the survivor interpreted the loved one as somehow not being whole. On the other hand, the same type of visual event could be interpreted in a positive way by another survivor. How one perceives the event is highly individual and heavily rooted in cultural beliefs and expectations about the extraordinary.

Sometimes fear is the product of negative perceptions of extraordinary or paranormal events as programmed by the media early in life. At other times, the experiences are diametrically opposed by one's philosophical or religious beliefs. (Some fundamentalists believe that any type of supposed contact from a deceased person is the work of the Prince of Darkness—the Devil.)

In the case of dreams, a not-uncommon scenario involves the deceased and the survivor's fear of death. For example, shortly after the death of the father of a teenager I knew, she had a terrifying dream in which she found herself at the cemetery. Her father took hold of her and was trying to pull her into the grave. Her fear became manageable when she came to see that her dream could be a reflection of her fear of dying which surfaced as a result of her father's sudden, unexpected death.

Another disturbing type of dream involves the deaths of other living family members, who may or may not be seen with the person who has recently died. Again, it is not unnatural to fear the deaths of others, especially if the recently deceased was a young person or the death was unexpected. When one experiences the death of a close family member, it is not unusual to entertain thoughts about someone else dying and thinking how difficult it would be to deal with the experience.

How should the negative experience be addressed? Actually, Corrine (see Chapter 8 and "Meg Came to Me and Put Her Arms around Me") has provided us with some very healthy guidelines. Initially, she shared her experience with her husband. An effective, universal method of conquering fear is to face it by open acknowledgment, exposing it to scrutiny with someone you love and trust. This is easier said than done, but it has been proven effective time and time again. In the face-to-face confrontation, one can show emotion and seek the nurturing which is commonly needed early in coping with fear. Harboring fear, allowing it to stay confined, is what gives it power to wreak havoc within. Share it, and its power to antagonize and heighten anxiety is neutralized.

Immediate discussion of the event also allows the prudent listener to help the survivor detail specific parts of the experience, which precipitate fear. Putting fear into words helps clarify its source, and provides both listener and survivor with a basis for deciding how to forge a plan to deal with it. Sometimes simply verbalizing the problem brings obvious solutions to your attention. It is clear that managing fear depends on changing your attitude toward it, and this occurs by choosing to adopt an alternative perception of it.

Not all friends or loved ones are able to give support to someone who has a negative experience. Try as they might, sometimes their own beliefs (and fears) get in the way of trying to understand the survivor's behavior. If potential helpers have strong convictions that all unusual experiences pertaining to the dead are products of overreaction, misinterpretation, or the work of the Devil, it will be difficult for them to be fully present to the survivor and allow for a completely open dialogue. There's a fine line between listening without judging and nonverbally showing disapproval of one's behavior, and it would be ludicrous to suggest that most loved ones are truly confident (or competent) in dealing with this type of dilemma. Because listening, particularly active listening, is the beginning of the healing process, all must learn to distinguish between a problem we can deal with and one which signals a search for professional assistance. It is a lamentable but inescapable truth that bereavement counselors are often the last persons the bereaved turn to when in need to share contact experiences. Thus, loved ones and friends should willingly suggest that the survivor seek assistance when they feel they are not prepared to render the necessary support.

In the final analysis, the negative experience should be dealt with in a patient, low-key manner by the support person. Refrain from providing quick interpretations. Listen to the mourner's story carefully. Repeat it back to him or her to be sure you have an accurate picture of the event. Together, consider each phase of the event and discuss alternative ways to interpret its meaning. Help the mourner clearly describe what particular part of the experience is most difficult to cope with. Do not make a judgment for the person. Allow for ongoing discussion over time. Do not take away their power to make the final decision on how they wish to deal with their fear. Make a plan together. Remember that as a support person, all of the above is immensely time consuming. Your greatest gift lies in your willingness to persist in being present to the mourner, and skillfully providing reassurance that the fear can be managed. This demands patience and love, which is the core of providing support.

A Final Note

You have begun a very important step in understanding that there is another reality, every bit as real as the one our culture touts. I have only scratched the surface of experiences that point to the ADC phenomena as an integral part of existence for many of the bereaved, a "final farewell until we meet again." ADCs are instrumental in forming a new inner representation of the deceased. There is no reason not to suggest that the experience may well be a purely natural occurrence, a part of the human condition not fully understood. At the very least, ADCs are an untapped source of wisdom for managing the many changes which are inevitable in the course of one's life. But they are also the stepping stones to becoming a whole person who feels an inherent spiritual longing for union with something greater than the self.

There is an ancient piece of wisdom that is appropriate here: What you tend to focus on expands and grows. St. Augustine put it a different way: "You become what you love." I urge you to consider continuing your study of the contact experience and its wide application for human happiness. As difficult as it may be, I urge you to resist the cultural bias toward the unexplainable, and make every effort to find out all you can about nonphysical reality. As you increase your awareness, it will not only assist you in your ability to help those in need, but as a by-product you will be forever changed in how you view the wonderful world in which we live. It will lead you to greater love and the realization that healing comes from the inside out. And in this realization you will begin to reach out and touch a most coveted prize—peace of mind.

AUTHOR'S REQUEST

If you have had an extraordinary experience when grieving and would be willing to share it, and perhaps have it chosen for publication at a future date, please contact me at the address listed below. I am continually updating my files and would be very interested in hearing from you and how your experience affected your grief work. Likewise, should you know of someone else who has had an extraordinary experience and would be willing to share it, please ask them to write to me. If it is a child who has had a contact, kindly ask the parent or guardian to contact me. Thank you for your help.

Louis E. LaGrand
Loss Education Associates
1605 Pine Tree Road
Cutchogue, NY 11935

ENDNOTES

Chapter One: The Bereaved and the Extraordinary

1. Although published more than fifteen years ago, *Attachment and Loss: Vol. 3. Loss: Sadness and Depression* (New York: Basic Books, 1980) is considered to be one of John Bowlby's most important contributions to understanding loss and grief. See pp. 86–87.

2. Colin Murray Parkes, *Bereavement: Studies of Grief in Adult Life:* (2nd ed., Madison, CT: International Universities Press, 1987): 57–63.

3. See Catherine M. Sanders, *Grief: The Mourning After* (New York: John Wiley, 1989): 95-96. Also, Margaret S. Miles, "The Search for Meaning and Its Potential for Affecting Growth in Bereaved Parents," in C. Corr, J. Stillion & M. Ribar (Eds.), *Creativity in Death Education and Counseling* (Lakewood, Ohio: Forum for Death Education and Counseling, 1983): 119–124.

4. W. Dewi Rees, "The Hallucinations of Widowhood," *British Medical Journal,* 4, (1971): 37–41.

5. Peter Marris, *Widows and Their Families* (London: Routledge & Kegan Paul, 1958).

6. P. Richard Olson, Joseph A. Suddeth, Patricia J. Peterson & Claudia Egelhoff, "Hallucinations of Widowhood," *Journal of the American Geriatrics Society, 33* (1985): 543–547.

Chapter Two: The Extraordinary Is Ordinary

1. Ian Wilson, *The After Death Experience* (New York: William Morrow & Co., 1987): 7.

2. Robert Burton, *The Anatomy of Melancholy* (London: G. Bell & Sons, Ltd., 1924): 476–481.

3. Beverly Raphael, *The Anatomy of Bereavement* (New York: Basic Books, 1983): 40.

4. Arthur Stanley Eddington, *Science and the Unseen World* (New York: Macmillan Co., 1929): 74–75.

5. Arthur Koestler, *The Act of Creation* (New York: Macmillan Co., 1964): 170.

6. Alfred Ribi, "Jungian Psychology and The Nature of Death," in Arthur Berger, ed., *Perspectives on Death and Dying: Cross-Cultural and Multi-Disciplinary*

Views (Philadelphia, PA: Charles Press, 1989): 189. This is an excellent article on the Jungian viewpoint about death as well as the role of the collective unconscious in paranormal events.

7. Charles Tart, "Compassion, Science and Consciousness Survival," *Noetic Sciences Review* (Spring, 1994, No. 29): 9–15.

8. Wilder Penfield, *The Mystery of the Mind: A Critical Study of Consciousness and the Human Brain* (Princeton, NJ: Princeton University Press, 1975).

9. Ralph W. Hood, Jr. "Eliciting Mystical States of Consciousness with Semi-structured Nature Experiences," *Journal for the Scientific Study of Religion* 16 (1977): 155–163.

10. Erlendur Haraldsson and Joop M. Houtkooper, "Psychic Experiences in the Multinational Human Values Study," *The Journal of the American Society of Psychical Research* 85 (April 1991): 145–165.

11. Andrew Greeley, "Mysticism Goes Mainstream," *American Health* 6 (1987): 47-49. See also, Andrew Greeley and William McCready, "Are We a Nation of Mystics?," *New York Times Magazine* (January 26, 1975): 12ff.

12. John Beloff, *Parapsychology: A Concise History* (New York: St. Martin's Press, 1993): x.

13. Ibid.

14. Andrew MacKenzie, *Hauntings and Apparitions* (London: Granada Publishing Ltd., 1983): 8–13.

15. Ibid., 10.

16. D. J. West, "A Mass-Observation Questionnaire on Hallucinations," *Journal of the Society for Psychical Research* 34 (1948): 187–196.

17. Peter Marris, *Widows and Their Families* (London: Routledge & Kegal Paul, 1958).

18. J. Yamamoto, K. Okonogi, T. Iwaski, et al, "Mourning in Japan," *American Journal of Psychiatry* 125 (1969): 12.

19. J. Palmer & M. Dennis, "A Community Mail Survey of Psychic Experiences," in J. D. Morris , ed., *Research in Parapsychology* (Metuchen, NJ: Scarecrow Press, 1974): 130.

20. Richard Kalish & D. Reynolds, "Phenomenological Reality and Post-Death Contact," *Journal for the Scientific Study of Religion* 12 (1973): 209.

21. Andrew Greeley, "The Paranormal Is Normal: A Sociologist Looks at Parapsychology," *The Journal of the American Society for Psychical Research* 85 (October, 1991): 367–374.

22. W. Dewi Rees, "The Hallucinations of Widowhood," *British Medical Journal* 4 (1971): 37–41.

23. P. Richard Olsen, Joe A. Suddeth, Patricia J. Peterson & Claudia Egelhoff, "Hallucinations of Widowhood," *Journal of the American Geriatric Society* 33 (1985): 543–547.

24. Andrew Greeley, "Hallucinations among the Widowed," *Sociology and Social Research* 71 (July, 1987): 258–265.

25. Andrew Greeley, "Mysticism Goes Mainstream," *American Health* 6 (1987): 49.

26. Ibid.

Chapter Three: The Contact Experience During Grief

1. Irving Oyle, "A Medical Doctor Diagnoses Reality," in Sy Safransky, (ed.), *A Bell Ringing in the Empty Sky: The Best of the Sun* (San Diego: Mho & Mho Works, 1987): 378.

2. Alan D. Wolfelt, "Dispelling 5 Common Myths About Grief," *Bereavement Magazine* (Fall 1989): 111–114.

3. A very practical approach to preparing for loss as well as a wealth of information on dealing with a variety of losses can be found in Bob Deits, *Life After Loss* (Tucson, Arizona: Fisher Books, 1988): 185.

4. See Samuel A. Schreiner, "Why Do We Cry?" *Reader's Digest* February 1987): 141–144 and William Gottlieb, *Prevention Magazine* (August, 1980): 126–129.

5. Therese A. Rando, *Grieving: How to Go on Living When Someone You Love Dies* (Lexington, MA: Lexington Books, 1988): 241–242. An excellent treatment of the grief process and very helpful suggestions for going on with one's life after the death of a loved one.

6. J. William Worden, *Grief Counseling & Grief Therapy*, 2nd ed., (New York: Springer Publishing Co., 1991): p. 25–26.

7. Daniel Goleman, "New Studies Find Many Myths About Mourning," *New York Times* (Fall 1989): C1 ff.

8. For an extended discussion of these response sets see Therese A. Rando, *Treatment of Complicated Mourning* (Champaign, IL: Research Press, 1993): 30–60.

9. John Bowlby, *Attachment and Loss: Vol 3. Loss: Sadness and Depression* (New York: Basic Books, 1980): 85–96.

10. Ira Glick, R. Weiss & C. Parkes, *The First Year of Bereavement* (New York: John Wiley, 1974): 147.

11. John Bowlby, *Attachment and Loss: Vol 3. Loss: Sadness and Depression* (New York: Basic Books, 1980): 92.

12. Catherine M. Sanders, *Grief: The Mourning After* (New York: John Wiley, 1989): 70. An excellent treatment of adult bereavement.

Chapter Four: The Intuitive Experience: Sensing the Presence of the Deceased

1. Quoted in William James, *The Varieties of Religious Experience* (New York: New American Library, 1958): 63–64.

2. C. G. Jung, *Memories, Dreams, Reflections* (New York: Vintage Books, 1965).

3. Frances E. Vaughan, *Awakening Intuition* (New York: Doubleday, 1979).

4. Philip Goldberg, *The Intuitive Edge* (Los Angeles: Jeremy P. Tarcher, Inc., 1983): 34.

5. C. S. Lewis, *A Grief Observed* (New York: Bantam, 1980): 85.

6. Ibid., 86-87.

Chapter Five: Postmortem Presence: The Visual Experience

1. Tom Hurley, "Dwelling with the Mystery of Death," *Noetic Sciences Review* (Spring, 1994): 6–7.

2. G. N. M. Tyrrell, *Science and Psychical Phenomena & Apparitions* (New Hyde Park, NY: University Books, 1961): ix.

3. Allen Spraggett, *The Unexplained* (New York: The New American Library, 1967): 32.

4. Tyrrell, *Science and Psychical Phenomena & Apparitions* (New Hyde Park, NY: University Books, 1961): p. 33.

5. Martin Ebon, *They Knew the Unknown* (New York: The World Publishing Co., 1971).

6. C. G. Jung, *Memories, Dreams, Reflections* (New York: Vintage Books, 1965): 312.

7. Ibid.

8. Judy Tatelbaum, *The Courage to Grieve* (New York: Harper & Row, 1980): 41.

9. Andrew MacKenzie, *Hauntings and Apparitions* (London: Grenada Publishing Limited, 1983).

10. Hoyt Edge, Robert Morris, John Palmer & Joseph Rush, *Foundations of Para-Psychology* (Boston: Routledge & Kegan Paul, 1986): 345

11. David C. Knight, *The ESP Reader* (New York: Grosset & Dunlap, 1969):88. This book is a must read for anyone interested in the extraordinary.

12. William Winter, *The Life of David Belasco* (New York: Benjamin Bloom, Inc., 1972): 466–467.

13. Ibid., 468.

Chapter Six: Auditory Contacts: Hearing the Deceased

1. *The Journal of the Society for Psychical Research*, Vol. 28, 253-255.

2. Martin Ebon, *They Knew the Unknown* (New York: The World Publishing Co., 1971): 16.

3. Sylvia Fraser, *The Quest for the Fourth Monkey* (Toronto: Key Porter Books Limited, 1992): 256.

4. C. G. Jung, *Memories, Dreams, Reflections* (New York: Vintage Books, 1965).

5. Patrick Huyghe, "Mind: Voices from Inner Space," *Hippocrates* (July/August 1988): 89.

Chapter Seven: Connections Big and Small: Animals and Birds

1. C. G. Jung, "The Structure and Dynamics of the Psyche," *Collected Works*, vol. 18 (Princeton, NJ: Princeton University Press, 1976): pars 96–97.

2. Cathy Griffin, "From the Heart," *Health* (May/June 1995) vol. 9, No. 3, 66–67.

3. C. G. Jung, *Collected Works* (Princeton, NJ: Princeton University Press, 1976)

4. John Beloff, *Parapsychology: A Concise History* (New York: St. Martin's Press, 1993): 221

5. Wayne Dyer, *You'll See It When You Believe It* (New York: Wm. Morrow & Co., 1989):203.

6. Richard Morsilli, "I Still See Him Everywhere," *Reader's Digest* (July 1984): 37.

7. Robert A. Baker & Joe Nickell, *Missing Pieces* (Buffalo, NY: Prometheus Books, 1992).

8. George O. Abell & Barry Singer, *Science and the Paranormal* (New York: Scribner, 1981).

9. James E. Alcock, "The Belief Engine," *Skeptical Inquirer* (May/June 1995):14–18

10. William V. Rauscher, *The Spiritual Frontier* (Garden City, NY: Doubleday & Company, Inc., 1975): 24–25.

Chapter Eight: The Experiences of Touch and Smell

1. Edmund Gurney, Frederic W.H. Meyers & Frank Podmore, *Phantasms of the Living* (London: Trubner & Co., Ludgate Hill, E.C., 1886): 506-507.

2. Alfred Ribi, "Jungian Psychology and the Nature of Death," in Arthur Berger, (ed.), *Perspectives on Death and Dying : Cross-Cultural and Multi-Disciplinary Views* (Philadelphia, PA: Charles Press, 1989): 190.

3. Ibid., 196–197.

4. Doris Jonas and David Jonas, *Other Senses, Other Worlds* (New York: Stein & Day Publishers, 1976).

5. Ruth Winter, *The Smell Book* (New York: J. B. Lippincott, 1976).

6. Ibid., 27.

7. Joan Wester Anderson, *Where Miracles Happen* (Brooklyn, NY: Brett Books Inc., 1994):128.

Chapter Nine: Symbols and Symbolic Thinking

1. Ed Lowe, "A Doctor's Twilight Zone at Dawn," *Newsday* (August 28, 1994): 43.

2. Dennis McCarthy, "One Golden Angel," *Catholic Digest* (August 1992): 107.

3. John Bramblett, *When Goodbye Is Forever: Learning to Live Again after the Loss of a Child* (New York: Ballantine Books, 1991): 145–146.

4. Ibid.

5. V. D. Volkan, *Linking Objects and Linking Phenomena* (New York: International Universities Press, 1981).

6. Dennis Klass, "Solace and Immortality: Bereaved Parents' Continuing Bond with Their Children," *Death Studies*, Vol. 17, 1993: 343–368.

7. Ibid.

8. Ibid.

9. William V. Rauscher, *The Spiritual Frontier* (Garden City, NY: Doubleday, 1975).

Chapter Ten: Third-Party Contacts

1. Louis E. LaGrand, *Coping with Separation and Loss as a Young Adult* (Springfield, IL: Charles C. Thomas, 1986): 93–94. Early in my research on extraordinary experiences of the bereaved, I originally classified this account as a visual experience. Since that time, I have come to classify it as a third-party experience to show the variety of contacts which occur.

2. *Spiritual Frontiers Fellowship International Newsletter*, December 1974, Vol. VIII, No. 10, p. 2. (Philadelphia, PA: Spiritual Frontiers Fellowship International).

3. John White (ed.), *Psychic Exploration: A Challenge for Science* (New York: G.P. Putnam, 1974): 380.

4. Alfred Ribi, "Jungian Psychology and the Nature of Death," *Perspectives on Death and Dying: Cross-Cultural and Multi-Disciplinary Views* (Philadelphia, PA: Charles Press, 1989).

5. Thelma Moss, *The Probability of the Impossible* (Los Angeles: J. P. Tarcher, 1974).

6. Kenneth Ring, *Heading Toward Omega* (New York: Wm. Morrow, 1985): 49. This is an eye-opening book on the NDE which is a must read for anyone interested in extraordinary experiences.

7. Edmund Gurney, with F.W.H. Meyers & F. Podmore, *Phantasms of the Living*, Vol. 2. (London: Kegan, Paul, 1886):216.

Chapter Eleven: Dreams of the Deceased

1. Ann Faraday, *Dream Power* (New York: Berkeley Books, 1980): 291.

2. Clyde H. Reid, *Dreams: Discovering your Inner Teacher* (Minneapolis: Winston Press, 1983): 42. This is an excellent book to help you learn how to use your dreams for greater self-understanding and decision-making.

3. Ann Faraday, *The Dream Game* (New York: Harper & Row, 1990); 267.

4. Ibid., 268.

5. Melvin Morse, *Parting Visions* (New York: Villard Books, 1994): 71. Must reading for anyone interested in learning more about nonphysical reality.

6. Erin Linn, *Premonitions, Visitations, and Dreams*. Incline Village, NV: The Publisher's Mark, 1991.

7. Dennis Ryan, *Dreams of Dead Relatives and Friends*. Paper presented at the Seventeenth Annual Conference of the Association for Death Education and Counseling, Miami, Florida, April 29, 1995.

8. J. E. Kennedy & H. Kanthamani, "An Exploratory Study of the Effects of Paranormal and Spiritual Experience on People's Lives and Well-Being," *The Journal of the American Society for Psychical Research* (Vol. 89, July 1995): 249–264.

Chapter Twelve: Skeptics All

1. Arthur Combs and the A.S.C.D. 1962 Yearbook Committee, *Perceiving, Behaving, Becoming* (Washington: Association for Supervision and Curriculum Development, 1962).

2. Melvin Morse, *Parting Visions* (New York: Villard Books, 1994): 109-110.

3. Willis Harman & Howard Rheingold, *Higher Creativity* (Los Angeles: Jeremy P. Tarcher, 1984): 62. This concept is an important one to study since its implications are far ranging for creative change and understanding our behavior. This book is clearly one of the best for increasing your awareness of the unconscious and the great source of wisdom that it holds.

4. See Norman Cousins, *Head First: The Biology of Hope* (New York: E.P. Dutton, 1989). In this book, some of the early work on the relationship between positive and negative thoughts and their biochemical counterparts is masterfully presented.

5. See H. J. Irwin, *An Introduction to Parapsychology* (Jefferson, NC: McFarland & Co., 1989). This is a text book for a college course and gives historical coverage as well as insight into research on parapsychological phenomena. Also see John Beloff, *Parapsychology: A Concise History* (New York: St. Martin's Press, 1993). Excellent historical coverage from Renaissance magic to recent developments in parapsychology.

6. Bernard Gittelson, *Intangible Evidence* (New York: Simon & Schuster, 1987).

7. Goethe, in Frederick Ungar, *Practical Wisdom: A Treasury of Aphorisms & Reflections from the German* (New York: Frederick Ungar Publishing Co., 1977): 25.

8. Marianne Williamson, *Return to Love* (Boston: G.K. Hall, 1993): XXI

9. Robert G. Jahn & Brenda J. Dunne, *Margins of Reality* (New York: Harcourt, Brace, Jovanovich, 1987): 308.

Chapter Thirteen: Helping a Person Who Experiences a Deceased Loved One

1. G. Scott Sparrow, *I Am With You Always* (New York: Bantam Books, 1995): 11.

2. Ken Czillinger, "Elements of Healing," *Compassionate Friends Newsletter* (Fall 1979, vol. 2, no. 4): 5.

3. Ken Czillinger, Personal letter.

4. Sophy Burnham, *A Book of Angels* (New York: Ballantine Books, 1990): 17.

SUGGESTED READING

Anderson. J. W. *Where Miracles Happen*. Brooklyn. NY: Brett Books, Inc., 1994.

Barrett, Sir William. *Deathbed Visions: The Psychical Experiences of Dying*. The Aquarian Press, 1986 (reprint of 1926 edition).

Broughton, R. *Parapsychology: The Controversial Science*. NY: Ballantine, 1991.

Cavendish, R. *Visions of Heaven and Hell*. NY: Harmony Books, 1977.

Devers, E. "Experiencing the Deceased." *Florida Nursing Review* 2 (January 1988): 7–13.

Dietz, B. *Life after Loss*. Tucson, AZ: Fisher Books, 1988.

Dossey, L. *Healing Words*. San Francisco: HarperCollins, 1993.

Finley, M. *Whispers of Love*. New York: Crossroads, 1995.

Greeley, A. "Mysticism Goes Mainstream." *American Health* 6 (1987): 47–49.

Greeley, A. "The Paranormal Is Normal: A Sociologist Looks at Parapsychology." *The Journal of the American Society for Psychical Research* 85 (1991): 367–374.

Greeley, A. *The Sociology of the Paranormal*. Beverley Hills, CA: Sage Publications, 1975.

Guggenheim, W. & J. Guggenheim. *Hello from Heaven*: Longwood, FL: The ADC Project, 1995.

Haraldson, E. "Survey of Claimed Encounters with the Dead." *Omega* 19 (1988–89):103–113.

Harman, W. & H. Rheingold. *Higher Creativity*. Los Angeles: Tarcher, 1984.

Hoyt, E., R. Morris, J. Palmer, & J. Rush. *Foundations of Parapsychology*. Boston: Routledge & Kegan Paul, 1986.

Hufford, D. J. "Paranormal Experiences in the General Population: A Commentary." *Journal of Mental and Nervous Disorders* 180 (1922): 362-368.

Hurley, T. "Dwelling with the Mystery of Death." *Noetic Sciences Review* (Spring 1994): 6–7.

Irwin, H. *An Introduction to Parapsychology*. Jefferson, NC: McFarland & Co., 1989.

Jung, C. *Memories, Dreams, Reflections*. NY: Random House, 1961.

Kelsey, M. *Dreams: A Way to Listen to God*. NY: Paulist Press, 1978.

Knight, D. C. (ed.) *The ESP Reader*. NY: Grosset & Dunlap, 1969.

Linn, E. *Premonitions, Visitations and Dreams*. The Publisher's Mark, P.O. Box 6939, Incline Village, Nevada, 89450, 1991.

Mackenzie, A. *Hauntings and Apparitions*. London: Grenada Publishing Ltd., 1983.

Moody, R. *Reunions: Visionary Encounters with Departed Loved Ones*. NY: Villard Books, 1994.

Moss, T. *The Probability of the Impossible*. Los Angeles: Tarcher, 1974.

Myers, F. W. H. *Human Personality and its Survival of Bodily Death*. NY: New Hyde Park, University Books, 1961.

Olsen, P., J. Suddeth, P. Petersen, & C. Egelhoff. "Hallucinations of Widowhood." *Journal of the American Geriatrics Society* 33 (1985): 543–547.

Rauscher, W. *The Spiritual Frontier*. Garden City, NY: Doubleday, 1975.

Rees, W .D. "The Hallucinations of Widowhood." *British Medical Journal* 4 (1971): 37–41.

Reid, C. *Dreams: Discovering Your Inner Teacher*. Minneapolis: Winston Press, 1983.

Sidgwick, E. *Phantasms of the Living*. New Hyde Park, NY: University Books, 1962.

Sidgwick, H. "Report on the Census of Hallucinations." *Proceedings of the Society for Psychical Research* 10 (1894).

Sparrow, G. *I Am With You Always*. NY: Bantam Books, 1995.

RESOURCE GUIDE

Our country was built on the efforts of self-help groups. People have been helping people in every human endeavor imaginable, from building homes and championing just causes to dealing with a host of health problems or gender issues. On the subject of support groups for those grieving the deaths of loved ones, there has been a near-exponential increase in organizations over the past two decades. The list that follows are some of the organizations that can provide direct support or guide you to someone who will assist you in your grief work.

If for some reason you are unable to find an organization you feel comfortable with, call your local hospice and ask to speak with the Bereavement Coordinator. This person will readily assist you in your search. Last but certainly not least, call your rabbi, priest, or minister for assistance. Many churches offer support groups for anyone in the community. Likewise, many funeral directors can provide sources of community help for the bereaved.

Aiding a Mother Experiencing Neonatal Death (AMEND)
4324 Berrywick Terrace
St. Louis, Missouri 63128
314-487-7528

American Association of Suicidology
2459 South Ash Street
Denver, Colorado 80222
313-692-0985

Center for Loss and Life Transition
3735 Broken Bow Road
Fort Collins, Colorado 80526
303-226-6050

Center for Sibling Loss
1700 West Irving Park
Chicago, Illinois 60613
312-883-0268

Children's Hospice International
1101 King Street, #131
Alexandria, Virginia 22314
800-24-CHILD

Compassionate Friends
P.O. Box 3696
Oak Brook, Illinois 60522–3696
708–990–0010
(This is a self-help support group for parents who have experienced the death of a child at any age or from any cause. There are chapters all over the country. I would recommend looking in your telephone book first for the possibility that a chapter is in your immediate area.)

Dougy Center
3909 Southeast 52nd Street
Portland, Oregon 97206
503–775–5683

Grief Recovery Institute
8306 Wilshire Blvd., Suite 21-A
Los Angeles, California 90211
800–445–4508

Helping Other Parents in Normal Grieving (HOPING)
Sparrow Hospital 1215 East Michigan Avenue
P.O. Box 30480
Lansing, Michigan 48909
Carolyn R. Wickham, Hospital Coordinator
517–483–3873

Miscarriage, Infant Death, Stillbirth (MIDS)
c/o Janet Tischler
16 Crescent Drive
Parsippany, New Jersey 07054
201–263–6730

Mothers Against Drunk Driving (MADD)
669 Airport Freeway, Suite 310
Hurst, Texas 76053
817–268–MADD

Mt. Vernon Center for Community Mental Health
Grief Program
8119 Holland Avenue
Alexandria, Virginia 22306
703–360–6910

National Association of Military Widows
4023 25th Road North
Arlington, Virginia 22207
703–527–4565

National Organization for Victims Assistance (NOVA)
717 "D" Street N.W.
Washington, D.C. 20004
202–393–NOVA

National Self-Help Clearinghouse
25 W. 43rd Street, Room 620
New York, New York 10036
212–840–1259

National Sudden Infant Death Syndrome (SIDS) Foundation
10500 Little Putuxent Parkway, Suite 420
Columbia, Maryland 21044
800–221–SIDS

Parents of Murdered Children (POMC)
100 East 8th Street, B-41
Cincinnati, Ohio 45202
Nancy Ruhe, Executive Director
513–721–5683

Pregnancy and Infant Loss Center (PILC)
1421 E. Wayzata Blvd., No. 30
Wayzata, Minnesota 55391
612–473–9372

Resolve, Inc.
5 Water Street
Arlington, Massachusetts 02174
617–643–2424

Saint Francis Center for Bereavement
5417 Sherier Place N.W.
Washington, D.C. 20016
202–363–8500

SHARE
Saint Elizabeth's Hospital
211 S. 3rd Street
Belleville, Illinois 62222
618–234–2415

SHARE - Pregnancy and Infant Loss Support
St. Joseph's Health Center
300 1st Capital Drive
St. Charles, Missouri 63301
Catherine Lammert, Executive Director
314–947–6164

Society of Military Widows
National Association of Uniformed Services
5535 Hempstead Way
Springfield, Virginia 22151–4094
703–750–1342

Teen Age Grief, Inc.
P.O. Box 4935
Panorama City, California 91412-4935
805-254-1501

THEOS Foundation (They Help Each Other Spiritually)
1301 Clark Building
717 Liberty Avenue
Pittsburgh, Pennsylvania 15222
412–471–7779

Tragedy Assistance Program for Survivors, Inc. (TAPS)
807 G Street, Suite 250
Anchorage, Alaska 99501
800–368–TAPS

Twinless Twins Support Group International
11220 St. Joe Road
Fort Wayne, Indiana 46835-9737
Dr. Raymond W. Brandt, Director
219–627–5414

UNITE
c/o Jeanes Hospital
7600 Central Avenue
Philadelphia, Pennsylvania 19111-2499
Janis Heil, Director
215–728–3777
(For those experiencing grief after miscarriage or infant death.)

Widowed Persons Services
American Association of Retired Persons (AARP)
1909 "K" Street N.W.
Washington, D.C. 20049
202–728–4370

For Information on Certified Grief Counselors

Association for Death Education and Counseling
638 Prospect Avenue
Hartford, CT 06105–4250
203–586–7503.
(This international organization has a list of certified grief counselors and therapists in every state and in some countries outside of the United States. These
counselors have been certified by ADEC.)

Magazines for the Bereaved

Bereavement: A Magazine of Hope and Healing
Bereavement Publishing
350 Gradle Avenue
Carmel, Indiana 46032
317–846–9429

Thanatos
Florida Funeral Directors Services, Inc.
P.O. Box 6009
Tallahassee, Florida 32314
904–224–1969

Bereavement and Hospice Support Netline

If you have access to the Internet, you can tap into the national on-line directory
of bereavement support groups and hospice bereavement services as follows:
URL: http:/www.ubalt.edu/www/bereavement
e-mail: bereavement@ubmail.ubalt.edu

ACTIVE LISTENING: The skill of understanding what another person is saying and feeling through body language, demeanor, and words, and then being able to reflect those feelings and thoughts back so the person knows he or she is truly understood. It is a much-needed skill to help others, especially children, and to establish trusting relationships.

APPARITION: A ghostly figure, a specter.

ANOMALY: Something that deviates from the normal or common order, is irregular, or is very difficult to classify.

BEREAVEMENT: An objective fact; the condition of having experienced a meaningful loss.

CHEMOTHERAPY: A treatment for cancer which uses certain chemicals or drugs to destroy malignant cells.

CLAIRVOYANCE: The ability to acquire information about objects or events at great distances by means not involving the known senses.

COLLECTIVE UNCONSCIOUS: In Jungian psychology, a part of the unconscious mind shared by all humanity.

COLLECTIVITY: A term used by parapsychologists to indicate that more than one person heard the voice of or a sound associated with a deceased person.

CRISIS APPARITION: The appearance of the deceased loved one at the moment of death or shortly after.

DÉJÀ VU EXPERIENCES: The experience of reliving an experience or of feeling you are in a place you have been before, although there is no way you could have been.

EMPIRICAL: That which is based on or derived from observation or experiment.

ENDOCRINE SYSTEM: A system of the body whose glands (often referred to as ductless glands) secrete hormones directly into the bloodstream. This system is intricately associated with our thought processes.

ESP: The acronym for extrasensory perception.

GHOST: The spirit of a dead person, especially one that appears in bodily likeness to living persons.

GRIEF: The normal physical and emotional response to any meaningful loss.

GRIEF WORK: The work of establishing new routines, priorities, and traditions in adjusting to the absence of a deceased loved one, including the difficult task of withdrawing the emotional investment (but not memories) in the deceased and reinvesting that emotion in life.

HALLUCINATION: A false or distorted perception of objects or events usually resulting from emotional disorganization or as a response to a drug.

HYPNAGOGIA: The point between being half asleep and still awake. It is considered to be a highly creative state.

LINKING OBJECTS: Any physical objects (and also memories) that are used by a grieving person to form a symbolic link with the deceased.

MOURNING: The active process of sharing one's grief with another in adapting to the absence of the loved one and establishing a new identity.

MYSTICAL EXPERIENCE: An experience having a spiritual quality involving direct communication with ultimate reality or God.

NATURALISM: A system of belief holding that all phenomena can be explained in terms of natural causes and laws without attributing moral, spiritual, or supernatural significance to them.

NEAR-DEATH EXPERIENCES: Unusual experiences reported by people believed to be on the brink of death, which may include out-of-body experiences, seeing deceased loved ones, going through a tunnel, seeing a being of light and the passage of one's consciousness into another dimension.

NOETIC SCIENCES REVIEW: A periodical published by the Institute of Noetic Sciences containing penetrating articles, research updates, reviews, and interviews on consciousness research and its application to the enhancement of quality of life.

PARAPSYCHOLOGY: The study of the evidence for psychological phenomena such as ESP or other unexplainable occurrences that are inexplicable by science.

PARADIGM: An example that serves as a pattern or model. Also used to indicate a particular worldview or way of looking at life.

PATHOLOGY: A departure or deviation from a normal condition. In terms of grieving, pathological grieving would be considered as complicated grief.

PLACEBO: An inert substance containing no medication and prescribed or given to a person to reinforce his or her expectation of getting well.

PRECOGNITION: Foreknowledge. The ability to randomly predict the future in a way other than through logical inference.

PRIMARY GRIEVER: One who is directly related to the deceased or who possesses a deep emotional investment in the deceased person.

PSI: The twenty-third letter in the Greek alphabet. It is commonly used to indicate the unknown. It is also used in collectively referring to telepathy, clairvoyance, precognition, and psychokinesis as psi phenomena.

PSYCHOKINESIS: The use of the mind to affect matter as in moving objects, inducing rapid healing, producing an image on unexposed film, or affecting the electrical circuits of machinery.

PSYCHONEUROIMMUNOLOGY: The area of study of the relationships between the brain, the endocrine system, and the immune system.

REPRESENTIVENESS FALLACY: A scientific theory stating that whenever anyone is confronted with an unexplainable event, immediate reasoning says that the event is representative of an unusual cause, not an ordinary one.

SCIENTIFIC METHOD: The principles and empirical processes of discovery and demonstration considered necessary for scientific investigation. It includes formulation of a hypothesis, the observation of phenomena, and experimentation to demonstrate or invalidate the truth of the hypothesis.

SCIENTISM: The belief that the scientific method used in investigating the natural sciences should be applied in all fields of inquiry.

SOCIETY FOR PSYCHICAL RESEARCH: Formed in London in 1882, it was the first organization of scholars, scientists, and other professionals to band together for systematic study of unusual or paranormal phenomena. The SPR has accumulated thousands of documented cases of the extraordinary over the years.

SUBCONSCIOUS MIND: The part of the mind below the level of conscious perception.

SYNCHRONICITY: A theory proposed by Carl Jung which suggests that the coincidence of events seem to be meaningfully although not causally related.

TELEPATHY: The transmission of information between two people by some means other than normal sensory perception.

UNCONSCIOUS MIND: A division of the mind in psychoanalytic theory containing elements, such as memories or repressed desires, that are not subject to conscious perception or control but that often affect conscious thought and behavior.

VISION: (1) The mystical experience of seeing as if with the eyes of a supernatural being. (2) A sight seen in a dream, ecstasy or trance-like state.

YEAR OF THE FIRSTS: A term used by grief counselors to designate the large number of significant dates, events, and social gatherings in which the survivor for the first time experiences those occasions without the deceased loved one. Consequently, these occasions are often times in which great emotional pain is experienced and the bereaved may need solace and comfort.

INDEX

A

AIDS, 1

Alternative explanations, 159, 164, 178

American Society for Psychical Research, 17

Anderson, Joan Wester, 75, 114, 127

Angels, 55, 76, 119, 121, 161, 182-185

Anger, 4, 29-31, 84, 153-154, 186

Animals and birds, 85, 87, 95

Apparitions, 12, 18, 53-54, 56-58, 62, 64-65, 68-69, 131-132, 161, 165, 186

    classifications of, 57, 69

    continuous, 62

    crisis, 57, 65, 68

Auditory experiences, 18, 77

B

Belief, 5, 7, 9, 11, 16, 26, 29, 44, 49, 56, 68, 85, 91-94, 104, 114, 122, 130, 143-145, 149, 160-162, 166

Bereavement, 4, 6-7, 11, 24-25, 41, 47, 54, 65, 97, 129, 166, 177, 188

    defined, 25

Bereavement coordinator, 54

Birds, 20-21, 85, 87-88, 92-97, 117, 122

Bowlby, John, 5, 30-31

Burton, Robert, 11

C

Christianity, 12, 55

Church authority, 162

Clairvoyance, 14, 17, 39, 162

Coincidence, 22, 41, 88-91, 93-94, 98, 116-117, 121, 123, 158, 184

Collective unconscious, 62, 105, 150, 155

Committee for the Scientific Investigation of Claims of the Paranormal, 163

Confidentiality, 9, 129, 172

Connectedness, 91-93

Contact experience, 2-4, 6-8, 17-18, 20-36, 38, 51-52, 54, 56, 58, 64, 69, 79, 91-92, 94, 96-98, 100-101, 103, 105, 109-113, 116, 126, 140, 143, 155, 164-165, 169-170, 173-176, 178-180, 182-183, 185-187, 189

    children and, 179

    nature and, 96-97

    negative, 186-187

    place in the grief process, 3-4, 30

    types of, 20

    what it is not, 32

Consciousness, 8, 11-12, 14, 33, 38, 40-42, 44, 55, 57, 65, 100, 144, 149

Coleridge, Samuel Taylor, 91, 139

Copernicus, Nicolaus, 161

Coping with loss, 24

Counseling, 23, 36, 42, 51

Crisis apparitions, 57, 65, 68-69

Crying, 10, 26-27, 43, 102, 104, 149, 160

Czillinger, Ken, 182

D

Death bed vision, 134-135

Deja vu experiences, 15

Denial, 30, 32, 177
Depression, 4, 26, 29-30, 75, 77
Descartes, 161
Devil, 187-188
Disbelief, 1, 30-32, 162, 180, 186
Divine intervention, 2
Dossey, Larry, 157, 170
Dreams, 4, 13, 20-21, 31, 55-56, 62, 100,
    105-106, 137, 139-155, 161, 181
  big, 145-146
  death and, 75, 144, 149, 187
  dying person and, 145
  creative solutions and, 141
  guidance, 11, 140, 142
  interpreting, 142
  recurrent, 152-153
Dyer, Wayne, 93

E

Eddington, Arthur, 12
Experience of touch, 100-101, 103, 106
  dreams and, 103, 106
Experience of smell, 109, 113
Expression of emotion, 25
Extraordinary experiences, 3-4, 15, 19,
    54, 87-88, 96, 98, 129, 163, 166-
    167, 170
  contact experiences, 3, 6, 15-16, 19,
    21-22, 162, 166, 169, 174, 186
  defined, 14-15
  if you have the experience, 2, 166,
    191
  types, 2, 54
  who believes in, 19

F

Fear, 10, 26, 34, 39, 46, 55, 60, 92, 96,
    104, 106, 115, 130, 144-145, 147,
    159-160, 165, 168, 170-171, 186-
    189
Fraud, 163

G

Gallup poll, 134
God, 7, 15, 21, 33, 40, 43, 51, 56, 59, 71,
    74, 76, 91, 93, 96, 104, 114, 116,
    118-119, 121-122, 127, 130, 132,
    143, 145, 147, 150, 155, 161, 182
Goethe, 165
Greeley, Andrew M., 1, 17-19
Grief, 2-4, 7, 10-11, 22-37, 44-45, 49,
    51, 56-57, 63-64, 68, 75, 77, 79-80,
    82, 89-90, 92-93, 101, 106-107,
    122, 127, 132, 135, 144, 150, 153-
    155, 160, 171, 173-177, 181, 191
  factors influencing, 4
  individuality of, 3
  normal, 24, 28-29, 31, 60, 65
  process, 3-4, 7, 22-25, 28, 30-31, 37,
    49, 60, 154-155, 173
Grief work, 22, 25, 27-28, 32, 35-36, 45,
    49, 51, 56-57, 68, 80, 82, 92-93, 95,
    106, 135, 150, 154, 176, 181, 191
Guilt, 4, 26, 29-30, 34, 147, 149, 154

H

Hallucinations, 1, 6-7, 17-18, 23, 28, 56,
    64-65, 72-73, 76, 131
Haraldsson, Erlendur, 16
Harman, Willis, 163
Helping, 3, 9, 16, 21, 46, 53, 64, 128,
    143, 147, 150, 171-189
  basic guidelines, 172
  the child, 179
Hope, 4, 8, 31, 43, 88-91, 96-97, 113,
    115, 117, 126, 167, 172, 182, 185
Hospice, 53-54, 94, 133, 166

I

Illusion, 103, 137, 168
Intuition, 13, 15, 36-41, 167
  psychic ability and, 39
  rational thought and, 38, 40

Intuitive experience, 2, 20, 36-52
Islam, 12

J
Jahn, Robert, 169
James, William, 17, 37, 57, 87, 97, 99
Joan of Arc, 55, 76
Judaism, 12
Jung, C. G., 13, 17, 39, 62-63, 65, 75, 87, 90-91, 184

K
Kekule, Freidrich August von, 13
Kelsey, Morton T., 9
Kubler-Ross, Elisabeth, 27, 108, 124, 136, 157, 180

L
Lewis, C. S., 44
Listening, 36, 73, 82, 89, 122, 188
Love, 24, 27-28, 34, 36, 42-45, 54, 56, 64, 71, 77, 83, 88-89, 92, 94, 99, 101-102, 107, 110, 113, 116, 123, 125, 127, 130, 143, 147-151, 167, 169, 175-176, 179, 185, 188-189

M
Mackenzie, Andrew, 53, 165
Merton, Thomas, 119
Messages and meanings, 84, 96
Miracles, 12, 71, 75, 87, 90-92, 114, 121, 127, 161-162, 186
Morse, Melvin, 65, 145, 159, 165
Mourning, 2, 4, 24-25, 29, 54, 80, 172-173, 181, 184
Music, 21, 71-72, 75-76, 114, 117, 143
Mystery, 15, 45, 139, 162, 168-170, 179
Mystical experience, 6, 50

N
Naturalism, 160
Nature, 4, 91, 96-97

Nichols, Jane, 177
Nonphysical reality, 38, 76, 101, 115, 117, 163, 167-168, 189

O
Opposing explanations, 130
Overdependence, 29

P
Parapsychology, 99, 158, 163-164
Paranormal, 6, 9, 12, 14-17, 19, 36, 49, 97, 116, 121, 148, 159, 161, 163, 174, 176, 180, 186-187
Pascal, Blaise, 115
Penfield, Wilder, 15
Perceptions, 7, 12, 28, 39, 55, 85, 98, 158, 160, 165, 187
Permission to grieve, 27, 184
Personal meaning, 14, 45, 63, 96, 106, 158-159, 170, 176
Physical reality, 163, 167-168, 170
Praying for a sign, 16, 71, 182
Precognition, 14, 162
Psychokinesis, 14, 162
Psychoneuroimmunology, 160

Q
Quantum physics, 68

R
Rando, Therese, 30, 176
Raphael, Beverley, 11
Rees, W. Dewi, 18
Remen, Rachel Naomi, 157
Ring, Kenneth, 13, 37, 134
Ryan, Dennis, 154

S
Sanity, 5, 34, 57, 60, 129, 178, 186
Searching for the deceased, 31
Search for meaning, 7

Science, 6, 11-13, 87, 93, 97, 131, 145, 157-159, 161-162, 164, 169-170
Scientific authority, 162
Scientific evidence, 164
Scientific method, 6, 12, 157, 161
Scientism, 160
Sense of presence, 17, 28, 31, 36-37, 39, 42-47, 50-52, 111-112
  twins and, 45
  life-long, 43, 52, 85
Sense of smell, 20-21, 109-110, 112, 114
Skepticism, 91, 155, 158-159, 164-165
  balancing, 158
Skeptics, 3, 17, 33, 97, 157-170
  and culture, 160
Society for Psychical Research, 17, 57, 65, 71, 100, 163
Socrates, 74-75
Space-time, 9, 186
Spirit, 6, 11, 15, 40, 56, 64, 74, 87, 114, 143, 157, 169, 180, 183-184, 186
Spiritual experiences, 69, 131
Stress, 6, 15, 23, 25, 27, 34, 57, 60, 79, 150, 168
Subconscious, 2, 104-105, 142, 155, 162, 167
Support systems, 5
Symbols, 20-21, 25, 92, 114-126, 141-142, 147
  messages and, 33, 150, 179
  of light, 125
Synchronicity, 90-91, 93

T
Tactile experiences, 18, 21
Tart, Charles, 14
Tatelbaum, Judy, 63
Telepathy, 14, 17, 39, 162
Third-party experiences, 20-21, 131
Threat, 103, 159, 170
  and perception, 159, 170

Touch experience, 102
  most common, 102
  dreams and, 9, 105, 187
Trust, 5, 28, 34, 37, 41, 43, 45, 117, 129, 139, 154, 175, 181, 188
  symbols and, 117
Tutankhamen, 11
Twins, 45-46, 166

U
Unconscious beliefs, 160

V
Visions, 11-13, 54-57, 60-61, 64-65, 160-161, 165, 167
  death bed, 134-135
  postmortem, 60
  meaning and, 64-65
Voices, 71, 73-76, 161
  Jung and, 62-63
  Socrates and, 74-75
  stigma and, 74

W
Western civilization, 55, 160
Widows, 1, 4, 11, 18-19, 31, 80, 150
Williamson, Ian, 169
Worden, J. William, 23, 28

PERMISSIONS

Stay in Touch . . .

Llewellyn publishes hundreds of books on your favorite subjects.

On the following pages you will find listed some books now available on related subjects. Your local bookstore stocks most of these and will stock new Llewellyn titles as they become available. We appreciate your patronage!

Order by Phone

Call toll-free within the U.S. and Canada, **1–800–THE MOON**.
In Minnesota call **(612) 291–1970**.
We accept Visa, MasterCard, and American Express.

Order by Mail

Send the full price of your order (MN residents add 7% sales tax) in U.S.funds to:

> **Llewellyn Worldwide**
> **P.O. Box 64383, Dept. K405-7**
> **St. Paul, MN 55164–0383, U.S.A.**

Postage and Handling

- $4.00 for orders $15.00 and under
- $5.00 for orders over $15.00
- No charge for orders over $100.00

We ship UPS in the continental United States. We cannot ship to P.O. boxes. Orders shipped to Alaska, Hawaii, Canada, Mexico, and Puerto Rico will be sent first-class mail.

International orders: Airmail—add freight equal to price of each book to the total price of order, plus $5.00 for each non-book item (audiotapes, etc.). Surface mail—Add $1.00 per item.

Allow 4–6 weeks for delivery. Postage and handling rates subject to change.

Group Discounts

We offer a 20% quantity discount to group leaders or agents. You must order a minimum of five copies of the same book to get our special quantity price.

Prices subject to change without notice.

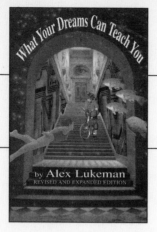

What Your Dreams Can Teach You
Alex Lukeman

Dreams are honest and do not lie. They have much to teach us, but the lessons are often difficult to understand. Confusion comes not from the dream but from the outer mind's attempt to understand it.

What Your Dreams Can Teach You is a workbook of self-discovery, with a systematic and proven approach to the understanding of dreams. It *does not* contain lists of meanings for dream symbols. Only you, the dreamer, can discover what the images in your dreams mean for you. The book *does* contain step-by-step information which can lead you to success with your dreams, success that will bear fruit in your waking hours. Learn to tap into the aspect of yourself that truly knows how to interpret dreams, the inner energy of understanding called the "Dreamer Within." This aspect of your consciousness will lead you to an accurate understanding of your dreams and even assist you with interpreting dreams of others.

0-87542-475-9, 288 pp., 6 x 9, softcover $14.95

The Secret Way of Wonder
Insights from the Silence
Guy Finley
Introduction by Desi Arnaz, Jr.

Discover an inner world of wisdom and make miracles happen! Here is a simple yet deeply effective system of illuminating and eliminating the problems of inner mental and emotional life.

The Secret Way of Wonder is an interactive spiritual workbook, offering guided practice for self-study. It is about Awakening the Power of Wonder in yourself. A series of 60 "Wonders" (meditations on a variety of subjects: "The Wonder of Change," "The Wonder of Attachments," etc.) will stir you in an indescribable manner. This is a bold and bright new kind of book that gently leads us on a journey of Spiritual Alchemy where the journey itself is the destination ... and the destination is our need to be spiritually whole men and women.

Most of all, you will find out through self investigation that we live in a friendly, intelligent and living universe that we can reach into and that can reach us.

0-87542-221-7, 192 pp., 5 1/4 x 8, softcover $9.95

Soul Healing
Dr. Bruce Goldberg

George overcame lung cancer and ended a lifelong smoking habit through hypnotic programming.

Mary tripled her immune system's effective response to AIDS with the help of age progression.

Now you, too, can learn to raise the vibrational rate of your soul (or subconscious mind) to stimulate your body's own natural healing processes. Explore several natural approaches to healing that include past life regression and future life progression, hypnotherapy, soulmates, angelic healing, near-death experiences, shamanic healing, acupuncture, meditation, yoga, and the new physics.

The miracle of healing comes from within. After reading *Soul Healing*, you will never view your life and the universe in the same way again.

1-56718-317-4, 304 pp., 6 x 9, softcover $14.95

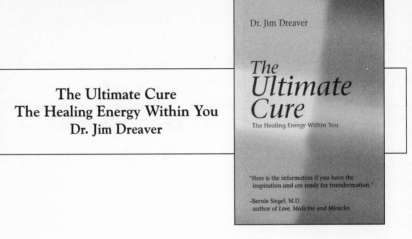

The Ultimate Cure
The Healing Energy Within You
Dr. Jim Dreaver

Dr. Jim Dreaver

The
Ultimate
Cure
The Healing Energy Within You

"Here is the information if you have the
inspiration and are ready for transformation."

-Bernie Siegel, M.D.
author of *Love, Medicine and Miracles*

The Ultimate Cure will open a door into consciousness and literally bring you into a direct, first-hand experience of illumination—an experience that will stimulate your mind, warm your heart and feed your soul.

Dr. Jim Dreaver provides a first-hand account of the spiritual journey and outlines the steps needed to live in the world with an authentic sense of wisdom, love and power. He addresses the issues of meditation, work as a spiritual exercise, harnessing the power of the mind, conscious breathing, and healing the wounds of the past. Dr. Dreaver's main theme is that spiritual presence, which is the source of all healing, is an actual, palpable reality that can be felt and tapped into.

To realize enlightenment, you must have a tremendous hunger for it. This delightfully honest and wonderfully human book will stimulate your appetite and, by the time you turn to the last page, will leave you feeling totally satisfied.

1-56718-244-5, 288 pp., 6 x 9, softcover   **$14.95**

Create Your Own Joy
A Guide for Transforming Your Life
Elizabeth Jean Rogers

Uncover the wisdom, energy and love of your higher self and discover the peace and joy for which you yearn! This highly structured journal-workbook is designed to guide you through the process of understanding how you create your own joy by how you choose to respond to people and situations in your life.

Each chapter offers guided meditations on overcoming blocks—such as guilt, grief, fear and destructive behavior—that keep happiness from you; thoughtful questions to help you focus your feelings; concrete suggestions for action; and affirmations to help you define and fulfill your deepest desires and true needs. As you record your responses to the author's questions, you will transform this book into a personal expression of your own experience.

Life is too short to waste your energy on negative thoughts and emotions—use the uncomplicated, dynamic ideas in this book to get a fresh outlook on current challenges in your life, and open the door to your joyful higher self.

1-56718-354-9, 240 pp., 6 x 9, illus., softcover   **$10.00**